"*America, Goddam* is the book we have been waiting for. A trenchant examination of the history and consequence of the particular overlap of anti-Blackness and misogyny—misogynoir—that has worked to undermine the life chances of all working-class and poor Black women. Unraveling easy narratives about progress and change in American history, *America, Goddam*'s focus on twenty-first-century iterations of the oppression and exploitation of Black women highlights both continuity and change. Treva Lindsey provides the historical and analytical tools necessary to make sense of the endless media and scholastic narratives of abuse and neglect in the coverage of Black women's stories. With extraordinary insight and elemental passion, *America, Goddam* is a critical contribution to the evolving cannon of Black feminist texts and scholarship."

—KEEANGA-YAMAHTTA TAYLOR, editor of *How We Get Free: Black Feminism and the Combahee River Collective*

"Written with insight, care, and verve, *America, Goddam* provides piercing insight into present-day movements including #BlackLives Matter, #SayHer Name, and #MeToo. Lindsey's voice orients us to the book's concerns through the lens of her own life experiences, making clear that *America, Goddam* achieves its effect through a brilliant and unbounded sense of how we can and should arrive at understandings about the origins, forces, and possibilities for resisting violence."

—MARTHA S. JONES, author of *Vanguard: How Black Women Broke Barriers, Won the Vote, and Insisted on Equality for All*

A **NAOMI SCHNEIDER** BOOK

Highlighting the lives and experiences of marginalized
communities, the select titles of this imprint draw
from sociology, anthropology, law, and history, as well
as from the traditions of journalism and advocacy, to reassess mainstream
history and promote unconventional thinking about contemporary
social and political issues. Their authors share the passion, commitment,
and creativity of Executive Editor Naomi Schneider.

The publisher and the University of California Press Foundation gratefully acknowledge the generous support of the George Gund Foundation Imprint in African American Studies.

America, Goddam

VIOLENCE, BLACK WOMEN, AND
THE STRUGGLE FOR JUSTICE

Treva B. Lindsey

UNIVERSITY OF CALIFORNIA PRESS

University of California Press
Oakland, California

© 2022 by Treva B. Lindsey

Library of Congress Cataloging-in-Publication Data

Names: Lindsey, Treva B., 1983– author.
Title: America, goddam : violence, black women, and the struggle for
    justice / Treva B. Lindsey.
Description: Oakland, California : University of California Press, [2022] |
    Includes bibliographical references and index.
Identifiers: LCCN 2021029665 (print) | LCCN 2021029666 (ebook) |
    ISBN 9780520384491 (cloth) | ISBN 9780520384507 (epub)
Subjects: LCSH: Women, Black—Violence against—United States. |
    Women, Black—Civil rights—United States. | Social justice—United
    States. | Anti-racism—United States.
Classification: LCC HV6250.4.W65 L565 2022 (print) |
    LCC HV6250.4.W65 (ebook) | DDC 362.88082—dc23
LC record available at https://lccn.loc.gov/2021029665
LC ebook record available at https://lccn.loc.gov/2021029666

Manufactured in the United States of America

31 30 29 28 27 26 25 24 23 22
10 9 8 7 6 5 4 3 2 1

For my father, the late ANTHONY WAYNE LINDSEY
And my mother, TREVA ANN STREETER LINDSEY
and
Black girls and women everywhere

Contents

Introduction

Goddam, Goddam, Goddam

As I finished this book, the trial of Derek Chauvin, the Minneapolis police officer who killed George Floyd, a forty-five-year-old Black man on May 25, 2020, by pressing his knee into Floyd's neck for almost ten minutes had just begun. On the second day of the trial, in March 2021, the prosecution called eighteen-year-old Darnella Frazier and her nine-year-old cousin—also a Black girl to testify about what they witnessed on that fateful day. My heart broke as I listened to Darnella, who was seventeen at the time she filmed Chauvin killing George. Her video went viral and sparked protests worldwide. This teenage Black girl cried as she testified and stated that she stayed up nights apologizing to George for not doing more.[1] I couldn't stomach the trauma and guilt she felt. Nor could I make it through the five-minute questioning of the nine-year-old Black girl who saw George's last moments as well. What she saw made her "sad and kind of mad."[2] Although both Black girls survived this horrific incident, what they endured as they bore witness is unbearable. They must live with the sounds and sights of a man's life being taken by a "peace officer" without an ounce of visible remorse. You don't shake off witnessing something like that; none of us do. The violence we endure as well as what we witness stays with and shapes us. All I could say as I witnessed their witnessing was Goddam.

On the evening of Saturday, March 21, 1964, legendary singer, songwriter, arranger, musician, and civil rights activist Nina Simone took the stage at Carnegie Hall in New York City. She performed and recorded what became the album *Nina Simone in Concert* over the course of three nonconsecutive nights at the storied venue. At the first show of the three-night engagement, one song reportedly shocked her captive, predominantly white, audience.[3] "The name of this tune is "Mississippi goddam / And I mean every word of it." "Mississippi Goddam" was Simone's first "civil rights anthem," a scathing chronicling of antiBlack racism released at the height of mid-twentieth-century Black freedom struggles in the U.S. and across the globe.[4] She had debuted the song a few nights before at the Village Gate nightclub in Greenwich Village, but it was the Carnegie performances that propelled the song to notoriety and infamy.[5]

It begins like a show tune, spritely and upbeat, but then quickly reveals itself to be fiercely political in its condemnation of racism. The music is almost playful, yet the lyrics indict a nation for its infinite crimes against Black people and convey Simone's furor with what she has endured and witnessed: "*Oh but this whole country is full of lies.*" Simone implores her audience to feel the weight of what being Black in the U.S. is. It's being chased, arrested and incarcerated, or fearing premature and violent deaths. "Mississippi Goddam" goes for the U.S.'s jugular. It's a callout, a presocial media dragging. The lightheartedness of the music intentionally and carefully belies its unrepentant message about injustice and anti-Black racial violence.

In an acerbic tone, Simone told the audience that the song is "a show tune, but the show hasn't been written for it yet." Reports indicate nervous laughter erupted from the crowd. "Mississippi Goddam" was banned in many places throughout the U.S. South. Radio stations returned the promotional single with the record literally cracked in half.[6] Those who viewed the song as a threat to a white supremacist status quo railed against the profanity of the song's title and lyrics and the possibility that it could further galvanize and intensify support for Black freedom struggles. In the song, Simone mentions only a few states, but what she describes is a long history that stretches into the present. The story she tells in just a few minutes is one of this nation's history of violence against Black people. It is woven into the fabric of this nation, one of its most prominent and defining features.

In Simone's autobiography, *I Put a Spell on You,* she talks about the assassination of civil rights activist Medgar Evers in Mississippi on June 12, 1963, as an inspiration for her first "protest" song.[7] Before writing "Mississippi Goddam," she pondered "How can you take the memory of a man like Medgar Evers and reduce all that he was to three and a half minutes and a simple tune?"[8] Evers was a prominent Black activist in one of the most violently racist areas of the country. Before being killed, he survived notable attempts on his life.[9] Shot in the heart in his own driveway after returning home from a meeting with NAACP lawyers, the thirty-seven-year-old Evers perished just fifty minutes after being admitted to an all-white hospital that initially refused him care.[10] His wife had been the first to find him after he was gunned down. His assassination sparked national outrage and protests. Deadly white supremacist violence left a widow (Myrlie Louise Evers) and three children—

Darrell Kenyatta, Reena Denise, and James Van Dyke—without their loved one. He was a prominent figure in the movement, but he was also beloved as a father, husband, and member of a community. How does one put all of that into a three-and-a-half-minute song?

The other catalyst for Simone penning and performing her first protest song was the Sixteenth Street Baptist Church bombing in Birmingham, Alabama. On Sunday, September 15, 1963, four members of the local Ku Klux Klan chapter planted dynamite on the east side of the church.[11] Five Black girls were changing into their choir robes in a basement bathroom in the church on what should've been an uneventful Sunday morning at their religious home. At approximately 10:23 a.m., the dynamite exploded and brutally killed eleven-year-old Carol Denise McNair, fourteen-year-old Carole Rosanond Robinson, fourteen-year-old Addie Mae Collins, and fourteen-year-old Cynthia Dionne Wesley. Those killed became known as the "Four Little Girls." Additionally, more than a dozen Black people were injured, including the younger sister of Addie Mae Collins, Sarah Collins, who was the fifth girl in that basement bathroom. The explosion blinded her in one eye and several pieces of glass embedded in her face.[12] The Sixteenth Street Baptist Church bombing was a gut-wrenching act of terror that shook civil rights activists, allies of Black freedom struggles, and everyday Black folks to their core.

History too often remembers Addie, Denise, Carole, and Cynthia as the "Four Little Girls" killed by white supremacists. When we talk about the bombing, we don't often say their names. We rarely talk about who they were before that fateful morning of unrepentant white supremacist violence. Denise loved baseball and was a Brownie. She also loved to perform and used her artistic gifts to raise money for muscular dystrophy research. Carole wanted to be a singer, so the choir was one of her beloved training grounds. She loved reading and dancing and played the clarinet. Addie Mae was also artistic and delighted in going door-to-door in white and Black neighborhoods to sell kitchen items made by her mother to help her large family make ends meet. Cynthia was an academic standout and thrived in math and reading. She was in her school band as well.[13] Among these young girls—Denise, Addie, Carole, and Cynthia—was an abundance of talent, laughter, and aspiration. Their lives were so much more than the seconds in which they were killed.

The murders of these girls and the broader attack on this haven within Birmingham's Black community combined with Evers's assassination, however, compelled Simone to write "Mississippi Goddam." Although she conceded that she "didn't like 'protest music' because a lot of it was so simple and unimaginative [that] it stripped the dignity away from the people it was trying to celebrate. But the Alabama church bombing, and the murder of Medgar Evers stopped that argument and with 'Mississippi Goddam,' I realized there was no turning back."[14] "Mississippi Goddam" is a mere glimpse into a violent history in which antiBlack violence is constant and ravenous. This song was her resistance—a forthright truth-telling.

The lyrics of "Mississippi Goddam" are also about collective resistance to racial injustice and violence and a history of Black protest. On March 24, 1965, Simone performed the song for thousands of people near the end of the Selma-to-Montgomery marches for voting rights. Notably, just a couple of weeks before her performance, protestors including activists such as the indomitable Amelia Boynton,[15] Student Non-Violent Coordinating

Committee member and future congressman John Lewis, and many others were brutally beaten by state troops and county posse men as they attempted to cross the Edmund Pettus Bridge during their march from Selma to the Alabama state capitol.[16] "Bloody Sunday," as it came be known exposed both a national and a global audience to the gravity of the brutality nonviolent protestors endured. Simone's participation at the historic final march was befitting and more firmly cemented her as a powerful voice of resistance and as an artist to whom we continue to return when we can't find our own words to capture the abundance of violence against us.

Simone followed up her first protest anthem with two more politically charged/themed songs: "Four Women," and "To Be Young, Gifted, and Black." "Mississippi Goddam" stands out among her cadre of anthems because it depicts both antiBlack violence and the struggle against it. She didn't just tell the story in terms of what happens to us; she sang about our fight against centuries of brutalization. Calling out those blocking the way to progress and those demanding that Black people be more gradual in their approach, Simone unequivocally rejected any efforts that didn't trumpet full equality or that kept the door open for violent acts like the murders of Medgar, Addie, Carole, Denise, and Cynthia.

It matters deeply that the deaths of four Black girls at the hands of racist violence propelled Simone to write a song so scathing in its critique of violence against Black people in the U.S. Frequently, how we talk about pivotal moments in both Black freedom struggles and America's history more broadly, ignores or limitedly acknowledges violence against Black women and girls as powerful catalysts. It's worth parsing through why violence against us time and again doesn't incite the kind of collective and sustained outrage expressed in this protest anthem. The nonnaming of the "Four Little Girls" and the erasure by some of their murders as catalysts for the release of "Mississippi Goddam" struck me as I reflected on how we talk about historical and contemporary antiBlack violence and Black freedom struggles. I always try to say their names when referencing what happened on that fateful Sunday. *Addie. Carole. Denise. Cynthia.*

I'm insistent about saying each of their names because their deaths at the hands of white supremacy reveal something I've always known to be true: antiBlack violence harms and kills Black people of all genders and ages. It may feel like I am stating the obvious, but far too often I find myself feeling like it's only Black women, girls, gender nonbinary, and gender-fluid folks who seem to acknowledge and rally around violence against us. I try to steer clear of sweeping statements about who cares and who doesn't. I remain convinced, however, both as a historian of Black women and as a Black woman who experienced multiple acts of violence throughout my life, that far too few who aren't Black girls, women, or gender nonbinary know or perhaps care about what has happened and is happening to us. A lot of folks refuse to invest in learning about our histories and traditions of resistance. This book, therefore, centers on those who have survived violence, those who were killed, and those who resist(ed). I don't reduce Black women and girls to *only* being casualties of antiBlack violence, although the focus of the book is violent encounters. I care deeply about the fullness of our lives and what exists that attempts to seize that fullness. We #SayHerName by telling our stories of surviving, dying, and struggling for justice.

America, Goddam explores contemporary violence against Black women and girls, as well as Black women's resistance to it in the United States. I look to the past to understand how we got here, where violence plays such an integral role in our lives. Whether 1708, 1964, or the present day, "Goddam" is a visceral and exacerbated response to the pervasiveness of violence against us. "Goddam" is also what I feel whenever I learn about yet another example of how compounding forces marginalize, harm, and kill Black women and girls. Words fail me time and time again as I search for a coherent response to the relentlessness. "Goddam" is typically all I can muster.

While I was writing this book in the spring of 2020, I, like so many other folks, learned about the brutal killing of Breonna Taylor by police officers in Louisville, Kentucky. Plainclothes officers Jonathan Mattingly, Brett Hankison, and Myles Cosgrove of the Louisville Metro Police Department (LMPD) forced entry into the apartment on March 13, 2020, as part of an investigation into an alleged drug dealing operation.[17] No drugs were found. Police fired thirty-two rounds into the home, awakening a sleeping Breonna and her boyfriend, Kenneth Walker. Six bullets struck Breonna. Her killing, for which no police officers were held legally accountable became a rare moment in which people continually galvanized around a Black woman's death at the hands of police.[18] We said her name. Something about the killing of Breonna Taylor struck a chord with millions of people. People sought out pictures of her in which you could see her vibrancy. Images of her flooded my social media for months after her killing. I can't recall a Black woman recently[19] killed by police galvanizing this kind of sustained public outcry. And even as I was heartened by this, I couldn't help but think about how often we don't say the names, know the stories of, or take to the streets for Black women and girls who experience violence. Our vulnerability and disposability are erased or, perhaps, illegible. The reality is that what happened to Addie, Carole, Cynthia, Denise, and Breonna illustrate a larger problem—a global one. White supremacy, after all, is a global reality.

America, Goddam also explores *unlivable living,* a Black life-centered riff on gender theorist Judith Butler's concept of unlivable lives.[20] In *Unlivable Lives: Violence and Identity in Transgender Activism,* sociologist Laurel Westbrook specifically looks at how to increase livability for trans people. Westbrook emphasizes what makes lives unlivable and even indicts existing activist and organizing practices for sometimes making lives for trans folks unlivable.[21] For Black women and girls, unlivable living is most emphatically felt at the intersection of poverty and economic deprivation. Capitalism wreaks a particular havoc on our lives. This deprivation and lack of access to basic necessities for surviving shapes the experiences of a disproportionate percentage of us. Unlivable living is a death-bound condition resulting from multisystem harm. Forcing Black women and girls into unlivable living is a form of state-sanctioned violence.[22]

Forms of oppression such as but not limited to racism, sexism, poverty, ableism, queerphobia, and transphobia as experienced by Black women and girls living in the U.S. conjoin to materialize as an interdependent, death-dealing superstructure. This superstructure includes seemingly less direct, but nonetheless devastating, forms of oppression, such as lack of housing, food insecurity, forced sterilization, extreme low wages, and lack of access to healthcare. *America, Goddam* underlines the brutal forms of subjugation that a significant portion of us experience and concludes by highlighting historical and contemporary resistance and activism practices as well. I aim to delineate a complex story of Black women's and girls' lives that encompasses the necessity of collective organizing and mobilization against oppression. Our resistance is a central part of how we have survived and, in some instances, prevailed.

Several questions drive this book: What are the particular forms of violence we've historically endured, and how does that legacy play out in more recent decades? What historical events and predominating ideas about Black womanhood and girlhood situate Black women and girls as distinctively violable to multiple forms of violence? Contemporary violence against us is what Saidiya Hartman identifies as an afterlife of slavery—antiBlackness normalized over five centuries on this occupied land. Key features of the afterlife of slavery are premature death and skewed life chances.[23] Our experiences with violence and unlivable living magnify how we, Black people of all genders, *are* the afterlife of slavery.

In the introduction to my first book, *Colored No More: Reinventing Black Womanhood in Washington, D.C.*, I wrote that "masculinist framings of anti-blackness during Jim Crow also contribute to contemporary discussions about anti-Black racial violence." I grappled with the problem of not acknowledging the numerous ways Black girls and women were victims and violable subjects in past eras. This lack of acknowledgment obscures "how and why gender mattered and continues to matter in the operations and praxes of antiBlackness."[24] In *Colored No More,* I put Black women in the nation's capital at the center of understanding the Jim Crow era. *America, Goddam* places Black women and girls in the U.S. at the forefront of understanding contemporary antiBlackness. Black women and girls incur disproportionate violence.[25] We are living, in-flesh embodiments of the interconnected oppressive systems of antiBlack racism, patriarchy, and capitalism. The history of anti-Black woman/girl terror in the United States encompasses multiple iterations of antiBlackness, misogyny, and economic exploitation. The inability to see Black women and girls as victims or as persons negotiating multiple forms of oppression and structural barriers is at the heart of chattel slavery, Jim Crow politics of exclusion, and contemporary antiBlack politics of disposability.[26] Understanding this history in conjunction with contemporary iterations of anti-Blackness renders visible why "Goddam" is one of the most apt and visceral responses to violence against us.

Like "Mississippi Goddam," this book concludes with a brief discussion of contemporary resistance to violence against Black women and girls. We are leading the charge in attempting to reshape the nation or, for some us, to abolish the nation as we know it.[27] Three of the most prominent rallying cries thus far this century, #BlackLivesMatter, #SayHerName, and #MeToo were coined by Black women.[28] Addressing antiBlack police violence and the pervasiveness of sexual violence, these hashtags and movements build on a legacy of Black women's resistance. Black women and girls have always been at the forefront of struggles for justice. As historian Martha Jones declared, we are the vanguard.[29]

It is in many ways unsurprising that these formidable, contemporary movements were formally founded and largely organized by Black women. Like Black women and girls of previous generations dating back to the transatlantic slave trade, today we fight back against multiple forms of violence and unlivable living through numerous organizations, campaigns, initiatives, and everyday acts of resistance. Contemporary Black women's activism in response to violence and unlivable living has a deliberate focus on those living at the margins. We continue to wrestle with and refuse to remain silent about violence against us. Our experiences as both victims and resisters constitute the archive I mine. This archive doesn't simply tell us what we've endured; it reveals many of the ways we push back and protest against the seemingly unending reality of violence against us. While we have not always been triumphant, a belief that "it is our duty to fight for our freedom," underpins an unflinching commitment to justice.[30]

The Archive of AntiBlack Violence

It's essential when studying violence against Black women and girls to look for the silences, the elisions, and the absences. This "looking" practice opened up the possibility of finding those on the margins and recognizing what political scientist Cathy Cohen identified as "the heightened stratification of marginal communities."[31] Because we exist on the margins, it's easy for us to be overlooked and written out of predominating narratives about how white supremacy, capitalism, and patriarchy operate in the United States. *America, Goddam* engages a looking practice that presumes violence as an ever-present reality or possibility for marginalized communities. Furthermore, I take seriously the specificity of unpacking how numerous oppressive systems operate interdependently in the lives of Black women and girls. The presumptions undergirding this excavation aren't unfounded. They connect to a history of violence as well as an archive too rarely used when uncovering harsh truths about white supremacy, patriarchy, and capitalism. The past provides us with a road map to now and insights for us to build new futures.

When it comes to the archive of antiBlack violence, I am struck by how infrequently many of us engage the inglorious history of violence against Black women and girls to illustrate the gravity of contemporary antiBlackness. It is the deaths and near-deaths of cisgender Black boys and men that predominate how we understand the ubiquity of antiBlackness. While it is not a matter of displacing the importance of what has happened and happens to Black men and boys, antiBlack violence against Black women and girls often fails to garner the kind of attention its gravity warrants. It is the assassinations of Medgar and the murder of Emmett Till that we reference to historicize antiBlack violence in the mid-twentieth century.[32] It's rarely the rape of Recy Taylor[33] or the murders of Denise, Carole, Addie, and Cynthia that serve as historical exemplars. To center Black women and girls in how we historicize Jim Crow–era violence isn't just about adding to and stirring existing narratives about antiBlack violence. The truth of antiBlack violence includes the experiences of Black people of all genders. There's something more at stake in remembering and documenting the depths and contours of what white supremacist and patriarchal violence did and does to Black communities.

The archive of antiBlack violence across all eras of U.S. history has an abundance of examples of what Black women and girls endured. The reality of Black womanhood and girlhood during slavery was that the body could be violated at any moment. In an interview with Fabiola Cineas for Vox about the *Vanity Fair* cover, historian Jessica M. Johnson asserted that "you don't need stripes to show the abject experience of slavery for the black feminine form. The exposed back, the exposed shoulder, and a lot of the archive of slavery will also expose the breasts—all of that was used to signal a kind of availability that was both hypersexualized and hyperviolent."[34] Abjection literally means the state of being cast off. Labeling Black women and girls as criminal, lascivious, and uncontrollable provides justifications for violence against us and for casting us off. This is the archive I engage to contextualize contemporary violence against us.

For many who at least recognize the pervasiveness of anti-Black violence, the enslaved Black body was male, the strange fruit hung from poplar trees were Black men, and the people being disproportionately killed by the police are *only* Black men and boys. *America, Goddam* does not dispute or refute the importance of this enduring and still unfolding history of violence against Black men and boys. My intention here is not to diminish or erase a distinct history of racial, gender, and sexual violence against Black men and boys either. I seek to expand how we think about state violence such as police brutality and how we address other forms of violence that Black women and girls encounter, such as intracommunal violence, which too often occurs at the hands of Black men and boys. When we survive intracommunal violence, we often risk being at the mercy of a broader criminalizing system.

To be clear, this is not an oppression Olympics. It's a call for specificity—an accounting of both the similar and distinct ways Black women and girls in the early twenty-first century experience violence and unlivable living. It means considering the shared experiences of police brutality and the criminalization of poverty alongside the distinct ways we are affected by those experiences.[35] A fuller, though not exhaustive accounting of what violence against Black women and girls looks like in the early twenty-first century requires naming the numerous institutions, groups, and systems that perpetrate harm against us. It would be dishonest and frankly inaccurate to leave intracommunal violence out of that discussion. Our stories with violence and unlivable living must and should be told, no matter who inflicts the harm. Patriarchy is a violent force that harms people of all genders and especially women and girls; it has operated and continues to operate alongside and in conjunction with white supremacy and capitalism to position Black women and girls as perpetually disposable and vulnerable to violence. When we look at the historical record, we can more clearly understand why Breonna Taylor's killing is illustrative as opposed to exceptional or why we rarely hear about missing Black girls. We can trace the trajectory of the interdependent death-dealing superstructure that's harmed and killed Black women and girls through hundreds of years in the United States.

History Unfolding: AntiBlackness, Misogynoir, and Multiple Jeopardy

There's a legible chronology from which we can learn about the depths and expanse of violence against Black women and girls in the United States. The subjection of Black women and girls in the U.S. to various forms of violence, surveillance, exploitation, and containment has formidable roots in the dank and dark spaces built to render captive Africans as a "commodity" for productive and reproductive labor. Enslaved Black women and girls forcibly labored as workers in numerous arenas and as reproducers of an enslaved workforce. What happened to captive African women embodied "what racial slavery actually meant."[36] Denigrating ideas about Blackness and womanhood formed during the transatlantic slave trade. These ideas morphed into new ideas that supported race-based and gendered subjugation in the colonial era. Enslaved women of African descent in the early modern period existed in a world that "came into being through innumerable acts of violence and violation."[37] These included assaults; torture; deprivation of food, water, and medical care; sexual violence; and the deliberate destruction of kinship and familial ties through punitive and lucrative separations. White supremacy, capitalism, and patriarchy converged into a powerful force in the lives of enslaved Africans. Conceptions of race, Blackness, and gender substantively evolved from the earliest years of the transatlantic slave trade through the 1800s in ways that reinforced the idea that Black women and girls were disposable.

The codification of antiBlackness led to gender-specific ways of maintaining white supremacy and patriarchy. The criminalization and negation of Black womanhood via the law resulted in rampant exploitation and brutalization. It barred these women from any form of legal redress.[38] Laws, social and cultural practices and customs, and the hyperexploitative demands of a newly established nation built on white supremacy, racial slavery, economic exploitation, Indigenous genocide, imperialist campaigns, as well as other forms of violence. The combination of these death-dealing, exclusionary, and harmful systems, customs, and practices rendered Black women and girls "unprotected" and easily criminalized for merely having the audacity to survive.

Afforded neither the protection of "womanhood" or "whiteness," the category of Black woman is predicated on an impossible negotiation of devalued statuses. Slave auctioneers and owners didn't flinch or show an ounce of compassion when mothers cried out as their children were sold away or when whipped for not calling the four-year-old child of a slave owner, "Marse."[39] Black women's anguish went unfelt. Their value as laborers conferred their "worth." We were and are deemed either perpetrators of violence or inviolable. To be inviolable meant that Black women were unassailable, unrapeable, and impervious to pain. The legacies of these figurations remain unflappably intact and are at the heart of many of the stories in this book.

In the aftermath of Emancipation, the maintenance of this devaluation resulted in remixed iterations of Black women's inviolability. From organized rapes to assaults of Black domestic laborers, Black women's bodies and their labor became primary sites on which Jim Crow–era antiBlackness manifested. As historians such as Sarah Haley detail, the criminalization of Black women and womanhood during the Jim Crow era exemplified and established a persisting legacy of Black women's humanity being illegible.[40] Black women and girls were further denied access to "womanhood" and "girlhood." Appeals to the pedestal of womanhood or girlhood for safety, protection, and vulnerability didn't work for Black women and girls in the Jim Crow era. It only kind of worked for white women and girls. The myth of "monstrous Black womanhood," which strove to defeminize Black women, took firm hold in the late nineteenth century and reverberates to the present.[41] It's easy to criminalize persons viewed as inherently monstrous. A monster doesn't get empathy, care, or love.

During the Jim Crow era, the criminal punishment system grew.[42] The system expanded alongside and in part because of the "stigmatization of crime as 'black.'"[43] As historian Khalil Gibran Muhammad asserts in *The Condemnation of Blackness: Race, Crime, and the Making of Modern Urban America,* "African American criminality became one of the most widely accepted bases for justifying prejudicial thinking, discriminatory treatment, and/or acceptance of racial violence as an instrument of public safety."[44] The Jim Crow-era criminal punishment system also built on racial and gender hierarchies entrenched from both the transatlantic slave trade and chattel slavery to perpetuate existing and to formulate new racist and sexist notions of protection.[45] Within each "era" in U.S. history, a shoring up of white supremacy and patriarchy via a reification of antiBlack and sexist myths about Black womanhood and girlhood occurs.

The technologies and practices of white supremacy adapt and evolve to remain entrenched. In the twenty-first century, Black women's and girls' status is one of perpetual vulnerability and disposability. Although it would be irresponsible to merely liken or compare ahistorically the experiences of Black women chained together on slave ships in the 1700s or on chain gangs in the early 1900s in the U.S. South to some of the experiences of Black women and girls I discuss in this book, understanding the fixity of disposability politics, their origins, and their afterlives is at the core of thinking about how we fit into a long history of violence. Our lives exist outside of any notion of legal protection and overindex as criminal. Violence against us lurks around every corner or while we are sleeping next to our partners in beds in Louisville, Kentucky. The inability to see Black women as victims or as actors negotiating multiple forms of oppression and structural barriers is at the heart of contemporary antiBlack politics of disposability. Understanding the historical politics of U.S. racial slavery and the Jim Crow era helps me contextualize a still-unfolding history of violent indifference toward Black women and girls.

The work to uncover this contemporary history requires a penetrative attention to silences and death-dealing logics that stretch back hundreds of years. This kind of historical approach offers possibility for hearing the more recent screams of those being killed softly and spectacularly. *Soft* killings refer to those that are slow and intentionally imperceptible. *Spectacular* killings are those fatal incidents when a life is snuffed out; they happen in an instant, a moment. Our screams of pain and resistance magnify how antiBlackness, misogynoir, and multiple jeopardy converge in the lives of Black women and girls. AntiBlackness, misogynoir, and multiple jeopardy are the primary lenses through which I contextualize the pervasiveness of violence against us. Individually, each of these forces can be death-dealing. The conjoining of these oppressive forces provides a pretext for everything from racist and sexist stereotypes to being killed by police while asleep in your own home.

AntiBlackness

Many definitions of racism exist, most of which account for the ways racial prejudice *and* power converge to facilitate discriminatory practices, beliefs, systems, and institutions. Although racism can exist without violence, it's important to understand racism, and particularly antiBlack racism, as a matter of life or death. In *Golden Gulag: Prisons, Surplus, Crisis, and Opposition in Globalizing California,* geographer and prison scholar Ruth Wilson Gilmore defines racism as "the state-sanctioned or extralegal production and exploitation of ground-differentiated vulnerability to premature death."[46] Gilmore's definition is compelling and worth unpacking. It indicts the state as well as other institutions and systems for producing and exploiting vulnerabilities based on race. Premature death as the endgame always strikes me when I return to Gilmore's definition. I immediately think of recent stories and data about the number of Black women dying while or soon after giving birth.[47] In the moment of giving life, we are losing ours. Violence and marginalization create conditions for premature deaths. This definition of racism not only offers the meaning; it emphasizes the stakes. Racism kills.

AntiBlackness is a more pointed and arguably, precise term for the violence and unlivable living Black people endure.[48] Yes, racism plays a huge role as well. But as kihana miraya ross noted in her June 4, 2020, op-ed in the *New York Times,* "'racism' falls short of fully capturing what Black people in this country are facing." Ross aptly assesses that "it's more than just 'racism against black people.' That oversimplifies and defangs it." AntiBlackness is "a theoretical framework that illuminates society's inability to recognize our humanity—the disdain, disregard and disgust for our existence."[49] AntiBlackness "is about the debasement of Black humanity, utter indifference to Black suffering, and the denial of Black people's right to exist."[50] Whereas Gilmore's definition of *racism* rightfully centers on premature death, *antiBlackness* helps us flesh out even further the ghastly history and far-reaching effects of that "disdain, disregard, and disgust" for Black folks simply living and breathing.

As Black studies scholar Rinaldo Walcott reminds us, "Any analysis that does not contend with antiblackness as central to modern life is blind to what exactly the modern means."[51] What I take away from this is that when we decenter antiBlackness in our understandings of the modern world, we willfully ignore one of its important and enduring features. Without question, violence against Black women and girls stems from this disregard, disdain, denial, and inability to acknowledge our personhood. The hashtag #BlackLivesMatter for example, directly responds to antiBlackness through asserting the worth of Black life in a white supremacist world that time and time again refuses our mattering. To even have to proclaim that "Black lives matter" and know that people will dispute it, or counter with "all lives matter," is a result of entrenched and learned antiBlackness. In what world would saying "Black lives matter" prompt a rejoinder? A fundamentally anti-Black one.

Misogynoir

Misogynoir, a term coined by Moya Bailey and co-popularized by @ thetrudz, "describes the anti-Black racist misogyny that Black women experience."[52] Misogynoir often plays a role in violence and other forms of violation against Black girls and women. It's extant in policing, medical/healthcare systems, and mass incarceration. A Black woman killed by police while sleeping in her bed can be regarded as a "threat" because of the particular form of racist misogyny we endure. Misogynoir also factors into intracommunal gender and sexual violence. Understanding the fear and hatred that people, even other Black people, have toward us is integral to grappling with our vulnerability to violence. Black women overindex as victims of gender and sexual violence, and in most cases, this violence occurs in domestic, intimate, and intracommunal settings.

Contempt and disdain also show up in places like our schools, where Black girls are disproportionately suspended, harshly disciplined, and dismissed as troublemakers.[53] In New York City, for example, Black girls were eleven times more likely to be suspended from school than their white peers.[54] A state-by-state analysis conducted by the ACLU in the late 2010s showed that in almost every U.S. state, Black girls were significantly more likely to be arrested at school than white girls.[55] Harsher disciplining and criminalization aren't occurring because Black girls misbehave more; misogynoir creates a context in which their behaviors are judged more harshly.[56] Cofounder of the National Black Women's Institute Monique W. Morris makes it painfully clear: "Black girls are being criminalized in and by the very places that should help them thrive."[57] Misogynoir doesn't wait until adulthood to show up in our lives. It starts early in shaping our lives. We learn and quite often internalize ruinous messages about ourselves.

In addition to misogynoir, Black trans women combat transmisogynoir, a distinct form of misogynoir rooted in transphobia and rigid gender binaries and policing.[58] Transmisogynoir is at the heart of dozens of vicious assaults and killings of Black trans women over the past few years. In December, actress and trans activist Laverne Cox went on Instagram Live to detail a transphobic attack she and her friend had recently survived.[59] Cox not only spoke about what happened that day; she linked what happened to her and her friend to a long history of antitrans violence. Despite being one of the most famous trans people in the U.S., she is still vulnerable to violence rooted in transmisogynoir. It is also notable that 2020 was the deadliest year so far for Black trans women in terms of homicides.[60] Accounting for the lack of reporting and misreporting, it's possible that even more Black trans women and nonbinary people have been killed than available data suggests.[61] It's a crisis compounded by conjoined oppressive forces. These compounding forces create a distinct context for Black women's and girls' violability.

Multiple Jeopardy

Black women and girls also experience what Deborah King identified as multiple jeopardy. The weight of several forms of oppression such as racism, sexism, poverty, ableism, queerphobia, and transphobia form an "interdependent control system."[62] Many of the Black women and girls I discuss in this book are multiply marginalized. We experience violence and unlivable living caused by the multiplicative combination of several forms of oppression.

Being a Black, poor, queer, and disabled woman means various systems of inequity and injustice combine to wage war against you. Policing sees each of these statuses and identities as "less-than," and consequently, Black women who occupy numerous "less-than" categories experience even more insidious politics of disposability. When we consider multiple jeopardy, it becomes more apparent why a poor Black queer disabled woman might be particularly vulnerable to everything from houselessness to police violence. Antipoor, antiqueer, antiBlack, misogynoiristic, and ableist ideas come together to create unlivable situations for those at the margins of the margins. The deep intertwining of multiple forms of oppression, therefore, makes it nearly impossible to identify a single cause for how Black women and girls experience violence. It's usually not just one oppressive force. It's the combination and their emboldening of one another.

The combined force of antiBlackness, misogynoir, and multiple jeopardy demands that we follow a death-dealing trail of violence and unlivable living from rapes aboard slave ships to Black women killed during recklessly executed mental wellness checks in their homes by police officers. The unique vulnerability of Black women and girls spans a nearly five-hundred-year history in the land that became the United States through Indigenous genocide and forced removal.[63] This vulnerability exists at the intersection of antiBlackness, misogynoir, and multiple jeopardy. Being multiply marginalized, however, can contribute to the emergence of multiple consciousness for justice. To understand how we are multiply situated as devalued and disposable opens up a possibility for struggling for justice in more robust and effective ways.

I use an intersectional approach, indebted to the work of legal scholar and #SayHerName report coauthor Kimberlé Crenshaw, to explore how people are multiply situated among differing structures of power.[64] Intersectionality, at its origins, took up violence against women of color and the response of the criminal punishment system to that violence. Contrary to popular misconceptions and widespread misusage, "to be intersectional" isn't an embodiment of multiple marginalized identities. As a Black feminist, I commit to accounting for where the power resides. An intersectional approach opens a necessary space to understand how power marginalizes, subordinates, exploits, or even erases the lived experiences of those whose lives are negatively affected by interconnected forms of oppression, namely Black women and girls. The concept of intersectionality, like multiple jeopardy, builds on a tremendous and diverse Black feminist tradition of Black women such as Maria Stewart, Anna Julia Cooper, Ida B. Wells, Charlotta Bass, Mary Church Terrell, Frances Beale, Toni Cade Bambara, Claudia Jones, and the cofounders of the Combahee River Collective, accounting for how structures and systems of power distinctly affect Black women. Throughout history, we've found ways to contextualize the reach and depth of violation. Contending with what renders us perpetually violable is a foundational step for comprehending a more recent history of antiBlack violence and unlivable living.

The Stakes: The Most Disrespected, Neglected, and Unprotected

America, Goddam is in an intergenerational dialogue with the Lady in Brown's opening poetic verse in Ntozake Shange's choreopoem *For Colored Girls Who Have Considered Suicide When the Rainbow Is Enuf.* Shange wrote about the "maddening screams & the soft strains of death."[65] What Shange identifies are screams unheard, unfelt, and unseen. She delineates the necessity of a multisensory response to "these soft strains of death." Black women and girls need to be heard, seen, and held. In the choreopoem, Shange also calls for someone to "sing a black girl's song" and to "let her be born / & handled warmly."[66] To be handled warmly is oppositional to the handling that occurs under conditions of antiBlackness, misogynoir, and multiple jeopardy. The Black feminist ethical framework of *America, Goddam* evolves out of the desire to comprehend and contextualize the "soft strains of death" and to handle Black people warmly through examining both still-evolving archives of violence against Black women and girls and our resistance. Handling this topic warmly also means attempting to remember the living, breathing joys of those assailed by the violence I discuss. It is imperative to me as a Black feminist to attempt to talk about all victims in life-affirming ways that do not reduce them to violent and sometimes death-dealing encounters. I take up this difficult subject as a Black feminist historian, which for me entails a robust ethical framework for engaging with an ever-expanding archive.

The impulse behind this book is also deeply personal. I have experienced violence and harm at the hands of the police, intimate partners, strangers, medical practitioners, and colleagues. Growing up, I also bore witness to numerous acts of violence against Black women and girls that haunt me to this day. Our stories didn't get mass media coverage or even widespread outrage from people I thought should or would care. The pain of screaming into a void while fighting alongside my fellow Black women and girls to merely be healthy, housed, fed, decriminalized, and valued is at the heart of this book. I felt compelled to use my training as a Black feminist historian to tell *some* of this heartbreaking and resistance-filled story.

The first "nonacademic" piece I ever wrote for a mainstream publication focused on the history of police violence and antiBlack violence, and more broadly against Black women and girls, in 2015. I went to archives I knew. I joined a gradually growing chorus of folks demanding that we don't erase the stories of violence against Black women and girls. In addition to the historical record, I knew all too well and too intimately how pervasive violence and other forms of systemic harm are among the Black women and girls in my life, including myself. What I knew as a historian of Black women and as a survivor of numerous acts of violence was that there is a heartrending story to tell. Telling this story demanded a willingness to engage an excruciating past and compelled me to look into my own life and lay bare *some* of my own truths as a Black woman. *America, Goddam* includes stories best told through the archival and the personal. It's one thing to write about Black women and girls; it's quite another to write from among us. I bear witness and withness to what's on these pages. As my fellow Black feminist scholar Alexis Pauline Gumbs reminded me as I finished writing this book, this is sacred work.

Early twenty-first-century experiences of Black women and girls with violence and unlivable living are part of a still-growing archive that reveals the systemic effects of misogynoir, antiBlackness, and multiple jeopardy on us. "Goddam" is an instinctive response to politics of disposability and the perniciousness of unlivable living. Each chapter of this book focuses on a particular form of violence Black women and girls experience in the twenty-first century in the U.S. This book is by no means exhaustive in terms of mapping *all* forms of recent violence against us. For example, I do not do an in-depth dive into the specific arena of violence against Black girls in schools. The work of scholars such as the aforementioned Monique Morris and Ruth Nicole Brown and Bettina Love brings into sharp focus the pervasiveness of school-based violence in the lives of Black girls. Black girls in K–12 schooling experience the carceral continuum, which is the broader nexus of state-based, criminalizing interventions into the lives of marginalized youth.[67] Schools too often play an integral role in harming Black girls.

Although this book focuses solely on the U.S., a global phenomenon of violence against us prevails. What's happening in the U.S. isn't singular or unmatched in terms of gravity. It's also important to acknowledge how U.S. imperialist and colonizing policies and interventions in places across the world contribute to and, in some cases, precipitate violence against Black women and girls in numerous nations. My "goddam" extends to all instances of us being impacted by how the U.S. operates around ideas and practices of antiBlackness and misogynoir both within and beyond our fictive borders. My expertise in U.S. history, coupled with most of my personal experiences with violence occurring in the United States, undergirds the U.S.-centric focus of this book. I strove to take a deep dive into a distinct geopolitical and personal context.

Doing well by Black women and girls means being specific and precise in the ways we discuss violability and vulnerability. This kind of specificity allows for making connections across places that acknowledge both similarities and differences. *America, Goddam* can and should be read alongside a growing body of work highlighting violence against Black women and girls across the world in places such as but not limited to Brazil, Canada, France, England, and South Africa. I am inspired by and indebted to scholars whose work wrestles with violence against Black women and girls on a global scale. The forms and experiences of violence centered in this book offer critical insights into the complex and vast terrain of violence against us in the United States and, hopefully, prompt and add to conversations about violence against us across the globe.

"Say Her Name: Policing Is Violence" builds on the growing body of work focused on police violence against Black women, girls, and nonbinary people. This chapter deals explicitly with how police violence manifests in the lives of Black women and girls in spaces often considered "safe." Police violence against us often occurs in our homes or the homes of our loved ones. Policing stretches beyond the public domain of streets and corners and into the spaces where we lay our heads to rest and escape the weariness of the world. "The Caged Bird Sings: The Criminal Punishment System" documents the unique effects of mass incarceration on Black women and girls through specific sites of twenty-first-century carceral encounters. I explore Black women's deaths in police custody and Black women and girls incarcerated for acts of self-defense. "Up against the Wind: Intracommunal Violence" homes in on Black intracommunal violence, specifically intraracial violence, that victimizes us. From domestic violence homicides to rape and sexual assault, we experience intracommunal violence at a rate that exceeds our white counterparts. Moving away from pathological arguments about inherently violent or aggressive Black men and boys, this chapter explores the contours and roles of misogyny, patriarchy, internalized antiBlackness, homophobia, and transphobia in intracommunal violent encounters.

"Violability Is a Preexisting Condition: Dying in the Medical Industrial Complex" centers on Black girls' and women's encounters with healthcare and, more specifically, the medical industrial complex. From alarming rates of maternal morbidity and infant mortality to being seen as impervious to pain and untrustworthy patients, we endure harrowing obstacles in the pursuit of healthcare. We are uncritically overdetermined as "unhealthy" and blamed for our premature deaths and chronic illnesses without any recognition of multiple factors contributing to our health and wellbeing. This chapter chronicles medical misogynoir, while tackling how antiBlackness in healthcare negatively affects outcomes for us. "Unlivable: The Deadly Consequences of Poverty" delves into the erasure of the social safety net. Whereas most of the violence presented in the previous chapters documents and contextualizes physical violence and specific encounters, this chapter digs into death-bound conditions. What does the reality of surviving as a poor Black woman or girl in this nation look like? The chapter also highlights efforts to connect unlivable living to more direct violence. Houselessness, food insecurity, and lack of access to clean water are just some of the ways poor Black women and girls experience unlivable living. Survival under these conditions literally requires making life or death choices daily.

"They Say I'm Hopeless"—a personal interlude—focuses on the damage caused by stereotypes and tropes. By using my own experiences with violence and how stereotypes and tropes affected my interpretation of what happened to me and others in my community, I unpack the power of words and images in normalizing violence against Black women and girls. The internalization of harmful narratives about myself and others like me kept me from identifying harm. In part, this chapter offers an even more personal dive into how I came to understand the pervasiveness of and complicity with violence in my life and those of Black women and girls in my life. Devaluing ideas about us that attempt to evacuate our personhood are harmful yet so common that they easily become undetectable.

"We Were Not Meant to Survive," the concluding chapter, offers some hope by briefly exploring the contemporary struggle for justice led by Black women and girls. We fight for ourselves, which, more often than not, means we fight for the actualization of justice for *all*. We struggle against violence, unlivable living, criminalization, and what Gilmore identifies as "organized abandonment."[68] We push back against systems predicated on casting us as disposable. Often because of enduring the weight of several simultaneous oppressive forces, we can develop a multiple consciousness.[69] An awareness of multiple systems of inequity working with one another enlivens how we can and do enter the struggle for justice. It's a moment of breath in a book that is in many ways unrelenting. While I remain unconvinced that we, as a nation and, more broadly, as a global community, invest in making this world safer, healthier, and more livable for Black women and girls, I remain steadfast in my belief in the collective power of oppressed people to change the world. More than that, I believe in our ability to make new worlds.

No matter what's stacked against us, I am undaunted in the audacity of dreaming and fighting for otherwise. I have faith in us—Black women, girls, gender nonconforming and nonbinary people. As I finished this book, I became even more emboldened in my convictions around the possibilities for envisioning, upending, and transforming. I found breath. Engaging the stories of Black women and girls is a prerequisite for divesting from death-dealing politics in the United States. "Goddam" is my gut response and my demand for us to be heard. We imagine a world not yet created. This imaginative force stands as a powerful weapon against a politics of inhumanity and disposability. That force brings together screams of pain and resistance across space and time. It affirms both the responsibility and right to struggle for justice. And to win, I hope.

1 *Say Her Name*

Policing Is Violence

Throughout my childhood, my car time with my dad was one of my favorite parts of the day. He would often stop by the liquor store down the street from our apartment in Northeast Washington, D.C., and get me a snack and play my mom's numbers. I knew he was in a good mood when he got a Reese's Cup and a bag of Grandma Utz chips. Driving down Benning Road in the shadow of the crumbling Washington Football Team's (then known as the Redskins) stadium, RFK, you could find me and him on any given afternoon in the 1980s listening to some grown ass music. Some days it was Al Green. Other days it was Run DMC and Salt'N'Pepa. My dad loved music and exposed me to a robust Black musical tradition. Unlike some of my friends' parents, he had an affinity for rap music. He even made sure I heard the more explicit songs.

One of those explicit songs was N.W.A.'s "Fuck Tha Police." The first time I recollect hearing it, I was riding with my dad. I bobbed my head as Ice Cube rapped:

Fuck the police comin' straight from the underground
A young nigga got it bad 'cause I'm brown

And not the other color so police think
They have the authority to kill a minority[1]

My dad looked at me as we both nodded our heads. He asked me if I understood what they were saying. I didn't fully get it at the tender age of six. I was clear though that these "boys didn't like the police." He laughed and said, "With good reason." Listening to "Fuck Tha Police" with my dad is perhaps one of the best examples of my parents using rap music to spark a conversation with me about the world around me. My dad worked in the criminal punishment system as both a corrections officer and a probation officer in the 1980s and 1990s. Knowing it was never too soon to begin educating his Black child about the realities of being Black in the U.S., he felt it was time for me to learn some harsh truths about policing.

Neither of my parents shielded me from the pulse of culture and politics, particularly the more controversial or "profane" parts. They embraced rap music and, at times, used it to teach me about race and racism in the United States. My dad knew I wouldn't encounter "Officer Friendly," a jovial, civil servant charged with the obligation to "protect and serve" me and my community. My dad also knew that more often than not, "protect and serve" didn't extend to me. He didn't want me to fear police officers per se; however, he did want me to understand the context for such an explicit callout of the folks I frequently saw patrolling my NE Washington, D.C., neighborhood. From then until I started using "cuss" words, it was "fudge the police."

Throughout my childhood and young adulthood, I personally bore witness to the violence of policing, to the point where saying "violent policing" felt redundant. Police equaled violence from what I gathered. I saw officers violently handle unhoused people on my block. Living just a short drive from the U.S. Capitol but clearly in another world, the police harassed young folks kicking it on corners. I heard cops call Black women in my neighborhood crack whores and their children crack babies. The ease with which they showed contempt and utter disgust for my neighbors stuck with me. They didn't see us as persons with loved ones, hopes, dreams, flaws, and struggles. We were the enemy. For me, it was never a few bad apples. Police signaled violence as much as if not more than the young boys in my neighborhood participating in the booming street drug economy of the late 1980s and early 1990s.

The presence of cops in my neighborhood and, eventually, in my schools didn't make me feel protected either. Although a lot of illicit activity went down in my poor/working-class Black neighborhood located near the corner of Benning Road and East Capitol Street, it became clear to me by the time I was a teenager that economic deprivation and stagnation and the public health crisis caused by crack cocaine was at the root of the violence I witnessed there. When I was growing up, cops seemed to be everywhere—in the parking lot in front of the corner store a couple of blocks from my apartment and at Benjamin Stoddert, the recreational center the kids in my neighborhood frequented. We couldn't get a quick snack at the corner store or play tag without being under the watchful eye of those incessantly arresting, deriding, and assaulting folks in our community. As a child, it made me feel under attack. My folks were overdetermined as criminal.

The neighborhoods of my peers at Sidwell Friends, the elite private school in upper Northwest Washington I attended from seventh grade to twelfth weren't surveilled in any way close to what I experienced growing up in D.C. or living in Prince George's County,

Maryland. When my mom got pregnant with me, she informed my dad that her baby was going to Sidwell. For her, Sidwell would put me in rooms and give me opportunities I would never have access to at my predominantly Black, poor, and working class-serving neighborhood school. My mom wanted to expose me to a world from which most people in my community were cut off. I wanted to go to school with my friends. I also thought I would never fit in with these "rich white kids" who lived west of Rock Creek Park, an invisible divide between the haves and have nots in a then-Chocolate City.

Most of my Sidwell folks lived in either affluent, predominantly white neighborhoods or historic, "old money" Black neighborhoods. When I got to Sidwell, I was in awe of how big my peers' houses were. Some of them had staff. Others mentioned vacation homes. Summer was both a verb and a noun for my peers whose primary and secondary residences were in some of the most expensive zip codes in the U.S. Some of my Sidwell friends were oddly curious about where I lived. In eighth grade, a white girl asked me "if I worried about getting shot every day." I laughed nervously and told her I was more worried about cute boys and fly clothes than getting shot. I tried to find ways to connect with my new peers, but some of their questions and what I'd seen growing up made it abundantly clear that we lived in different worlds.

Funny enough, I saw a lot of illegal drug use at high school parties thrown in affluent neighborhoods, but guess where I could always find the police? Not to dry snitch or anything, but in high school I saw white kids do everything from mushrooms to cocaine. Although a lot of my private school peers just engaged in heavy drinking and some occasional weed, drug and alcohol consumption were weekly activities. A few of their parties got broken up by police. There were a couple of memorable nights where they even got citations for underage drinking. For the most part though, their neighborhoods weren't policed. They faced little to no consequences for seemingly clear violations of the law. If anything, the police gladly looked the other way and considered their behavior "youthful transgressions." They were never in danger of being seen as criminals. By my sophomore year at Sidwell, I came to understand that there were those who police committed to protecting and serving. Then there was us, the targeted and criminalized.

One of the other defining moments that shaped my perception of policing occurred before I arrived at Sidwell—the beating of Rodney King. My parents could've shielded eight-year-old me from watching the video of four Los Angeles Police Department (LAPD) officers—Stacey Koon, Laurence Powell, Timothy Wind, and Theodore Briseno—viciously beat King, but they opted to let me see this previral, viral video as further evidence of the violence of policing. I'd seen this kind of police violence before, but now the world could see what I, my parents, and my community saw on a far too regular basis. This confirmation anchored my growing fear, disdain, and anxiety about police. The uprising that followed the acquittal of these officers was my first encounter with watching the rage of marginalized people set cities on fire in response to police violence. It wouldn't be the last time. Burned out buildings can be rebuilt though. There's no justice for those grievously harmed or killed by police.

As my consciousness evolved regarding police violence, I noted how few of the victims discussed in mainstream media were Black women and girls. I also recognized comparatively less community mobilization when police violated Black women and girls in my neighborhood. What I witnessed personally and what I saw on television greatly differed. Black people of all genders were treated as enemy combatants by police officers. The most significant uprising of my childhood pivoted around police assaulting a Black man, but with my own eyes I'd seen cops assault Black sex workers and women living with debilitating drug addiction in my neighborhood. On both a local and a national level, I rarely saw coverage of that or campaigns highlighting police violence against us. This chapter speaks into the void I felt then and adds to a growing number of voices demanding that we grapple with police brutality against Black women and girls right now.

Apart from the response to the nonindictment of the officers who killed twenty-six-year-old Breonna Taylor, cities seemingly only burned in response to direct police violence against *some* cisgender Black men and boys. The killings of Michael Brown, Eric Garner, Tamir Rice, and George Floyd compelled folks to take to the streets using the "language of the unheard."[2] Although the founder of @seenblackgirls, @simimoonlught, tweeted, "I see you, black girl. You'll never be invisible to me. I'll burn cities down in your name," back in July 2017, the response to the nonindictment of the cops who killed Breonna was the first time I saw a groundswell of people willing to see the murder of a Black woman as a catalyst for a sustained national uprising. This rallying around a Black woman was unusual given what political theorist Shatema Threadcraft identifies as a "spectacular violent death deficit," whereby the killings of Black women and girls rarely garner the organizing and mobilizing efforts around Black people killed by police.[3] While still not as widespread as the unrest that occurred in the aftermath of some of the more well-known and spectacular incidents of fatal police violence, Breonna's murder and the nonindictment of the cops responsible for it did bring tens of thousands of people into the streets to proclaim the unjustness of U.S. policing.

Police violence has not only cost billions of dollars in settlements to the loved ones of those harmed or killed by cops. It's also cost us billions of dollars in rebuilding in the aftermath of these fatal encounters with government-paid and protected employees.[4] It's important to explicitly call out police violence as the root cause of uprisings in the aftermath of yet another Black person killed by police. The destruction of property doesn't occur if someone's life hadn't ended at the hands of violent policing. While it may be easy to dismiss the efficacy of setting cities on fire, policing lit the matches and provided the lighter fluid for those responding to an unchanging pattern. In a criminal punishment system in which property matters more than the lives of Black people, many folks condemn uprisings as unwarranted and unjustifiable responses to police violence. Even those who recognize systemic issues in U.S. policing make false equivalencies between police violence and rebellions against it.[5] The refusal to see police violence for what it is and the ripple effects it has on communities resurfaces every time an uprising against fatal police brutality against Black men and boys occurs.

The Ferguson Uprising, which included thousands of people led by residents of Ferguson, Missouri, who erupted in protest in the aftermath of Michael Brown's killing by Officer Darren Wilson, was my first experience as an adult witnessing a rebellion against antiBlack, racist policing.[6] From decrying racism in policing to reports, books, articles, and studies about the criminalization of Black men and boys, I saw a growing abundance of compelling takes on the state of policing in the United States. It was refreshing to see more folks raising questions and concerns about both the origins and state of policing in this nation. What pushed me to say something, however, was how few of these reinvigorated conversations included police violence against Black women and girls. Nevertheless, it finally felt like we approached a moment of semi-collective consciousness around this issue.

In May 2015, the African American Policy Forum and the Center for Intersectionality and Policy Studies led by writer, attorney, and activist Andrea Ritchie and critical legal studies and race theory scholar Kimberlé Crenshaw released the *Say Her Name: Resisting Police Brutality against Black Women* report. They not only gave us names of Black women and girls killed by police; they offered a framework for understanding the unique susceptibility of Black women and girls to police brutality and suggestions about how to work with communities to achieve racial justice.[7] The report detailed the killing of Black women and girls in recent history and emphasized how infrequently we hear their names or learn about their encounters with fatal police violence. The report was a reckoning. It shed light on the violent premature deaths of dozens of Black women and girls for whom we did not set cities on fire.

Reading the report and revisiting some of my earlier work and the work of other scholars and activists on the history of violence against Black women and girls pushed me further into questioning why cities didn't burn when police harmed and killed us. For the one-year anniversary of the killing of Michael Brown and the Ferguson Uprising, I contributed a piece entitled "Race in the US: Herstory" to a special issue of *Al Jazeera* about the history of state violence against Black women and girls. I ended the piece by proclaiming that "Black women and girls have always been victims of racist terrorising. This is why we must emphatically #SayHerName."[8] I didn't mention that cities hadn't burned in the wake of our deaths at the hands of police, although I acknowledged that the killing of Black women and girls doesn't garner nearly as much attention from media or as much energy from some racial justice activists and organizers as it should. I regret not being more forceful in my denouncement of this erasure. I delicately called on folks, when what needed to be and continues to need to be done is a "callout" of police violence against us.

Here, I build off my 2015 piece and the tremendous work by folks such as Ritchie, Crenshaw, Threadcraft, Monique Morris, Emily Thuma, Joy James, and Beth Richie to grapple with how police violence manifests in the lives of Black women and girls. "Masculinist explorations of racism and policing," as political philosopher Joy James discusses in *Resisting State Violence: Radicalism, Gender, and Race in U.S. Culture,* often minimize the impact of racist police violence on noncisgender men.[9] Police violence against us takes many forms. Police violence frequently occurs in places often considered "private"—our homes and the homes of loved ones. The police killings discussed in this chapter all occurred in a domestic space. The "home" isn't viewed widely as a site for spectacular violence; consequently, even the killings of Black women and girls by police tends to resound as a "more private death."[10] The private rarely galvanizes. Yet Black women are 1.4 times more likely to be killed by police than white women.[11] In other spaces such as classrooms, Black girls encounter criminalization that often leads to police violence in their schools at alarming levels as well.[12]

Without question, police violence against Black women and girls occurs in other spaces, too. It's the allusion of protection that certain settings provide, nevertheless, that stuck out to me. The violence of policing reaches into and beyond our homes in death-dealing ways. It assaults, sexually violates, and kills us with impunity. From a cop demanding, on a public street, that a Black woman remove her tampon during an illegal search to waking up to a storm of bullets barreling into your home as you sleep, police violence against us takes on multiple injurious and sometimes fatal forms.[13] Cities may not burn for us, but our blood is all over the hands of the enforcers of the criminal punishment system.

A Brief History of Policing

Like so many things pertaining to how white supremacy operates in the U.S. in the twenty-first century, policing has roots in the enslavement of captive Africans. One of the first forms of policing in the U.S. was slave patrols, which began in the 1700s.[14] In an effort to maintain the white supremacist and capitalistic order of chattel slavery, white volunteers formed squadrons to brutally reprimand enslaved people for "violations" of plantation rules, trouncing rebellions led by enslaved people, and searching for, capturing, and returning fugitive enslaved people.[15] These patrols were violent arbiters and enforcers of racial capitalism.[16] The wealth generated from the exploitation of enslaved people, as political theorist and Black studies scholar Cedric Robinson argued in *Black Marxism: The Making of the Black Radical Tradition,* intertwined with various forms of racial oppression and produced a social order that embraced the criminalizing and policing of Black people.[17] Capitalism's survival relied and relies on and exploits an "unequal differentiation of human value."[18] Slavery in the Americas epitomized the unjust and inequitable treatment of Black people for the purpose of extracting tremendous economic value. Slave patrols therefore played an integral role in protecting and serving the extractive aims of slave societies.[19]

Free and enslaved Black people feared slave patrols, as these forces could violently stop and search, beat, sexually assault, reenslave, newly enslave, and even kill Black people with impunity.[20] The protection of white wealth was at the heart of slave patrols, as was the brutalization of enslaved people. Some people may challenge whether these patrols formally count as precursors to modern-day law enforcement, but the record and legacy of these patrols are clear. Slave patrols protected and served the interests of white land- and business owners by surveilling, criminalizing, and subjugating enslaved people. The enforcers of the racial and economic order of U.S. society in the eighteenth and early nineteenth centuries designated those who would be protected and served and those who would be criminalized and brutalized. Without question, this designation lives in the blood and bone of modern U.S. policing. As historian W. Marvin Dulaney emphasizes in *Black Police in America,* "the slave patrol was the first distinctly American police system, and it set the pattern of policing that Americans of African descent would experience throughout their history in America."[21] This pattern thrives on violence.

In Boston in 1838, the first publicly funded police force with full-time officers was established. These officers protected the property of businesses. Slave patrols, emboldened by laws that viewed Black people as property, operated with similar intentions as the publicly funded police forces that emerged in the mid-nineteenth century. Even after the Civil War and the emancipation of millions of enslaved people, policing continued to serve the economic interests of white businessmen and landowners. Sheriffs in cities and towns across the nation enforced racial segregation and the legal and extralegal disenfranchisement of recently freed African Americans through intimidation, violence, and threats of incarceration.[22] Businesses, particularly those in rapidly growing cities, used newly formed police forces to crush labor strikes and target those in the workforce who were seen as potential threats to a business's economic interests.[23] Recent immigrant communities joining the U.S. workforce were viewed as potential disruptors of law and order, a laboring "Other," necessitating targeted surveillance. Consequently, law enforcement treated immigrant communities with suspicion, fear, and disdain. Systemic anti-immigrant practices are part of the rotten core of U.S. policing. One need only scratch the surface of the violence U.S. Immigration and Customs Enforcement (ICE) has wreaked in less than two decades thus far to see its roots in anti-immigrant policing that emerged in the nineteenth century.[24]

AntiBlack racism, xenophobia, and economic exploitation undergirded the expansion of law enforcement throughout the late nineteenth and early twentieth centuries. Campaigns to further professionalize police intensified during Prohibition and continued throughout the mid-twentieth century.[25] The spread of police precincts and evolving standards for law and order built on a foundation of violent, unjust, and prejudicial enforcement. The professionalization of U.S. policing didn't alter these core elements; it codified and reified them as integral values and standards. Policing continued to grow in the U.S. throughout the mid- to late twentieth century, as the rampant politicization of "law and order" powered mass incarceration, as well as the hypercriminalization of people of color, poor people, and people with disabilities.[26] The Safe Streets Act of 1968, a key part of President Lyndon B. Johnson's Great Society, invested hundreds of millions of dollars into the "War on Crime."[27] With this funding, Johnson strove to modernize law enforcement and to assist each state in building what historian

Elizabeth Hinton identified as "respective state apparatuses."[28] States also invested their own funds to the collective tune of hundreds of billions of dollars in all aspects of the criminal punishment system, including law enforcement.[29] This rapid expansion increased the number of police encounters with civilians. More sheriffs and more police officers meant more opportunities for criminalizing encounters.

For Black people, this meant an increase in potentially violent contact with police. Although white people are slightly more likely than Black people to have contact with police, Black people encounter a higher rate of the threat of or use of physical force by police officers than do white people.[30] Violent policing leads to mass incarceration, injuries, and deaths. Policing is an essential component of "a massive system of racial and social control."[31] Policing drags people, particularly marginalized people, into the criminal punishment system and brands them as "criminals and felons" deserving of being policed in a way that denies them the most basic civil and human rights.[32] This system demands policing that actively seeks to criminalize, with a pointed focus on those living on the margins. Black women and girls occupy those margins.

Black Women and Policing

For Black women and girls, specifically, though not exclusively, policing rested on a demonization of Black personhood. Prior to the U.S. becoming a nation-state through genocidal violence, laws existed that relied on dehumanizing racial, gender, and sexual stereotypes about captive Black people.[33] The designation of Black women and girls as animalistic and monstrous was embedded in laws and, subsequently, law enforcement during the early eighteenth century.[34] The early modern culture of policing in the U.S. sought to maintain a white supremacist and patriarchal order in which Black women and girls figured prominently as a controlled and exploited, productive and reproductive labor force.[35] Enslaved Black women and girls had value for slave owners because of their work and their ability to give birth to new enslaved people. Slave patrols helped keep this order intact by tracking, capturing, and returning fugitive enslaved people.[36] After the passage of the Act Prohibiting Importation of Slaves of 1807, the reproductive capacity of Black women and girls became even more valuable to a booming economy intimately tied to enslaving and criminalizing Black people.[37] The policing of enslaved Black women and girls contributed to the sustaining and further development of racial capitalism. This is the history on which more recent police violence against women and girls should be contextualized.

One of the more well-publicized cases of fatal police violence against Black women was that of Eula May Love.[38] Killed by LAPD officers in the front yard of her own home in the West Athens/Watts neighborhood of South Los Angeles in January of 1979, Eula's story reveals numerous systemic failures that led to her death. Just six months prior to her violent demise, Eula's husband passed away from sickle cell anemia.[39] Poor Black women don't get any time to grieve though; there's no breath or pause for such a tremendous loss of love, companionship, and semblance of stability. She became a widowed parent of three young daughters and quickly accrued a mountain of debt from medical, utility, and mortgage bills.[40] The struggle to survive in the aftermath of her husband's death placed the thirty-nine-year-old Black woman in a precarious position.

On January 3, 1979, the Southern California Gas Company sent a utility worker to Eula's home to shut off her gas. Her unpaid bill at the time totaled $66.[41] When the worker arrived at her home, reports indicate that a distraught Eula attacked the worker with a shovel and successfully chased him away from her home.[42] This confrontation prompted Eula to head to a nearby store to acquire a few money orders, including one for the minimum payment for her gas bill: $22.09.[43] By getting this money order, Eula attempted to avoid any further confrontations with utility workers. In the time between her encounter with the utility worker and her trip to the store for money orders, the utility worker called the police and his employer to inform them of what transpired.[44] Southern Gas Company sent two new utility workers.[45] Whether they came to collect the bill or to once again attempt to shut off her gas remains unclear. Unsurprisingly, the arrival of more workers further agitated Eula as she returned home with a money order for the minimum payment.[46] She was ready to pay but they were not at her home to de-escalate.

According to reports from utility workers, Eula entered her home and retrieved an eleven-inch boning knife.[47] Police arrived on the scene to "aid" the new utility workers sent to this West Athens home and allegedly witnessed her with the knife in her hand. LAPD officers Lloyd O'Callaghan and Edward Hopson ordered her to drop the knife. She refused and turned to walk back into her modest home. The officers stated that Eula then turned around and tossed her knife towards them.[48] The toss wasn't potentially injurious. Also, once the knife was out of her hand, she was no longer a physical threat. She was unarmed and could've been subdued in a less violent manner. Without hesitation, however, the officers fired several shots at Eula at relatively close range. They shot her all over her lower body. The fatal shot pierced her chest.[49] After the barrage of bullets from these officers' guns, she collapsed onto the grass in her front yard. Her lifeless, bullet-ridden body was then handcuffed. The money order for the minimum payment to keep her gas on remained in her purse.[50] The very thing that brought utility workers to her home in the first place was right there. But police chose to kill this distressed and unarmed poor Black woman anyway.

Seemingly contradictory to police accounts of the event, no fingerprints were found on the knife Eula supposedly threw toward the officers.[51] Even if she did have a knife, the officers were eight to twelve feet away from Love when they shot and killed her.[52] There was no immediate or grave threat to their well-being from what they characterized as a "knife-wielding" suspect. But allegedly throwing a knife on the ground near police amounted to "deadly assault" and, therefore, offered pretext for the officer's fatal actions.[53] Their reaction to her supposedly "violent" behavior rendered her death justifiable. A little more than three months after her murder, the Los Angeles District Attorney exonerated Officers Hopson and O'Callaghan.[54] Their actions aligned with established policy. Eula's murder occurred within a criminal punishment system in which an overdue gas bill became a capital offense.

Widespread community outrage followed the exoneration.[55] The Los Angeles Police Commission found that the killing of Eula Love failed to meet department standards. Although this commission asserted that the officers "exercised poor judgment," their assessment of the incident carried no legal weight.[56] The commission wasn't backed by any legal law enforcement entity and therefore had no say in any effort to hold the officers accountable for killing her. An assertion of poor judgment is by no means a murder indictment, but it is the closest any "official" body came to recognizing the fatal actions of two officers. The criminal punishment system determined that no one would be held accountable for killing Eula Love and that $66 was worth more than a widowed Black mother's life. The system decided that although she was killed, the officers didn't act with malice aforethought. The criminal punishment system was incapable of seeing the killing of a poor Black woman as an act that warranted accountability. Without any formal accountability assigned, it feels like the system said, "No one killed Eula Love."

I learned about Eula not too long after the four LAPD officers assaulted Rodney King. I overheard my parents and their friends talking about Rodney, and someone mentioned her. They talked about a pattern of racist policing and how cops killed a Black woman over a few measly dollars. I remember being shocked and asking probative questions about her death. I didn't get many answers then, but I knew from their conversation and their responses to my questions that Eula's murder was not an exceptional occurrence for Black women. Her story stuck with me for years. I returned to her story as I began to learn the names and engage the stories of other Black women and girls killed by police.

It wasn't until 2016, however, that I fully grasped the significance of Eula's death within the broader context of how we talk about antiBlack police violence. In an article written by John Patrick Leary for the *Jacobin,* I learned of a particularly fascinating detail about the coverage of Eula's death and its effect on how we talk about police violence. Leary pinpointed the origins of the now commonly used phrase "officer-involved shooting," to the LAPD's Robbery and Homicide Division. The phrase derived directly from the Officer-Involved Shooting Team within this division of the

LAPD.[57] This team investigated incidents in which officers discharged their weapons on civilians. As police violence intensified throughout the 1970s, local media began covering police violence against civilians. By the mid-1970s, local papers in Los Angeles interchangeably used "officer-involved" and "police-involved" shooting to report on police officers shooting and, in some cases, killing civilians. The killing of Eula Love solidified the usage of the term by mainstream media outlets as the go-to for describing police shooting civilians. Leary noted that with exception of a single local Black newspaper in Los Angeles, the city's press identified the killing of Eula as an "officer-involved shooting."

Why is the language used to describe police violence so important? "Officer-involved" is passive. It doesn't tell us the role the officer or officers played in the shooting. There's a world of difference between Treva shot someone and Treva was involved in a shooting. Being involved could also mean I was the victim. The passive description of a violent act works to evacuate responsibility or accountability from police officers who shoot and kill people. Mainstream publications across the U.S. adopted the term and became complicit in what Leary and others identify as an obfuscation of the reality of fatal police violence. The rhetoric of "officer-involved shooting" tells us that police killings are victimless crimes. Ask the family and friends of those killed by police how offensive the language of "officer-involved shooting" is. The phrase refuses to acknowledge their loved ones as victims.

By the time the story of Eula Love reached the *New York Times*, the usage of "officer-involved" to describe the fatal encounter had effectively erased her victimhood.[58] The term embeds bias into how the general public views, processes, and responds to the killing of a thirty-nine-year-old Black woman in her own yard.

"Officer-involved" leaves the door open for many questions about who ultimately was responsible for the assailed or dead person. The built-in police bias of the phrase also implies that the shooting was justifiable. If one believes that the police "protect and serve," then their involvement in a shooting would suggest an attempt to fulfill their duties. When you are part of communities being disproportionately gunned down by police, the use of the phrase "officer-involved shooting" is yet another example of police being able to terrorize marginalized communities with impunity and unequivocal support from those it does protect.

Every time I read a story with the words "officer-involved shooting," I cringe. It bothered me before I knew the origins, but I feel another level of anger knowing that it was the killing of a Black woman my age that catalyzed the mainstreaming of such a purposefully ambiguous, biased, and evasive phrase for police violence. "Officer-involved shooting" entered our public discourse because the Los Angeles Police Department wanted the public to believe that its officers were justified in shooting a Black woman in her own yard over an unpaid gas bill. Despite the term's application to victims of police violence irrespective of race, the disproportionate rate at which police shoot and kill Black people means we most commonly see the term when yet another police officer kills a Black person. The killing of Eula Love was undeniably a heartbreaking loss for her loved ones and her community. It was also a definitive moment for the discourse around fatal police violence. At the convergence of antiBlackness, misogynoir, and, in numerous cases, ableism and poverty are Black women and girls killed by police.

For me and so many in my generation—those who came of age in the 1980s and 1990s—the ferocious assault of Rodney King by the LAPD was a crucial moment of witnessing police violence. I didn't know about Love's murder back then or the names or stories of Black women killed by police in that era. Growing up, I was unaware of the report released by the Center for Law and Social Justice in 1988 titled "Black Women under Siege by the New York City Police."[59] This report would've refuted my internalization of the idea that police violence only *really* affected Black men and boys. My parents taught me about police violence as something that could happen to me. I just don't recall learning about any Black women or girls who were victims of fatal police violence until my twenties.

After watching the Ferguson Uprising in response to the killing of Michael Brown, like so many others, I strove to deepen my understanding of police violence against Black people. By 2014, I knew that Black women were experiencing police violence and that we were being left out of national conversations and debates about police brutality. It became abundantly clear that far too many didn't know the recent history of police violence against us and could only comprehend antiBlack police violence as spectacularly violent acts against Black men and boys. Whether thinking about police violence in the late twentieth century or in the last few years, a notable percentage of Black women and girls have been killed by police in their homes. The fact that many of the killings of Black women and girls occur "outside of public view" facilitates the ease with which we maintain a masculinist framing of antiBlack policing.[60] If we don't see it, or if it doesn't occur in ways that we can readily recognize, these cases become exceptional as opposed to illustrative of the depths of antiBlack police violence.

In Her Own Home

One of the more prominent incidents that prompted the "Black Women under Siege by the New York City Police" report was the fatal shooting of Eleanor Bumpurs on October 24, 1984, by New York Police Department (NYPD) officer Stephen Sullivan during an attempted eviction. Eleanor was a sixty-six-year-old, disabled Black woman living in Sedgwick Homes, a public housing complex in the Bronx. She fell five months behind on her monthly rent of $89.45.[61] For a grand total of less than four hundred dollars, city housing officials authorized her eviction from her home. Prior to the attempt to evict this elderly woman, Eleanor informed her daughter about someone in the building harassing her.[62] She also told the city's housing authority about maintenance issues and refused to pay rent because of what she felt was ongoing neglect of her concerns as a tenant. In one conversation with a housing authority manager, Eleanor allegedly expressed that people had ripped her off and had come through the walls, floor, and windows.[63] This particular exchange with the housing authority indicated, in the very least, serious emotional and mental distress.

She eventually relented with regard to allowing maintenance workers into her home.[64] They arrived on October 12, 1984, and found no issues with the state of her appliances. They did, however, report finding several cans of feces in her bathtub.[65] According to them, Eleanor blamed "Reagan and his people" for what they saw in her tub.[66] A little more than a week after maintenance workers visited her apartment, the city of New York sent a psychiatrist to her home to evaluate her mental health. The psychiatrist deemed Eleanor "unfit to manage her affairs" and identified her as "psychotic."[67] Despite the psychiatrist's alarming diagnosis, a Social

Services supervisor made the decision to evict her prior to a recommended hospitalization. The supervisor prioritized a punitive response over aiding and supporting this elderly, disabled Black woman. Given her recent history of documented agitation with even the idea of people entering her home, it's notable that a supervisor opted to proceed with an eviction as the first course of action.

On the crisp autumn morning of October 29, 1984, city marshals sent by the New York City Housing Authority arrived to serve an eviction notice. The marshals reported that she made numerous hostile threats and that they considered her possibly "dangerous."[68] They stated that Eleanor threatened to throw boiling lye on anyone who entered her home.[69] Housing Authority officials then called the police, which included the NYPD Emergency Service Unit. This unit specializes in "subduing emotionally distressed people."[70] They proved unsuccessful in convincing her to open her door. Officers then proceeded to drill out the lock on her door. Through the drilled hole officers noted that she was naked and holding what appeared to be a ten-inch knife in her hand.[71] They knocked down the door and immediately attempted to restrain her with a Y-shaped bar and plastic shields.[72] Eleanor broke free and allegedly continued to wave her knife in a slashing motion at the officers who had broken down the door of her home. After a very brief struggle with her, Officer Sullivan fired two shots at Eleanor from a twelve-gauge shotgun. While one pellet from the first shot struck her hand, a total of nine pellets from the second shot hit her chest.[73] Those pellets proved fatal. She died on the floor of her own apartment.

On January 30, 1985, a grand jury indicted Officer Sullivan on charges of second-degree manslaughter.[74] Just a couple of months after the grand jury returned an indictment, State Supreme Court

Judge Vincent A. Vitale dismissed the indictment, citing Sullivan's conformity with established procedures and guidelines of NYPD's Emergency Service Unit.[75] Over eighteen months later, in November of 1986, the New York Court of Appeals reinstated the grand jury's indictment of second-degree manslaughter.[76] Sullivan waived his right to a jury trial, opting for a bench trial.[77] The trial commenced in January of 1987. Just a little more than six weeks after the trial started, Judge Fred W. Eggert acquitted Officer Sullivan on the manslaughter charge.[78] That summer, federal prosecutors declined any further investigation of the killing of Eleanor Bumpurs.

Once again, the message sent from no officers being held accountable was that "no one" killed this disabled elderly Black woman. The family sought $10 million in restitution from the city for killing their loved one. It wasn't until 1990 that the city agreed to "awarding" $200,000 to the Bumpurs estate.[79] The only other people held accountable for anything that transpired with regard to Eleanor was the demotion of two supervisors at the city's social services administration. The supervisors had failed to seek an emergency rent grant and appropriate psychiatric aid for her, which in the least were precipitating failures that led to her death at the hands of police.[80] They didn't lose their jobs though, as the city didn't find itself culpable for killing a person in distress. The killing of Eleanor Bumpurs sparked outrage throughout the city.[81] She was among the more well-known victims of fatal police violence in the 1980s in New York City. Her killing, like many others, resulted in little to no accountability for those who failed to protect or serve her. Multiple agencies, including the NYPD, the Social Services Administration, and the New York Housing Authority, criminalized her disability and her economic status. It's hard to imagine any of these entities treating an elderly white woman as disposable and with such violent contempt. Her vulnerability was illegible to those with the power of life and death.

When talking about fatal police violence in the twenty-first century and connecting to what occurred in the last three decades of the twentieth century, the killing of Eleanor Bumpurs may not be invoked as an exemplifier of a violent pattern. The 2016 police killing of Deborah Danner, a disabled elderly Black woman in New York, however, brought Eleanor's killing back into sharp focus as we once again bore witness to the cruelty and carelessness with which police engage disabled Black women and girls.[82] Disability and mental illness, in particular and in conjunction with Deborah's Black womanhood, exacerbated her vulnerability. A 2016 study conducted by the Ruderman Family Foundation, found that disabled people account for between one-third and one-half of all victims of police violence in the United States.[83] The compounding forces of ableism, antiBlack racism, and misogyny rendered Eleanor, Deborah, and others in the late twentieth and early twenty-first centuries multiply jeopardized by violent criminalization. The existence of a deadly pattern of police violence against disabled Black women warrants excavation.

Deborah Danner had been hospitalized in relation to her mental illness at least ten times in her life prior to her killing.[84] The IT/MIS professional lived in an apartment in the Bronx, to which police had been called on more than a few occasions.[85] On October 18, 2016, a neighbor called the NYPD to report her "erratic" behavior.[86] Not too long after this call, five officers came and entered Deborah's apartment. According to one of the officers who responded to the call, they found her "sitting on her bed, holding a pair of scissors and threatening to fight police if they entered the room."[87] Officers spent just a few minutes attempting to convince her to put down the scissors. After a brief, unsuccessful attempt, Sergeant Hugh Barry of the NYPD entered the bedroom with the goal of taking Deborah into custody. At this point, she reached for a baseball bat and allegedly raised it into the air as though she may swing it.[88] Barry pulled out his gun and commanded Deborah to put the bat down. She stepped closer to Barry and he shot her twice. Danner succumbed to her injuries at Jacobi Hospital.

Outrage from the city and from some folks across the nation swiftly followed her tragic death.[89] In May 2017, Barry was charged with second-degree murder, first- and second-degree manslaughter, and criminally negligent homicide. Less than a year later, in February 2018, the State Supreme Court acquitted Barry on all charges.[90] Deborah's family received a $2 million settlement for the killing of their loved one—a settlement for a killing apparently no one committed. The similarities between the killings of Eleanor and Deborah are striking. From the location, their age, and the impunity with which officers killed these disabled Black women, it's hard not to compare these murderous incidents. The criminalizing of Blackness, womanhood, and disability led to these killings. The criminal punishment system refused to take any responsibility for them. A system that couldn't see either of these elderly, disabled Black women in distress as victims is perhaps one worth dismantling.

One of the most heartbreaking parts of the case of Deborah Danner was that she wrote about living with schizophrenia, policing, and the criminalization of mental illness. In 2012, she published a piece entitled "Living with Schizophrenia." One of the eeriest and prescient parts of the piece spoke directly to the grave fate Deborah met in 2016. She wrote, "We are all aware of the all too frequent news stories about the mentally ill who come up against law enforcement instead of mental health professionals and end up dead."[91] She even went on to referencing the case of Eleanor Bumpurs in her calling out of law enforcement's failures at protecting and serving people with disabilities, and more specifically people living with mental illnesses. Deborah pointed out that "many years ago, here in NY, a very large woman named Gompers [*sic*] was killed [by] police by shotgun because she was perceived as a 'threat to the safety' of several grown men who were also police officers. They used deadly force to subdue her because they were not trained sufficiently in how to engage the mentally ill in crisis. This was not an isolated incident."[92]

In the #SayHerName report, Crenshaw and Ritchie identify five Black women who were in or perceived to be in mental distress who were killed by the police in the 2010s alone.[93] Although Deborah doesn't single out disabled Black women in her analysis, it's notable that she uses the killing of a Black woman as the example for illustrating how police engage people with disabilities and in mental distress.

As Ritchie argues in the first book-length study of contemporary police violence against women and gender-expansive[94] people of color, *Invisible No More: Police Violence against Black Women and Women of Color,* Black women broadly, but particularly disabled Black women, are "met with deadly force rather than compassion."[95] The lack of empathy or concern, however, is emboldened by a criminal punishment system that historically and contemporarily denies Black women and girls' full personhood. Disability situates us even further from a kind of personhood police attempt to protect and serve. While it may seem like police officers should view disabled individuals as more vulnerable to violence and victimization, the reality is that police have "their own preconceptions and fears, and either no knowledge of mental health and other disabilities, or just enough garbled 'knowledge' to amp up their own anxieties."[96] Ableism heightens the possibility of police violence. Intersecting prejudices coupled with the tendency for police to profile people with physical, sensory, intellectual, or mental disabilities as a danger to the public, or as some kind of "public nuisance," means that an estimated one-third to one-half of people killed by police in the U.S. every year are disabled.[97] Disability further calcifies Black women and girls' status of being perpetually criminalized and potentially at risk for fatal police violence.

The vulnerability of disabled Black women and girls to fatal police violence hit close to home for me in 2014. In a year many won't soon forget because of the killings of Michael Brown in Ferguson, Eric Garner in Staten Island, and twelve-year-old Tamir Rice in Cleveland, as well as the Ferguson Uprising that connected to struggles against policing and white supremacy, a young disabled Black woman was killed by police outside of her home just two hours away from where I lived. Her story didn't become as mainstream as the higher-profile victims of police violence that year, but her loved ones, her community, and activists and organizers who do focus on Black women and girls amplified her death at the hands of police. She wasn't forgotten by a lot of us, though her death certainly wasn't one of the police killings around which people around the nation mobilized.

Tanisha Anderson dreamt of becoming a broadcast journalist. She was beloved by her family. Her brother Joell took pride in looking after both of his sisters growing up and saw himself as their protector. In her twenties, Tanisha was diagnosed by mental health practitioners as having bipolar disorder. She began taking medicine for her mental illness shortly after her diagnosis. The intensity of her symptoms varied over the years. Although her family noted that they called the police in past years to assist with her, they had not called 911 in quite some time in regard to her health and well-being. On November 13, 2014, however, Tanisha's behavior alarmed her family. Her sister Jennifer noted that Tanisha was having what her loved ones identified as "one of her 'bad days.'"[98] Without shoes and dressed only in a nightgown, a disoriented Tanisha kept attempting to leave the house. With few other options for assistance, her brother Joell called 911, hoping an ambulance or someone trained in helping folks in mental distress would arrive.

Two different sets of police arrived at their home in east Cleveland that evening. Upon the arrival of the first set of cops, Tanisha calmed briefly. Not long after their departure, she became distressed again. Her family called 911 again, hoping for meaningful support. The second set of police officers came and according to her family were immediately rude and brusque. Officers Brian Meyers and Scott Aldridge told the family to stay in the house and escorted Tanisha to their patrol car. At this point in the encounter, the story of what happened according to police varies wildly from what her family witnessed. What is indisputable is that the officers restrained Tanisha by placing her in handcuffs. Her family asserted that these officers slammed her onto the pavement, which effectively lifted her nightgown up over her hips. Less than thirty minutes after Officers Meyers and Aldridge arrived, Tanisha stopped breathing. Her listless body was in the middle of the street, handcuffed, exposed, and criminalized.

By the time she got to the hospital, she was in full cardiopulmonary arrest. Doctors couldn't revive her. The coroner ruled her death a homicide. The cause listed was "'sudden death associated with physical restraint in a prone position'" in association with ischemic "heart disease and bipolar disorder" with agitation.[99] According to the office of the Cuyahoga County Medical Examiner, Tanisha's preexisting heart disease and bipolar disorder increased her risk for sudden death from physical restraint in a prone position.[100] The cause of death not listed was police violence. Her family had simply sought help. Instead, they had to bear witness to the violent last moments of her life in front of their home. Tanisha's sixteen-year-old daughter, Mauvion, watched helplessly "from a window" as two officers killed her mother.[101]

The officers who killed Tanisha Anderson criminalized her the moment they arrived on the scene. They handled her as though she were a threat to their lives. They refused to see her family's concern or Tanisha's history of mental illness. Officers Meyers and Aldridge saw a vulnerable Black woman as disposable and her loved ones as collateral damage. How does a mother, brother, sister, or daughter make sense not only of their loved one being killed but of personally witnessing the fatal edge of misogynoir, ableism, and anti-Blackness? Her family reached out for support, and instead their loved one became an in-memoriam hashtag. Tanisha became yet another example of policing's systemic cruelty toward disabled Black women and girls. Tanisha was only thirty-seven years old when police killed her with impunity. More than three years after her violent death, a special grand jury decided not to indict the officers who killed her.[102] A civil lawsuit against the city awarded Tanisha's family a $2.8 million settlement; however, the criminal punishment system failed to hold anyone accountable. The system protected itself against culpability. And once again, "no one" killed this disabled Black woman.

The deaths of these disabled Black women show the distinct and fatal intersection of ableism, antiBlackness, and misogynoir in policing. These women, who were killed in or right outside of their homes, are an important part of a larger cadre of Black women killed "outside of public view." In 2020, however, something shifted, if only temporarily. People took to the streets to protest the "outside of public view" killing of a Black woman by police officers. Breonna Taylor is a somewhat exceptional contemporary historical figure in that the killing of Black women by police rarely gets extensive coverage, sustained investment, or mobilized collective outrage.[103]

When interviewed about this surprising response to the killing of Breonna, I didn't know what to say. The more I got asked to talk about her death, the more I found myself fighting to talk about her life. Like me, she loved Mary J. Blige's "My Everything" and reruns of *Martin*.[104] I loved seeing pictures of her in sexy dresses, as well as in her E.M.T. uniform. I imagine her loved ones' responses to numerous images of Breonna circulating may have conjured a flood of mixed emotions. Witnessing their deceased loved one's picture everywhere could be simultaneously painful and heartening. I couldn't pin down what made her killing become a cause célèbre in ways almost no other case of fatal police violence against a Black woman arguably ever had. What was so different about Breonna's killing? The May 2020 viral video of a Minneapolis police officer killing George Floyd was an immediate catalyst for the uprisings of 2020. Although Louisville police officers killed Breonna around two months prior to Floyd's death, Breonna emerged as one of the more prominent and recent illustrative figures of anti-Black policing. Breonna was killed during a controversial "no-knock raid," and her violent death became a flashpoint for both those arguing for police reform and those demanding the defunding and abolishing of the police.

The city of Louisville awarded Taylor's family a $12 million settlement for a killing for which "no one" would be held accountable.[105] The killing of Breonna Taylor stuck with and energized so many people outside of her family and local community. Her likeness could be found on the covers of major magazines. She even became a meme. Some folks, including myself, became increasingly uncomfortable with this memeification, fetishization, and commodification of Breonna.[106] It's not that I didn't want folks rallying around her death and her family, but I couldn't put my finger on what made me uncomfortable with this abundance of gestures of solidarity and awareness for this young Black woman. Perhaps I was skeptical because I'd never seen anything like it before when it came to responding to police killing someone who looked like me. The death of Sandra Bland is probably the moment when I felt the most collective rage around police violence against a Black woman in my lifetime. Without question, Breonna and every other person killed by police across the globe deserve campaigns, protests, and mass media coverage. I just couldn't understand what made *this* case resonate with so many people.

At a national level, we didn't take to the streets after a seven-year-old Black girl named Aiyana Stanley-Jones was shot and killed in Detroit during a horribly executed raid on the wrong apartment.[107] Aiyana was asleep on the couch at around midnight on May 16, 2020, in her grandmother's house when six officers from Detroit's version of SWAT, the Special Response Team with an A&E television network crew in tow to film the raid for *The First 48*, threw a grenade into the apartment. Within seconds, Officer

Joseph Weekley fired a single fatal shot that struck Aiyana in the head and exited her neck. Cities didn't burn for her, although her death is probably referenced more now in the wake of the killing of Breonna Taylor.

Atatiana Jefferson, who was killed in her home by Fort Worth Texas police officer Aaron Dean in the early morning of October 12, 2019, didn't become a meme.[108] Atatiana hasn't been the primary subject of a national conversation about fatal police violence. A neighbor called a number in the phonebook for a wellness check because he noticed the front door open and the lights on in his neighbor's home. He knew his neighbor was in the hospital. He didn't know his neighbor's daughter and grandson were in the house when he called to report his concerns about what might have happened to his neighbor. When police arrived at the home Atatiana came to her window, allegedly with a handgun. Police didn't identify themselves. Within seconds, Officer Dean shot through the window and killed her with her eight-year-old nephew close by. There was an outcry over Atatiana's death, but nothing sustained outside of a more localized context.[109] Cities didn't burn for her. Notably, it's one of very few cases in which a grand jury returned a murder indictment for an officer who killed a Black person.[110] Nevertheless, it's rare that I hear or see Atatiana's name featured in national conversations about fatal police violence. Beyond her loved ones, her community, and those deeply committed to #SayHerName, too many of us don't know or mobilize around stories like Atatiana's. At best, her name becomes part of a roll call of those killed by police. We learn so little about her life before this fatal encounter. On one hand, these stories profoundly show how deadly policing can be in the lives of Black women and girls. On the other hand, these stories still fall short of memorializing the lives of these women and girls—who they were and who they may have become.

Nonfatal Police Violence

Although fatal police violence understandably garners the most attention in discussions about police brutality, nonfatal police violence is even more common.[111] It leaves scars that often don't heal, physically or emotionally. Frankly, violent encounters with police can be soul-crushing. The first time I felt compelled to write in a mainstream publication about police violence, I focused on a case of police sexual misconduct against Black women and girls. Given my personal experience with police sexual violence, I intimately knew how devastating and life-changing that experience can be.

In my first article for *Cosmopolitan*,[112] I discussed a 2015 report conducted by the Associated Press on sexual misconduct by U.S. law enforcement over a six-year period. The yearlong study found that nearly one thousand officers lost their jobs during that period for acts of sexual misconduct, including rape and sexual assault. Notably, the researchers who conducted the study stressed that "the number is unquestionably an undercount because it represents only those officers whose licenses to work in law enforcement were revoked, and not all states take such action."[113] States with some of the largest law enforcement agencies in the nation weren't fully accounted for in the study because they don't have a statewide system for decertifying officers. Furthermore, the records used for the study only indicate officers who lost their jobs because of sexual misconduct. Even a police chief acknowledged that "it's so underreported and people are scared that if they call and complain about a police officer, they think every other police officer is going to be then out to get them."[114] The lack of victims reporting alongside less-than-adequate data collection for allegations and disciplinary actions make it quite difficult to assess the magnitude of police sexual violence in the U.S. What we do know is that violent policing disproportionately affects Black women and girls.

The release of the Associated Press's study came on the heels of a case about an officer accused of multiple acts of sexual violence. In the early summer of 2014, news broke regarding an Oklahoma City police officer sexually violating more than a dozen Black women and girls.[115] A fifty-seven-year-old Black woman named Jannie Ligons reported to police that then-officer Daniel Holtzclaw forced her to expose her breasts and perform oral sex on him during a traffic stop.[116] Another victim accused ex-officer Holtzclaw of forcing her to perform oral sex after finding a crack pipe in her purse.[117] In total, thirteen Black women and girls, mostly poor, some living with drug addiction and others suspected of being sex workers, came forward with accusations of sexual misconduct against Holtzclaw.[118] After an extensive investigation, a grand jury indicted him on thirty-six offenses, including sexual battery, forcible oral sodomy, stalking, and rape in November 2014.[119] Holtzclaw's trial began on November 2, 2015.

I first wrote about the accusations in a piece for a special issue of *Feminist Studies* in which I argued for taking a "herstorical" approach to studying antiBlack police violence against Black women and girls.[120] At the time, mostly local news outlets and only a few major national media outlets reported on the case. As the trial approached, I became more and more incensed by the lack of collective outrage with regard to an alleged serial sexual predator who used his authority as a police officer to target Black women and girls. My first public piece on the Holtzclaw case was entitled "The Rape Trial Everyone in America Should Be Watching." At the time it felt like only Black women and a few other folks cared. In light of the increased attention to police violence against Black people, it infuriated me that more people weren't connecting what happened to these Black women and girls to an ongoing history of antiBlack police brutality.

I wrote two more stories about the case; the final one came after I attended the sentencing of Holtzclaw in Oklahoma City. I remember sitting in the courtroom with activists, scholars, community members, and some of his victims as the judge sentenced him to 263 years on eighteen of the thirty-six charges on which he was actually convicted.[121] Cries went out throughout the sentencing but none more piercing than the one I heard outside of the courtroom immediately following the proceedings. I went over to this crying middle-aged Black woman and just held her. Tearfully, she explained to me how Holtzclaw ruined her life. She wasn't one of the victims for whom charges were brought; however, she came to the courthouse that day to face him. She conveyed both relief and fury. Like so many of the victims who came forward, she remarked that she never thought anyone would believe her because she was a Black woman.

The testimonies of his accusers stuck with me. They're still with me as I write this book. The words of the Black woman outside the courtroom haunt me in a distinct way. She was right. Holtzclaw seemed to choose his victims because they were Black women and girls. He knew that the criminal punishment system viewed us as unrapeable, as untrustworthy, and as criminals. He chose to terrorize Black women and girls with criminal records and those suspected of living with drug addiction. Holtzclaw knew he could victimize with impunity those that the criminal punishment system sees and treats as disposable. The fact that he was held accountable for his actions by the very system that rarely if ever recognizes Black women and girls as victims was anomalous—a one-off in a system predicated on criminalizing, violating, and disposing of Black people.

Holtzclaw understood that he was in a profession where he could brutally assault a Black teenage girl in a classroom without facing any consequences.[122] Or, he could've followed in the footsteps of McKinney, Texas, police officer Eric Casebolt and drag a fifteen-year-old Black girl in a bikini outside of a pool party by her hair, slam her to the ground, and handcuff and pin her without facing any criminal charges or personal liability.[123] One of his fellow officers in 2019 was on tape tackling and pinning down an eleven-year-old Black girl with special needs at a middle school in New Mexico while telling those around him he wasn't using "excessive force."[124] If Holtzclaw had worked in a school with Black students as a school resource officer, he could've broken the jaw of a seventeen-year-old Black girl falsely accused of possessing mace and had people defend his actions.[125] Although Holtzclaw's violent behavior preceded many of these incidents, it is in this context of widespread police violence against Black girls and women that he understandably thought he would never face any consequences. History told him he could. The numerous cases of cops assaulting and sexually violating Black women and girls since Holtzclaw's conviction reveals how irregularly the criminal punishment system provides any semblance of accountability for those of us victimized by police violence.

Fuck Tha Police as Concept

For those who survive and those who witness violent policing, "Fuck the Police" is a refusal to accept the status quo of embracing police officers as necessary arbiters for protecting and serving communities. A lot of us don't experience police officers in those capacities. The full-throated declaration also recognizes that one of the unsaid mantras of U.S. policing includes "Fuck Black People." Police departments and unions that frame "Black Lives Matter" as antipolice or that refuse to work with organizations that amplify or support #BlackLivesMatter shamelessly show their hands. For example, in October 2020 Barron County, Wisconsin, officials voted to strip funding from Embrace, a domestic violence organization that hung Black Lives Matter signs at four of its locations in northwestern Wisconsin.[126] After complaints from local law enforcement about these signs being antipolice, the elected/appointed officials in Barron County took actions to defund Embrace. Most of the seventeen different law enforcement agencies in the area that work with Embrace severed ties with the organization as well. These law enforcement agencies were so opposed to the mere assertion that Black lives matter that they put domestic violence victims of all races at risk for not receiving support, counseling, and other care services. It was more important for them to be anti–Black Lives Matter than to protect and serve victims of domestic violence.

By these law enforcement agencies' own logic, you can't support policing and affirm that Black lives matter. It may be one of the only things on which I personally agree with U.S. police about policing. It's impossible to reconcile supporting U.S. policing as it exists and wanting to protect and serve Black communities. The boldness with which these agencies moved unveiled an institutional disdain for Black life. They doubled down on sustaining a system that can harm Black lives with impunity. What happened in northwestern Wisconsin isn't exceptional either; law enforcement agencies and departments across the nation severed ties with and called for the defunding of antiviolence organizations, programs, and initiatives that supported #BlackLivesMatter to any extent.[127]

The logics of policing uphold an anti-Black life orientation. For Black women and girls, though not singularly, both fatal and nonfatal manifestations of police violence are an outgrowth of this orientation coupled with a distinct entanglement with misogynoir. Ableism, transphobia, and poverty also often intertwine with anti-Black policing that leads to cops assaulting, sexually violating, or killing us. Policing in the U.S. is predicated on an already criminalized Black subject—the fugitive enslaved person. This criminalization doesn't stop at the police encounter, if we survive it. It carries into every crevice of the U.S. criminal punishment system. It often leads to our dying in police custody or being punished for surviving violence against us.

2 *The Caged Bird Sings*

The Criminal Punishment System

The first time I was stopped by police while driving I was seventeen years old. I was lost in a recently gentrified neighborhood in my hometown, the formerly Chocolate City, Washington, D.C. It was almost midnight and pitch black on the street. The streetlights were inoperable. After circling the block at about ten miles per hour, I noticed a cop car in my rearview mirror. I immediately swelled with fear. I'd been in the car when my parents had been stopped and knew all too well how quickly things could escalate. Within seconds I heard the siren and saw the lights. I froze. After a few more seconds, I pulled over to an empty spot on the street. Two cops walked slowly over to my car, one came to my window, the other shined a bright light on the passenger side.

Immediately the cop's demeanor was hostile. Before I could even finish saying, "Good evening, officer," this white man with a gun forcefully asked me, "What are you doing around here?" I explained that I was lost. Exasperated and seemingly somewhat titillated, he then asked if I had been drinking. I told him that I had not. I kept my hands on the steering wheel just like my parents taught me. He asked again, "Are you sure you haven't been drinking?" I assured him that I hadn't been drinking and that I was only seventeen. It felt like my fear excited him. The other officer on the passenger side of the car continued to shine the light in search of who knows what. Without asking for my license or registration, he told me to get out of the car. I briefly hesitated because his demeanor was aggressive. I was seventeen, lost, alone, Black, and girl. It never crossed his mind to help me. My mind raced as I tried to figure out how to de-escalate. With tears slowly rolling down my face I stepped out of the car.

I can't recall or perhaps have deliberately forgotten every detail after that moment. I do remember the way he slowly ran his hands over my body "searching for something." Once I got out of the car, the other officer went back to the patrol car. I didn't see him again. I smelled the officer's stale cigarette-infused breath. I'm not sure how long it took for him to "frisk" me several times. It felt like an eternity. My legs trembled as he groped them from my ankles to my inner thighs underneath my sun dress. As his sweaty fingers got closer and began to fondle my vulva, he pressed the full weight of his body against mine. He inserted two fingers into my vagina slowly. I felt his hard penis on my back as he moaned. It was at that moment that I couldn't hold it in for a second longer. It took everything in me to ask the officer, "Sir, do you need to see my license and registration?" He slowly leaned back away from my body and told me to get back in my car. "Tonight's your lucky night," he said. As I got back in the car, my body still shaking, he closed the door. He leaned back over to tell me, "Next time bring a map." I rolled up my window and sat in the car crying until I could calm myself. I needed to get home. I was still lost, but I knew I had to get away from the scene of the crime.

When I finally made it home that night, I couldn't bring myself to tell my parents what had happened. I didn't tell anybody. I was ashamed that I hadn't done more. I didn't acknowledge this as a sexual assault for years. I suppressed the memory for as long as I could. It wasn't until I wrote about Daniel Holtzclaw that I began to come to grips with what happened to me back in 2001. While not death-dealing, that officer killed something within me that I didn't begin to recover until I named what he did. For too many Black women though, the outcomes of police encounters are far worse.

I called my parents immediately after I heard about the death of Sandra Bland in 2015. I was inconsolable. My voice trembled as I told my parents I was scared, angry, and hurting. I saw Sandra's face everywhere—her smile, the texture of her hair, her dark brown eyes. I saw so much of me in her or rather her in me. I took her death personally, as though I knew her beyond the story of her suspicious death.[1] Perhaps it hit me harder because I saw myself in her. She looked like she could be my cousin. Her short natural twists reminded me of my hair when I started my locs journey. As pictures of her surfaced on the internet, I noticed that she changed her hairstyle quite often, just like me and many of my Black homegirls. I didn't know her, of course, but I felt like I knew her.

What happened to her aligned with more recent, viral accounts of antiBlack policing such as the killings of Michael Brown, Eric Garner, and Tamir Rice. Sandra's death in a jail cell, however, brought up new public debates about Black women, antiBlackness, and the U.S. criminal punishment system. It also intensified my commitment to the struggle to end violence against Black women and girls. As a historian and as a Black woman who has had numerous encounters with police officers, I knew Bland's story wasn't singular. Although she became a symbolic figure in how people discuss antiBlack police violence against Black women and girls, I and others such as the coauthors of the #SayHerName report knew her story was illustrative of a systemic and underreported problem. We also knew that she was singularly important to those who loved her or those who watched her "Sandy Speaks" video blog where Sandra spoke about racism and left inspiring messages for those watching.[2]

The events leading up to Sandra's death in that jail cell in Waller County, Texas, epitomizes antiBlackness as an unrelenting force rendering trite "transgressions" of the law fatal for Black people. Historically and contemporarily, punitive responses to perceived "transgressions" of Black people against white supremacy include violence—sometimes fatal violence. Under the auspices of law and order, which crystalized in the early nineteenth century as a way to police enslaved people and protect the property (which included enslaved people) of white business owners, Sandra Bland became another casualty in the entrenchment of legalized antiBlack terror.[3] Within the framework of "law and order," Black lives are and have always been disposable.

Sandra's death in police custody was a reminder of what anthropologist Marc Lamont Hill identifies as a "broken criminal justice system that criminalizes vulnerability and, more specifically, Black womanhood."[4] Hill rightfully notes the criminalization of Black womanhood within the criminal punishment system, but I would argue, as he and others have elsewhere, that the system isn't broken. In fact, it operates as intended. In *In the Wake: On Blackness and Being,* Christina Sharpe posed a question that speaks directly to how we respond to a system grounded in antiBlackness: "What happens when instead of becoming enraged and shocked every time a black person is killed in the United States, we recognize Black death as a predictable and constitutive aspect of this democracy?"[5] In this framing, Sandra's death was predictable. It's a damning though accurate assessment of U.S. democracy that a prominent and inextricable feature of the criminal punishment system's design is antiBlackness. The criminalization of Black people is an origin story for this system.

Other deeply entrenched aspects of this system include misogyny and patriarchy. As Black Studies scholar Imani Perry explains, "The multiplicity of people who were unrecognized legally were not, as many who speak simplistically of slavery, deemed 'nonhuman.' Rather, personhood and patriarchy became a way to determine who counted and who did not among the human."[6] Enslaved women had neither sovereignty, property, or personhood, which afforded primarily property-owning white men in the U.S. with patriarchal power and legal standing within the criminal and civil legal systems.[7] Misogyny, at the systemic level, devalued women and positioned them as subordinates to male authority. Black women and girls experience the intersection of the systemic attributes of antiBlackness, patriarchy, and misogyny when encountering the criminal punishment system. Sandra Bland existed at this intersection.

Sandra's mug shot was ubiquitous on social media—on Twitter, Facebook, and Instagram. Her eyes looked lifeless and pierced with indescribable pain. Theories swirled about what led to her death; many people did not and still do not believe Sandra took her own life. Rumors swirled about her being deceased in the mug shot. For those unconvinced that she would take her own life, the notion of foul play quickly gained traction.[8] The handling of her death only added to a growing fury about what *really* happened to Sandra Bland. Her mug shot, coupled with the police dashboard camera's video of her with arresting officer Brian Encinia, stoked the flames of dissent of those inquiring about the events before her death.[9] Officer Encinia told Sandra he would "light her up," during a traffic stop.[10] His overt contempt for her, coupled with his authority as a police officer, created a lethal combination. Only three days after this violent and unnecessary encounter, formally attributed to her failing to signal a lane change, Sandra died alone, in a jail cell. An alleged traffic violation was the catalyst for a death-bound set of events. This was being Black here. This was the fatal edge of misogynoir—a distinct hatred for Black women.

Perhaps the visual "evidence" of her demise inserted her more firmly into #BlackLivesMatter-era protests and national debates about antiBlack racism and policing. The video of her encounter with Officer Encinia replayed on social media and in mainstream news coverage.[11] People cited her name alongside those of contemporaneous Black victims of police-initiated shootings such as Mike Brown, Eric Garner, and Tamir Rice. For those rallying around her death, Bland exemplified antiBlack policing. She became one of the first Black female victims of the 2010s to resonate as a galvanizing example of racist policing. In 2018, HBO released the documentary *Say Her Name: The Life and Death of Sandra Bland,* which followed Sandra's family on their long journey to find out what really happened.[12] The moving and emotionally wrenching documentary offers more questions than answers as it pertains to the formal cause of death; however, it indicts "the criminal justice system in which Bland became ensnared."[13]

Sandra was not the only one. As I pored over records of Black women's arrests, convictions, and imprisonment, it became blaringly apparent that dozens of Black women died in police custody or were imprisoned for fighting back, for speaking up, or for refusing to endure violence at the hands of loved ones, strangers, or law enforcement. These mostly invisible Black women and girls suffered and sometimes died at the hands of the State. By learning about who these women are and were and what they've experienced, we get a sense of the depth and gravity of the problems we face in the criminal punishment system, particularly after being arrested.

The same month of Sandra's death, reports surfaced of five other women, four of them Black, dying in police custody. Kindra Chapman of Alabama, Joyce Curnell of South Carolina, Ralkina Jones of Ohio, Alexis McGovern of Missouri, and Raynette Turner of New York all died in police custody in July 2015.[14] Although Sandra's story became the most well-known, each of these women's deaths raises questions about the treatment of Black women in police custody. The stories of these women, however, went largely unheard. With only a few outlets covering their deaths, primarily in their respective local contexts, their stories did not enter the national conversation on police violence. Despite their potential importance to a broader understanding of the effects of the criminal punishment system on Black girls and women, their names are largely forgotten amid the #hashtag-centered roll call of antiBlack violence at the hands of policing. Their stories, alongside more recent examples of Black women dying in police custody, offer a point of entry for parsing out why Black women's stories remain on the periphery. Even at a historical and cultural moment in which the deaths of Black people at the hands of the criminal punishment system inform how we talk about racism, policing, and mass incarceration, Black women and girls are not central to a mainstream dialogue about the reality of antiBlack policing or the failures of the U.S. criminal punishment system. Without question, gender matters.

The lack of a formidable uproar about Black women who died in police custody in July 2015 sits at the intersection of how we understand antiBlack policing and the incarceration of Black people. Both inexplicable deaths in the custody of the state and the criminalization of Black womanhood and girlhood are essential to grasping how racism and sexism combine and operate in the criminal punishment system. Important connections exist between incarcerated Black women who die in the custody of the state and Black women and girls whose defense of themselves against physical/sexual abuse precipitate their incarceration. These particular experiences expose the inability of the U.S. criminal punishment system to see Black women and girls as victims of abuse, as well as the system's carelessness with those of us in its custody. Callousness and fatal indifference—primary features of misogynoir—are evident in the stories of those who die in police custody, as well as the stories of a cadre of Black girls and women whom organizations like the Survived and Punished Collective identify as "hyper-criminalized for surviving domestic, sexual, or interpersonal violence."[15]

The violent relationship between the criminal punishment system and Black women and girls magnifies what historian Kali N. Gross identifies as an "exclusionary politics of protection."[16] These politics undergird the treatment of Black women in police custody and the vilification of those who survive violent encounters; their experiences exemplify antiBlack violence. Black women in police custody aren't protected, and neither are those of us who survive assaults, abuse, and sexual violence. The stories of those who died in police custody and those incarcerated for defending themselves tell us a new story of life "behind the wall." Deaths in custody and the criminalization of Black women and girls for acts of self-defense provide distinct entry points for centering us in conversations about the far-reaching effects of mass incarceration. Their stories reveal the inhumanity of disposability and the perniciousness of white supremacy. They also connect us to a distinct history of carceral practices.

Locked Up

The United States has the largest prison population in the world. As reported by the Bureau of Justice Statistics in 2013, more than 6.8 million people were under some form of correctional supervision, which includes prison, jail, probation, or parole.[17] In 2019, nearly 1.3 million women and girls were under correctional supervision.[18] Around 18 percent of women and girls under correctional supervision are incarcerated in federal and state prisons and jails, local jails, juvenile detention centers, and immigrant detention centers.[19] Almost seven thousand girls are confined in juvenile facilities.[20] Sixty-one thousand women currently confined in local jails haven't been convicted of anything. Of the girls locked up in juvenile facilities, 10 percent "are held because of status offenses such as running away, truancy, and incorrigibility."[21] According to the report *The Sexual Abuse to Prison Pipeline: The Girls' Story,* most status offenses are often tied to abuse.[22]

These data points exist at the core of what scholar Beth Richie identifies as "America's prison nation." This kind of nation comes into existence through ideologies and public policies that criminalize communities of color and that routinely undercut the rights of disenfranchised and marginalized groups.[23] The convergence of the power of public policy, law, and institutional practices in deciding what constitutes criminality and violation within civil society disproportionately criminalizes Black people.[24] The U.S.'s prison nation, as noted by scholars, activists, and artists such as Richie, Andrea Ritchie, Mariame Kaba, Angela Davis, Emily Thuma, Julia Sudbury, Regina Arnold, and many others has a particularly carnivorous appetite for us. Although men, especially men of color, make up a disproportionate percentage of those under correctional supervision, "increasingly, black women and women of colour are the raw material that fuel the prison industrial complex."[25] Tough-on-crime approaches coupled with the criminalization of poverty render Black women and girls particularly vulnerable to incarceration.[26]

Black women are imprisoned at twice the rate of white women in the U.S.[27] Black girls constitute a disproportionate percentage of those in juvenile detention centers, as well.[28] Criminalizing Black womanhood and girlhood not only reinforces long-standing racist and sexist stereotypes about us; it is profitable.[29] The U.S. prison nation comes to life via a criminal punishment system shamelessly committed to taking lives and livelihoods of those it never intended to protect. The U.S. prison nation also exploits the labor of those trapped within it; this nearly unpaid labor helps to generate billions of dollars for those profiting off the prison industrial complex.[30]

It may seem cliché to acknowledge that the criminal justice system isn't broken but, in fact, is working exactly as it was designed. Although I agree with this sentiment, many of us remain unfamiliar with the core design elements and features of this system and believe in the future possibility of it delivering justice. It's why we demand the arrest of police officers who assault or even kill people. It's also why we often turn to the criminal punishment system for "justice" for Black women and girls who've been harmed. Far too frequently, many of us perhaps misremember or overlook the antiBlack and misogynist origins of the criminal punishment system. We struggle to make sense of a system where five Black women could die in police custody in a single month or where we incarcerate a woman who fired a warning shot into the air to defend herself from an abusive ex-partner.

Captivity and, more specifically, the transatlantic slave trade and chattel slavery are inextricable parts of the origins of the U.S. system of criminalization. So, when some, including myself, say that "the criminal punishment system is rotten to its core," we root that assertion in an acute understanding of how the forced removal and genocide of millions of Indigenous people, the transport of captive Africans and the enslavement of Africans and people of African descent, patriarchy, sexism, and economic exploitation live at the heart of the system. For captive Africans of all genders transported during the transatlantic slave trade, slave ships took them on what Stephanie Smallwood pinpointed as a "one-way route of terror."[31] Laws, codes, and prevailing ideas about the inferiority of African people normalized this "terror" and embedded it into undergirding logics for subordinating, marginalizing, criminalizing, and eventually incarcerating Black people in the United States. The stories of most Black women and girls in the U.S. from the sixteenth century until abolition commence in bondage.[32] While I resist drawing a straight line from plantations to prisons, the enslavement of Africans and people of African descent is in an origin story for U.S. carceral logics. These logics feed a carceral imagination predicated on how the criminal punishment system adjudicates who should be contained and deemed unfit for civil society.[33]

Postslavery, it was Jim Crow laws, as well as the creative remixing of bondage practices and criminalizing and racist and sexist ideologies, that rendered Black people in the United States distinctly vulnerable to carceral technologies, systems, and institutions. The vestiges of slavery were manifested in post-Emancipation systems such as convict leasing, a racialized form of involuntary servitude.[34] African American women and girls were among those criminalized and subsequently surveilled and incarcerated by a rapidly expanding criminal punishment system. Each era of anti-Blackness has distinct features and technologies, but the penchant for forcibly containing Black women and girls cuts across eras. Whether historically or more recently, the archive often requires a deeper penetration to uncover our stories from behind the wall. It's rare that an accurate report detailing what happened to a Black woman even exists. The criminal punishment system writes the story, and we try to fill in the blanks. When we do get a video, a letter, or some other "evidence" of how vicious this system is toward Black women and girls, it can be seen as exceptional or even unprecedented. Peeking intently behind the wall, however, tells a very different story about a centuries-old normalization of anti-Black, sexist, economically exploitative, and oftentimes ableist criminalization.

What Really Happened . . .

The world witnessed Officer Encinia yelling at Sandra Bland about what he could and would do to her. Unlike the other five Black women who died in police custody in July 2015, footage exists of her initial police encounter on July 10, 2015. The summer before Sandra's death, footage of the killings of Eric Garner in Staten Island, New York; John Crawford in Beavercreek, Ohio; and Kajieme Powell in St. Louis had gone viral. Videos of their violent deaths at the hands of police officers, coupled with a historic uprising in Ferguson, Missouri, after the killing of Michael Brown by Officer Darren Wilson in August 2014, helped galvanize a national uproar about antiBlack racist policing. In November 2014, footage of Cleveland police officer Timothy Loehmann killing twelve-year-old Tamir Rice and the announcement of the nonindictment of Officer Wilson for killing Brown sparked further outrage about police officers killing Black men and boys with impunity.[35]

In December 2014, #SayHerName, a campaign launched by the African American Policy Forum and the Center for Intersectionality and Social Policy Studies, sought to "bring awareness to the names and stories of Black women and girls who have been victimized by racist police violence, and to provide support to their families."[36] Acknowledging the rarity of Black girls and women's stories and names being included in discussions about police violence, this campaign sought to unequivocally insert Black women and girls into conversations and campaigns on police violence experienced by Black people. Nearly two months prior to the death of Bland, the campaign released the *Say Her Name: Resisting Police Brutality against Black Women* report. The framework outlined in this report is an entry point for contextualizing what happened in the encounter between Sandra and Encinia. *How does a "routine" traffic stop lead to the death of a Black woman three days later?* In Encinia's recollection of the events that led to Sandra's arrest, Sandra was a volatile, noncompliant, irrational, and physically aggressive person. She was an "angry Black woman" who didn't know her place and who should've managed her response to align with racist and sexist expectations. The long-standing stereotype of the "angry Black woman" undergirds how police officers engage Black women who don't comport to racialized notions of femininity.[37]

Nearly a year prior to Sandra's arrest, two videos capturing white police officers violently engaging Black women went viral. In Tempe, Arizona, Officer Stewart Ferrin violently manhandled Ersula Ore for allegedly jaywalking on the university campus at which she taught.[38] In Los Angeles, Daniel Andrew repeatedly punched a Black woman named Marlene Pinnock to "protect" her from wandering into freeway traffic. While these videos alarmed many throughout the nation, the question of whether these officers justifiably and reasonably used force polarized onlookers. Numerous responses to these violent, viral videos either normalized or justified the actions of these arresting officers. These police assaults resulted in no substantial consequences for the officers. Within the criminal punishment system, Ore and Pinnock were merely "angry Black women" who needed to be disciplined by any means necessary.

Encinia threatened and violated Sandra and knew that he could violently engage a Black woman with impunity. Her police encounter was a death-bound event, one all too common for Black people interacting with police officers. Her experience with Encinia cannot be separated from her untimely death, which was officially ruled a suicide. Suicide, as a designation of cause of death for Sandra, however, is insufficient. The circumstances surrounding her death expose the state's callousness and neglect toward this Black woman. A criminal punishment system rooted in misogynoir is a culprit in her death. Its role in taking her life cannot be ignored. A failure to signal a lane change resulted in a Black woman dying alone in a jail cell in Waller County, Texas.

When new footage of Sandra's violent encounter with Officer Encinia surfaced, it provided visual confirmation of what some already suspected or knew: antiBlack, racist policing doesn't impact only Black boys and men; it also has devastating, even fatal, ramifications for Black women and girls. In May 2019, more footage circulated of Sandra's death-bound encounter: a video from her own mobile phone.[39] This video showed Bland calm, knowledgeable of her rights, and compliant. The police officer quickly and without hesitation became aggressive with her. From this video, Officer Encinia's anger, threats of violence, and encroachment on her body establish a context in which she would be found dead in her jail cell three days later.

The Texas Department of Public Safety claimed that Sandra's arrest stemmed from her kicking Officer Encinia.[40] Claiming Sandra was argumentative and uncooperative during the arrest, they charged her with assaulting a public servant.[41] They also deemed her a "high-risk" to others and placed her in a jail cell by herself.[42] Only Encinia's version of events mattered. The dashboard camera footage captured his rapidly shifting temperament, his forceful grabbing of Sandra after he received a response he did not like, and his threat to "light her up." He enacted and attempted to incite violence.

Sandra's story resonated in a way that few stories about Black women's and girls' encounters with police had. Her name became integral to conversations about racist policing. She was a prime example of how Black women experience antiBlack policing and carceral violence. In the 2010s, if there was a Black woman cited as an example of fatal police violence, it was Sandra Bland. With the exception of perhaps Breonna Taylor, Sandra Bland is the name we know, cite, and rally around when talking about police violence against Black women in the early twenty-first century. The singling out of these two women means we still see their cases as exceptional as opposed to illustrative of a larger issue.

Only Encinia is armed and has already violated and threatened violence against Sandra. In a separate bystander video of the encounter, after she exited her car, Sandra can be seen lying on the ground as Encinia and another cop stand above her.[43] This video captured her pleading that she can't hear and that Officer Encinia slammed her head onto the ground. Eventually, Encinia ordered this bystander to leave the area.[44] Both the dashboard camera and bystander footage show Encinia as aggressive and angry. Sandra became increasingly emotional in her responses, but Encinia never opted to de-escalate or disengage. He viewed her—a Black woman who allegedly failed to signal a lane change and expressed irritation at being pulled over for such a minor infraction—as a threat.

Encinia's contempt for and fear of Sandra stem from misogynoir. Her Black womanhood, irritation, and Sandra's questions were a "problem" he chose to address through threats of physical violence and, ultimately, placing her in the custody of the state. An everyday minor transgression made by many led her to a jail cell in Waller County, Texas. The quotidian for this Black woman rendered her vulnerable to the racist and sexist whims of an officer operating from the inhumane logics of misogynoir. Encinia threatened and violated her with the knowledge that his account of the encounter would trump her story. Even with visual evidence, he could rely on the criminal punishment system's penchant for permitting police officers to violently engage Black women with impunity. The footage of her encounter with Encinia entered the growing visual archive of state-sanctioned antiBlack violence. Her screams were and remain available to hear. Arguably, the "evidence" of her fateful encounter positioned Sandra as a rallying figure within the broader Movement for Black Lives and other Black-led racial justice campaigns. To this day, her story resonates in a way that so few stories about Black women's and girls' encounters with police have.

The coverage of and organizing around the death of Sandra Bland, nevertheless, is somewhat singular in moving us to think about misogynoir and policing. Sandra's death emerged as both symbolic and singular. Many people talking about and enraged by what happened to Sandra were unaware of the four other Black women who died in police custody in July 2015. Their stories, both individually and collectively, show an underdiscussed facet of violence in jails and prisons: preventable deaths in police or the state's custody. The stories of Raynette Turner, Ralkina Jones, Joyce Curnell, and Kindra Chapman compellingly show the significance of not viewing Sandra's death as exceptional or isolated but as illustrative of a recurring violent actualization of misogynoir within the criminal punishment system.

Only one day after a Waller County jailer found Bland deceased in her cell, officers returning an inmate from court to a jail cell in Homewood, Alabama, found eighteen-year-old inmate Kindra Chapman hanging in that cell.[45] Primarily local news outlets covered her death and the events leading up to that fateful evening. Footage of Kindra taking her life in that jail cell exists, yet suicide as cause of death fails to fully capture what occurred. She died by suicide just two hours after arriving at the Homewood City Jail.[46] Many questions remain unanswered about why this young Black woman took her own life. One of the most important lingering questions is if and how the Homewood City Jail staff assessed the mental state of Kindra before leaving her alone in a jail cell. If assessed, what did they miss?

On the evening of July 14, 2015, Homewood police responded to a call about a person with a gun. The call eventually shifted to attempted robbery. Officers gathered a description of the suspect and shortly thereafter encountered Kindra in a nearby apartment complex. Police picked her up and, having her in custody, brought her back to the scene of the alleged crime for the accuser to identify. The accuser identified Kindra as the person who attempted to steal his iPhone. Consequently, police took her to the Homewood City Jail. According to police documentation, Kindra arrived at the jail at 6:14 p.m.[47] After being unable to contact anyone regarding bail, police placed her in a jail cell alone at 6:30 p.m. In those sixteen minutes, it remains unknown whether officers assessed her mental state and well-being. Footage reveals that Kindra appears physically unharmed.[48] It is, however, unlikely that in such a short period of time that officers did due diligence regarding her psychological and emotional well-being. Even if officers followed protocol, existing police procedure for assessing mental health too often allows for cops to miss critical signs of trauma, illness, or invisible disabilities.[49] Furthermore, few if any widely accepted practices and procedures for assessing mental health wholly acknowledge how race, and more specifically Blackness, as well as gender affect perceptions of health, wellness, and vulnerability.[50]

Once in the jail cell, Kindra became visibly agitated.[51] She knocked over the water cooler and removed the bed sheet. Kindra stood on the water cooler, tied the bed sheet to a wall support rail extended from the ceiling, and then tied the sheet around her neck. Just a little more than an hour after she had been put in the jail cell, officers found her hanging and unresponsive. Those who found her immediately began resuscitation efforts. Medical emergency personnel arrived soon after and transported her to Brookwood Hospital. The hospital pronounced Kindra Chapman dead at

8:36 p.m. A mere two hours and six minutes transpired between her first steps into a jail cell and the declaration of her death.

The footage confirmed death by suicide but does not absolve the arresting officers or the jail staff of any culpability for Kindra's death. No one responded to her agitation in real time or properly assessed her state of being. It's difficult not to wonder if her intake forms included questions about depression, suicidal thoughts, or ideations about self-inflicted harm. Did Kindra's history of encounters with police stemming from allegations of marijuana possession or damaging a police patrol car affect how they engaged her once she was in police custody? Did antiBlack or antiqueer sentiments regarding this young, Black lesbian woman shape the decision to not evaluate her mental and emotional state before putting her in that jail cell?[52] Black women are typically viewed by the criminal punishment system and society more broadly as combative and impervious to physical and emotional pain; it leaves a lot of room for cops to use those assumptions to justify their failure to care about their well-being. The answers to these questions are unknowable, despite resonating as potentially key aspects of what happened in the eighty minutes between Kindra's jailing and her being found unresponsive. Her rapid demise leaves many unanswered queries for loved ones and for those organizing around the treatment of Black women in police custody. The lack of definitive answers to these questions leads far too many to ignore extant racist and sexist dynamics in the criminal punishment system. What is knowable, however, is the deep entrenchment of misogynoir within policing and criminalizing systems. What we also know is that her family described her as a "wonderful soul" and a person with so much ahead of her.[53]

A little over a week after Kindra Chapman's death, Joyce Curnell died in police custody in Charleston County, South Carolina. The official cause of death for the fifty-year-old woman was dehydration.[54] She died in a housing unit in the Charleston County's jail facility. Before arriving at the jail, Joyce suffered from an existing stomach illness, coupled with intestinal irritation.[55] Her sudden incarceration ultimately contributed to her untimely death. In the days before her death, Joyce endured both nausea and vomiting.[56] An ambulance came to her home on Edisto Island, South Carolina, and took her to Roper Hospital. An emergency room doctor diagnosed her with gastroenteritis, an inflammation of the stomach and intestines.[57] Although not a fatal diagnosis, this viral or bacterial infection can cause extreme pain and discomfort. Hydration is one of the main lines of defense for those with this condition.

At some point during her stay at Roper Hospital, her son notified law enforcement of an open bench warrant for her arrest.[58] The circumstances under which police acquired this information about Joyce remain unclear. Her son has not confirmed whether police asked specific questions or if he volunteered the information.[59] The existence of the bench warrant, however, catalyzed a chain of events that led to the preventable death of Joyce Curnell. Three years prior to her death, Joyce was placed on a payment plan to pay the fines related to a shoplifting case.[60] The shoplifting case: Joyce and an acquaintance stole $20 worth of beer and candy bars from a neighborhood convenience store.[61] She made payments until January of 2013, leaving her with a balance of $1,184.90 still owed. Like so many poor Black women struggling to make ends meet, Joyce worked numerous low-wage jobs to simply stay afloat, including "deveining shrimp at a local restaurant" and cleaning houses on Edisto Island.[62] A warrant for her arrest followed in August 2014. Police arrested her at the hospital and took her to Charleston County Jail. Instead of being taken to the jail's medical facility, Joyce was placed in a normal housing unit and allegedly provided with a trash bag for vomiting.[63] Joyce was too weak to use the bathroom. The morning following her arrest, she was too ill to eat breakfast and continued to be visibly symptomatic.[64] While jailed, Joyce did not receive water or intravenous fluids.[65] Just twenty-seven hours after arriving at the jail, Joyce perished. The official and preventable cause of death was dehydration.

Everyone from those who arrested her to the jail's medical contractor, Carolina Center for Occupational Health, failed to provide Joyce with life-saving medical treatment. The inmate's Bill of Rights and South Carolina state law respectively require humane treatment of incarcerated persons and medical care for inmates in need.[66] Police arrested her as she was undergoing treatment for an illness.[67] Their awareness of her condition and her continued professions of pain, as well as her inability to eat or drink, were more than sufficient reasons to place her in the medical care unit of the jail. Instead, all involved from the arrest to the jailing ignored or dismissed her pain. Without curative or palliative treatment, Joyce suffered tremendously in her last few hours before dying.[68]

Joyce's death rests at the intersection of Black women's pain not being believed by medical professionals and the willful neglect of the police and jailers.[69] The failure to pay fines is not a capital offense, yet this minor transgression resulted in a preventable death. Her battle with alcoholism compromised her overall health, yet independent medical professionals reviewing her case concluded that dehydration and the failure to treat her gastroenteritis caused her death.[70] Punishing Joyce trumped caring for an ailing middle-aged Black woman. Those culpable either believed her and didn't care, or they didn't believe her despite arresting her in a hospital and deliberately denied care. Willful neglect or disavowal of Joyce's pain exemplifies the deadly effects of misogynoir on those in police custody. The events leading up to her death reveal negligence, inhumanity, and a subpar level of care too often afforded Black women in both the U.S. healthcare and criminal punishment systems.

On July 25, 2015, Ralkina Jones of Cleveland Heights, Ohio, was arrested for attacking her abusive ex-husband.[71] Ralkina was cooperative during the arrest and was peacefully taken to a Cleveland area jail.[72] During intake, she informed officers about her multiple medical conditions, including postural orthostatic tachycardia syndrome, depression, and ADHD. Ralkina also took medication for seizures. She also noted that she had suffered a brain injury that evening during her altercation with her ex-husband. Her sister informed cops at the scene that Ralkina suffered from a heart murmur as well. The combination of these illnesses and health challenges made her particularly vulnerable in a jail setting, where medical treatment is often subpar.

A few hours after interviewing Ralkina, police took her to HealthSpan medical clinic. After three and a half hours, officers brought her back to the jail. Only two hours after returning to her cell, jail personnel called paramedics to check her vitals. At some point while detained, Ralkina uttered "I don't want to die in your cell."[73] By 7:30 a.m. the next day, Ralkina was found nonresponsive in her cell. Emergency Medical Services pronounced her dead at the scene.[74] Gaps in recording, differing log reports regarding the administering of her medication, and infrequent checks throughout the evening make piecing together her last hours challenging. What is clear, however, is that those working at the jail let her die in the cell despite her cry for help.

The official cause of death was sudden cardiac death in association with postural tachycardia syndrome and obesity with amphetamine therapy.[75] The comorbidity not identified as a cause of death was medical neglect. Ralkina's multiple health challenges didn't compel jail staff to check on her condition more often than an arrestee with no known illnesses. Her cries were not met with compassion or reasonable consideration. Although recordings show initially respectful interactions between officers and Ralkina, the rapid demise of her health shows a glaring indifference toward her well-being after she was returned to jail from the clinic. At the time of her death, Ralkina had a twelve-year-old daughter waiting for her to come home. Although her family settled with the city in January 2018, many questions remain about what happened in those last hours and why she received only infrequent checks after her return from the medical clinic.[76] While not directly violent, Ralkina's death could possibly have been prevented if officers had taken seriously the severity of her multiple health issues. Like Joyce, Ralkina's death also resulted from willful neglect. Those officers didn't see Ralkina as a domestic violence victim, as the mother of a preteen, or as a vulnerable person in distress. She was criminalized and disregarded. She died alone in a cell.

One day after Ralkina died in Cleveland Heights, Ohio, a forty-two-year-old mother of eight, Raynette Turner, died in a holding cell in Mt. Vernon, New York. Arrested for allegedly stealing crab legs from Restaurant Depot in the Bronx, Raynette faced a petty larceny charge.[77] Officers could've given her a desk appearance ticket to appear in court at a later date. After all, it was only $40 worth of crab legs allegedly stolen.[78] It was a Saturday and the police opted not to call a judge to conduct a brief arraignment, which would've allowed Raynette to return home to her family. Even more shockingly, her name was not found on the court calendar for the following Monday's court session, begging the question, was a formal complaint ever filed?[79] Instead of choosing any of the options that would've permitted Turner to return to her family, officers placed her in a holding cell. Not only did Turner indicate that she did not feel well; she vomited while in custody. Police finally relented and took her to Montefiore Mount Vernon Hospital for treatment of her nausea.[80] Montefiore briefly treated her, and police took her back to jail.[81] Officers also reportedly knew about existing health conditions beyond her visible symptoms, including hypertension and possible complications from a recent bariatric surgery.[82] She suffered for hours before her eventual death as a result of medical neglect.

The official cause of death was an enlarged heart, the result of long-term cocaine and morphine use.[83] Consequently, the arresting and detaining officers were found not criminally culpable for her death.[84] While her health conditions undeniably contributed to her death, her pleas for help went unanswered. Neither the cops nor the medical personnel on that fateful day in July 2015 took seriously the gravity of Raynette's pain. Whether they thought she was exaggerating or "faking," she repeatedly indicated her deteriorating condition. Medical neglect too often befalls Black women, both within and outside of the criminal punishment system. The inability to believe Raynette was in pain fits into a long racist and sexist American tradition of treating Black women as impervious to pain. The unlisted comorbidities for Turner were misogynoir and antiBlackness.

Although July 2015 was a particularly harrowing month for reports of Black women dying in police custody, there's no shortage of examples in more recent years. In August 2018 in Dallas, Texas, local police were called in response to a domestic disturbance. During their encounter with Diamond Ross, police suspected she was under the influence of a substance. Police reported that Diamond became combative when they attempted to arrest her. Throughout the encounter, Diamond proclaimed that she needed water and that "I can't breathe."[85] The refrain "I can't breathe" has been the last words too many Black folks utter during violent encounters with police.[86] They were the words of Eric Garner in July 2014 and of George Floyd in May 2020. The videos of these Black men's deaths went viral and caused a global outcry. While videos do exist of Diamond's arrest, confirming that she informed the officers of her inability to breathe, her story prompted no national outrage.

After the arrest, they placed her in a squad car and took her to the City of Dallas Detention Center. Before literally carrying her into the jail, they left her restrained and nearly lifeless on the pavement.[87] They then dragged her into a holding cell and left. Officers made no attempt at CPR. Eventually, they placed Diamond in a wheelchair.[88] Several minutes passed before paramedics arrived and took her to Baylor Hospital. She was declared dead the next day, and cause of death was listed as an accidental overdose.[89] Toxicology reports confirmed the presence of PCP.[90] The lack of care that officers afforded her, despite her repeated calls for help, contributed to her death. If they listened to her or saw her as a person in distress, perhaps her life could've been saved. They ignored her cries for help because they could. They saw her as a violent "junkie," not as a person struggling with drug addiction who couldn't breathe.

In June 2019, a well-known Afro-Latinx trans woman, Layleen Xtravaganza Cubilette-Polanco, was found dead in her cell at Rikers Island Jail in New York.[91] Layleen was part of the vibrant New York City underground ballroom scene and a member of the beloved and globally renowned House of Xtravaganza.[92] Although described as bubbly by her loved ones, her sister noted a shift in Layleen's demeanor in the months before her death. Layleen had been looking for jobs and trying to get into school but continued to encounter transphobia in her search for employment.[93] This vivacious young woman struggled, like so many others, to survive in an antiBlack, antitrans, antipoor, and misogynistic world. She was trying to survive, live, and thrive by any means necessary, which rendered her particularly vulnerable to participating in illicit economies and to being criminalized for surviving and coping with the realities of multiple jeopardy.

In the immediate aftermath of her death, details were scant. An inability to pay bail for minor offenses pertaining to sex work and drug possession meant Layleen could not be released from jail. With her bail set at $500, Layleen remained in solitary confinement in the notoriously repressive and violent Rikers facility.[94] Black trans women, especially those engaged in sex work, are particularly vulnerable to criminalization.[95] Layleen existed at the intersection of antiBlack racism, sexism, transphobia, and hatred of sex workers. Layleen's death in police custody could have been prevented had any of the officers bothered to check on her well-being. Although the official cause of death was listed as complications from epilepsy, the negligence of officers compounded her medical distress.[96]

Layleen's story garnered very little media coverage and only a handful of local protests, led by Black/and Latinx LGBTQ organizers. She deserved more. The deaths of Black trans women rarely, if ever, gain widespread attention, even from Black-centered media. The burden to amplify their stories typically falls on other Black trans folks and a handful of committed allies. Transphobia and, in some cases, devaluation of sex work and sex workers affect how people organize and mobilize around the deaths of Black trans women.[97] The story of Black women's deaths in police custody, however, is incomplete without including stories like Layleen's encounter with the criminal punishment system.

At the intersection of a politics of disposability and misogynoir are the deaths of Diamond, Layleen, Sandra, Raynette, Ralkina, Kindra, and Joyce. "Deaths in police custody are often associated with excessive force, medical neglect, or failure to prevent suicide, and they are more common than they should be."[98] The five Black women who died in police custody in July 2015 and those who have died since that time not only exemplify this harsh reality; they reveal a distinct and systemic cruelty against Black women. Medical neglect led to the deaths of Joyce, Raynette, Ralkina, Diamond, and Layleen. Jail personnel did not work to prevent the suicide of Kindra or the suspicious death of Sandra. Most of these Black women died within three days of being jailed for allegedly committing minor offenses. Shoplifting, unpaid fines, drug use, sex work, or a failure to signal are not capital offenses, yet these violations contributed to deaths in police custody. The criminalization of these Black women for relatively minor offenses encapsulates the structural effects of misogynoir. Cash bail, systemic lack of empathy, and the hypercriminalization of minor offenses disproportionately affect Black women and girls encountering the criminal punishment system. The combined weight of these realities can and often does have violent and even fateful outcomes. Criminalization kills Black women and girls.

Criminalizing Black Womanhood

The criminalization of victimized Black women and girls who defend themselves against violence also exemplifies another facet of misogynoir. In her 1991 germinal article, "Mapping the Margins: Intersectionality, Identity Politics, and Violence against Women of Color," Kimberlé Crenshaw affirmed the necessity of exploring the race and gender dynamics of violence against women of color. Intersectionality offered a lens for both individuals and systems to reckon with how racism and sexism coconstitutively contribute to violence against these women.[99] The inability of Black women and girls to claim self-defense when fending for their lives or the lives of their loved ones stems from their marginalization. We can't claim self-defense in a system that overdetermines us as criminal or incapable of being violated. The criminal punishment system historically and contemporarily renders racially disparate outcomes for cases involving Black victims.[100] Self-defense emerges as one of few vehicles for surviving violent encounters. Black women and girls have no legal reprieve from being terrorized. We aren't allowed to defend ourselves without being criminalized for it.

Self-defense exists as an affirmative defense to provide those "reasonably fearing for their lives."[101] This defense often does not extend to black girls and women who've been raped or beaten; it does extend, however, to almost all police officers and vigilantes killing unarmed Black people.[102] What constitutes a reasonable fear for one's life, and how is reasonable fear delineated for people of differing racial, socioeconomic, occupational, gender, religious, or sexual identities? For the numerous police officers who have killed Black people in the twenty-first century, an officer's belief of being in "imminent danger of grievous injury or death" is the legal standard for a justifiable homicide.[103] Although "trained" to de-escalate and to minimize harm to all parties, police officers receive the widest latitude for determining what constitutes imminent danger. A battered Black woman or girl faces a far harsher and less compassionate criminal punishment system when she details the imminent danger she has faced. Police officers, who undergo training to appropriately assess danger, are given more space to be wrong about imminent danger than an untrained Black woman being violently attacked.

Black women and girls defending themselves against abuse occurs in cases of forced sex work, transphobic attacks, family violence, and intimate partner violence. Although several recent examples of each of these "survived and punished" circumstances exist, the four discussed here attempt to capture the range of criminalization of Black women and girls. Bresha Meadows, Cyntoia Brown, CeCe McDonald, and Marissa Alexander survived various forms of violence and were punished for defending themselves against violent perpetrators. Digging into the similarities and differences among their stories should give us a deeper understanding of the systemic criminalization of Black girlhood and womanhood. Their stories also unveil understudied parts of mass incarceration and the limitations of self-defense as a mitigating factor in their treatment by the criminal punishment system. Criminalizing Black women and girls' survival is a distinct form of devaluing Black life, as well as a unique form of racial and gender terror.

In Defense of Ourselves

He told me he'd kill me. He knows where my mom lives. And I know if a dude choked me until I almost passed out, he's not afraid to kill me.

—CYNTOIA BROWN

These words haunted sixteen-year-old Cyntoia Brown. Reportedly her pimp, Garion "Kutthroat" McGlothen, regularly threatened and brutally assaulted her as a way to control her.[104] Although unable to consent to many of the sexual acts her pimp ordered her to perform, Cyntoia became one of the millions of children around the world trafficked for the purpose of rape and sexual assault.[105] Kutthroat's alleged abuse also included berating her, calling her a whore and a slut.[106] He repeatedly asserted that no one would want her but him.[107] In sex trafficking, this process of devaluation and dehumanization is referred to as "breaking a bitch." Creating dependency emboldens the sense of control a pimp has over a young victim. By the time Cyntoia killed one of her many rapists, Kutthroat had broken her.

According to Cyntoia, the evening of the killing transpired as follows. After she arrived at the home of Johnny Michael Allen, he showed her his gun collection.[108] Identifying himself as a former army sharpshooter intensified her nervousness. They ate dinner and watched television before heading to his bed. They got into the bed, and he forcefully grabbed her vagina. This further exacerbated her fear of a violent encounter. In the immediate aftermath of this aggressive act, a statutory rape occurred. Allen paid her and went to sleep. Cyntoia left the room and retrieved a gun from his collection. She returned to the bedroom with the gun and shot Allen in the back of the head. She fled the scene of the killing with Allen's wallet, gun, and car.[109]

The prosecution in Cyntoia's trial successfully convinced a jury that her actions constituted premeditated murder, robbery, and prostitution.[110] For the prosecution, a sleeping Allen did not pose a threat to her. Their depiction of Cyntoia omitted her rape at the hands of Allen. Those demanding she be labeled a calculating murderer invalidated her experiences of serial violence both in her family and at the hands of her pimp. Her trauma was invisible. She did not choose to be raped by Allen or to be choked by Kutthroat, yet her history of victimization did not result in leniency or any modicum of compassion. She was tried as an adult and sentenced to life in prison. A nearly lifelong victim of rape and sexual and physical assaults, Cyntoia would not be eligible for parole until she is sixty-nine years old. Her victimization as a Black girl was meaningless as part of her defense. The only victim visible in this trial and conviction was a forty-three-year-old rapist.

In the 2010s, Cyntoia Brown's story and conviction became a cause célèbre. People expressed renewed outrage at the criminal punishment system's inability to account for the extraordinary trauma and violence Brown experienced in her life before turning eighteen. The combination of advocacy and activism was led by Black women; a 2011 documentary, *Me Facing Life: Cyntoia's Story*, chronicling both her experiences and her trial; a 2017 petition for her release; and the public support of celebrities such as Rihanna and LeBron James.[111] The foundational work of Black women brought Cyntoia's harrowing story and her conviction for murder into the national spotlight. Public pressure and heightened interest in her case led to a clemency hearing in May 2018.[112]

A parole board split on whether to grant her clemency, to reduce her sentence, or to uphold her original sentence.[113] Two members of the board voted to grant clemency. Two other members voted to reduce her sentence and make her eligible for parole after serving twenty-five years. The remaining members of the board voted to uphold her original sentence. During the hearing, Cyntoia expressed gratitude for the board granting a hearing. The split among the board members reflected three distinct interpretations of Cyntoia's 2004 actions: (1) she committed premeditated murder of a sleeping man; (2) she killed a man, but there were mitigating circumstances that warranted a modicum of compassion and leniency; (3) she killed her rapist, and this killing was directly related to her subjection to years of physical and sexual violation.[114] Tennessee governor Bill Haslam had the final word on Cyntoia's future. In early January 2019, he granted executive clemency. She was released on parole for ten years on August 7, 2019. While no longer incarcerated, she had to wait an additional eight months to be released after being granted clemency and will be under the hypersurveillance of the state until 2029.[115]

What became clear to many throughout the trial and the clemency hearing was that Cyntoia was a victim of multiple acts of sexual violence in her childhood via forced sex work. Her struggle to survive played an undeniable role in her conviction and subsequent incarceration. She was a victim of sex trafficking—not to be conflated with consensual sex work.[116] The tendency, even among those advocating and organizing for victims of trafficking, is to conflate consensual sex work with the stark global phenomenon of sex trafficking. This is not a matter of semantics but an insistence on appropriately identifying violence inflicted on trafficking victims and distinguishing that from consenting adults working within sexual and gray economies, who are also vulnerable to sexual violence.[117] Like the one million children and teenagers under eighteen throughout the world being trafficked for the purpose of sexual violence, Cyntoia could not consent to many of the acts she was paid to participate in or perform.[118] Every client over the age of eighteen with whom she engaged committed an act of sexual violence.

Cyntoia emerged as yet another example of the unjustness of the U.S. criminal punishment system, as well as its unique callousness toward Black girls, and more broadly Black women and girls victimized by violence. Her story sits at the intersection of rape culture, gender violence, antiBlack racism, patriarchy, misogyny, and the prison industrial complex. The incarceration of battered, brutalized, and sexually violated Black women and girls for defending themselves results from the endemic structural precarity that we encounter within this system. Unable to be seen as "true" victims and stereotyped as overly aggressive, hypersexual, and irrationally angry, those of us who endure abuse within this system have little recourse.

Battered women syndrome—a condition often asserted by defense teams seeking a not guilty verdict for clients with "provable" histories of violent victimization—is disturbingly limited in its application.[119] Cases such as Cyntoia's illuminate the racial limitations on which battered women can lay claim to self-defense.[120] Legally, self-defense acts can also result from extreme emotional distress.[121] Within our criminal punishment system Black girls, like Cyntoia, who have endured ongoing violence are not viewed as being in extreme emotional distress. Their victimization does not factor into their trials. Years of sexual violence fail to convince juries and judges that Black girls like Cyntoia reasonably feared for their lives.

Unfortunately, she is not exceptional in experiencing antiBlack and sexist treatment by the criminal punishment system.

Two months before fourteen-year-old Bresha Meadows shot and killed her father, she ran away from her home in Warren, Ohio, to stay with an aunt in nearby Cleveland, Ohio. After witnessing her father, Jonathan Meadows, routinely beat her mother, Brandi Meadows, and hearing his threats to kill her whole family, Bresha resorted to running away as her only viable and potentially life-saving option.[122] According to her mother, Bresha witnessed daily physical and mental abuse at the hands of her husband. Brandi Meadows also recalled more than a dozen visits to hospitals, urgent care, and other outpatient medical facilities throughout her twenty-two-year marriage to Jonathan.[123] Evidence of his violence includes holes and marks in the kitchen wall of their home—made by his fists as well as by Brandi's head being shoved into it.[124] A 2011 police report and civil restraining order cited Brandi's fear for her life and the lives of her three children and Jonathan Meadow's potential for "extreme violence."[125] Brandi even noted shifts in her daughter's disposition toward one of fear, sadness, and uncertainty. Bresha pleaded on numerous occasions for her mother to leave her father, fearing his abuse would turn fatal.

When Bresha ran away in May 2016, she was attempting to escape a violent norm in her household. Her mother's understandable expressions of fear about leaving her husband or of calling authorities compounded a sense of helplessness when she returned home from school each day and locked herself in her room. Back in 2011, her mother dropped the civil restraining order under pressure from her husband. Bresha's options for ending a cycle of violence or even a brief reprieve from it lessened each day she remained in her household. While staying with her aunt, she proclaimed that she would rather kill herself than live in a house with her father.[126] After she returned from her brief stay with her aunt, Bresha went right back to the frightening reality that compelled her to run away in the first place.

Despite Jonathan's family's insistence that his abusive behavior ceased years ago, considerable evidence including accounts of family members in the household, as well as house damage caused by physical assaults, tells a different story.[127] Even Bresha's best friend, Saquoya, witnessed the effects of Jonathan's violence on her friend. Saquoya thought Bresha suffered from depression because of seeing her mom repeatedly abused.[128] Although there was no official diagnosis of Bresha's mental state leading up to the killing, depression is a common condition for those directly and indirectly experiencing domestic abuse. Exposure to violence in the household has long-term effects on the physical, emotional, and mental well-being of children.[129]

In many ways, evidence confirms Bresha's account of events leading up to the night she killed her father. The terror that Jonathan wreaked on his family took Bresha to a point where she felt only his complete removal from their lives would end the violence against her family. Like her mother, she feared what would happen if she reported him to authorities or if authorities issued another restraining order. What in her history with her father would suggest that his response to police involvement would be anything but violent? Her fears echoed those of many people living in abusive households as both children and adults.

In the early morning hours of July 28, 2016, Bresha Meadows took her father's .45-caliber, semiautomatic handgun. After retrieving the gun, she went into the living room of their home, where he was sleeping. She shot and killed her sleeping father. In that moment, the violence her family endured ended with her father's last breath. Bresha was immediately arrested. Police transported her to a juvenile detention center in Warren.[130] This was the last time Bresha saw her home until February 2018. The killing sent shockwaves through her family and their community. Whereas her mother publicly expressed relief and called Bresha her hero, Jonathan's family felt the murder was calculated.[131] They challenged the veracity of claims of years of ongoing abuse. Bresha's act of self- and familial preservation divided her family. Although her father could no longer terrorize her family, Bresha faced harsh consequences for defending herself and her loved ones.

Bresha Meadows is one of the youngest examples of the criminal punishment system's failure to reckon with the impact of domestic violence on Black girls and women. Convicting Meadows for killing her serially abusive father, despite overwhelming evidence of the numerous ways he terrorized her and her family for years, represents a tendency to criminalize a Black girl's act of self-defense. Although eventually released back to a mental health facility and the care of her family after a slightly early release from the detention center, her prosecution and incarceration reflect a perniciousness far too many Black girls and women experience within this system.[132] Depicted as murderous and vengeful, Meadows was convicted of involuntary manslaughter; her conviction and subsequent incarceration in a juvenile detention center displayed the illegibility of the victimization of a Black girl. This illegibility is systemic and evident in case after case involving Black women and girls defending themselves against violence.

The 2012 case of Marissa Alexander also speaks to this pervasive illegibility. On August 1, 2010, Marissa was in the Florida home of her estranged husband, Rico Gray. She asserted that Gray threatened her life via texts and in-person.[133] Given his history of abusive behavior, Marissa feared for her life. She attempted to escape through the garage but could not open it. She then got a gun from her car in the garage, returned to the kitchen, and fired a warning shot into the air. Her attempt to defend herself against someone she reasonably believed might kill her did not cause harm to any person. She tried to stand her ground against a violent partner. Her documented history with him included a restraining order, multiple accounts of abuse not disputed by Gray, and a belief that she had the right to use lethal force if she feared for her life. What she did not know, however, was that a "warning shot" was not legal.[134]

It is worth noting the alarming rate at which black women are victims of domestic violence homicides. Black women are the victims of domestic violence homicide at 2.5 times the rate of white women.[135] Later in this book, I delve more deeply into the realities of intimate partner and domestic violence in the lives of Black women and girls. Beyond statistics and headlines, the reality of Black women and girls being assaulted, sexually violated, or even killed in familial and intimate spaces further contextualizes the mortal fear and hopelessness suffered by Marissa and several other Black women and girls as they fought to survive. Given what Marissa endured at the hands of her ex-partner, firing a warning shot was both an act of self-defense and an attempt to not harm the person who harmed her. She opted for one of the least violent options available to her as a survivor of intimate partner violence.

The court did not agree that Marissa had a right to save her own life and those of her family. She was convicted of aggravated assault with a lethal weapon and sentenced to twenty years in prison.[136] After an appellate court overturned the first trial and sentencing, the prosecuting attorney, Angela Corey, sought to have Marissa sentenced to three consecutive twenty-year sentences. Corey insisted that Marissa shot at her ex-husband out of anger, not fear.[137] Fearing for her life should have been a mitigating factor. Corey, however, saw this abuse victim as an irrational, angry Black woman who put the lives of the children in the home and her abusive ex-husband in danger. Despite the ex-husband confirming his abusive behavior toward Marissa, Corey refused to see her as a terrified victim, who didn't want to harm anyone. The "angry Black woman" stereotype is entrenched in the criminal punishment system. Marissa ran up against a system unable to identify her as a battered woman. Furthermore, this system failed, as writer and emotional justice activist Esther Armah contends "to grapple with the cumulative impact of domestic violence on a survivor's sense of fear and notion of threat."[138] Existing laws provided legal grounding for hypercriminalizing a domestic violence victim. In July 2015, Marissa took a plea deal, which included time already served, and was released from a Jacksonville prison.[139] Additionally, she served two years under house arrest with an ankle monitor.

In the same state where unauthorized neighborhood watchman George Zimmerman was found not guilty of murdering seventeen-year-old Trayvon Martin, an unarmed seventeen-year-old black boy, because Zimmerman "feared for his life," Marissa could not stand her ground.[140] Corey served as the prosecuting attorney in the Zimmerman trial. Corey failed to convince a jury of Zimmerman's guilt in the killing of a Black teenager being pursued by a vigilante, yet she sought the maximum sentence for Alexander's act of self-defense.[141] The disparate outcomes in cases tried by the same district attorney help illuminate the role misogynoir plays in the criminal punishment system. A jury believed that an unarmed Black boy posed a threat to an armed adult, while another jury could not believe that a Black woman reasonably feared for her life and the life of her children from an abusive ex-partner. A warning shot fired by a Black woman is a violent act; the unauthorized pursuit and murder of a Black boy is an act of self-defense. The fact these two "Stand Your Ground" incidents occurred within the same year makes the comparison even more apt. It allows for a pointed assessment of the racist and sexist (de)valuation Black women experience when they claim "self-defense." Whose fears rise to the standard of reasonable?

The legal system's misogynoir also has particularly stark effects for Black trans women.[142] The case of CeCe McDonald garnered more mainstream attention than nearly any case involving the violent victimization of Black trans women prior to her surviving a vicious assault on June 6, 2011. CeCe and her friends were confronted by a mixed-gender group including Dean Schmitz, Jenny Thoreson, and Megan Flaherty outside of Schooner Tavern.[143] According to CeCe, the group hurled racist and transphobic slurs at her and her friends as they stood outside smoking cigarettes. After enduring a barrage of insults, she and her friends attempted to leave. The group escalated their attacks to a physical level shortly thereafter.

Reportedly, Flaherty smashed a bottle of alcohol on CeCe's face, resulting in her needing eleven stitches.[144] Thoreson told police that after that, Flaherty threw the first punch. At this point, CeCe and her friends retaliated in self-defense, physically attacking Flaherty. Schmitz pulled CeCe off of Flaherty, and they became engaged in a fight. CeCe asserts that she tried to move away from Schmitz, but that he charged her.[145] The fight ceased when it became clear that Schmitz had been stabbed with a pair of scissors. Differing accounts attribute his stabbing to CeCe, as well as another person in her group. She and a friend fled the scene to a nearby grocery store.[146] Schmitz died in the ambulance. As police circled the area, CeCe exited the store, flagged the officers down, and ultimately confessed to stabbing Schmitz. Still bleeding from wounds inflicted during the brawl, she affirmed that she feared for her life.[147]

Hennepin County prosecutor Michael Freeman reviewed the evidence, which included a taped confession from CeCe, and charged her with second-degree murder.[148] He argued that Schmitz didn't pose a threat to her and therefore killing him was not an act of self-defense. Freeman further asserted that CeCe didn't exercise her "duty to retreat." Lastly, Freeman declared that no evidence existed to prove Schmitz assaulted her. The case against CeCe was strong, particularly in a system that devalues and criminalizes Black trans women. The racist, sexist, and transphobic stereotypes about Black trans women are bountiful. The legal system struggled to grasp why CeCe feared for her life, despite clear evidence of her having been attacked. This system didn't even acknowledge a bloody history of transphobic assaults and murders in the United States.[149] CeCe knew that history and moved through the world with an understanding of how vulnerable she was to transphobic violence, especially as a Black trans woman. Not long before the altercation provoked by racist and transphobic slurs, a police officer briefly stopped, questioned, and followed CeCe and her friends.[150] This was nothing new for her, as police regularly surveil and criminalize Black trans women.[151] CeCe was vulnerable not only to the group who attacked her but to an officer who identified her as potentially criminal. Self-defense is a constant state of being for Black trans women who face the threat of violence on a painfully consistent basis.

In 2012, CeCe accepted a plea bargain under which second-degree murder charges were dropped to second-degree manslaughter.[152] This reduction compelled her to admit to criminal negligence rather than murder. Media coverage of CeCe's case prompted outrage from some who could not fathom how this wasn't a clear case of self-defense. CeCe, like Cyntoia, Bresha, and Marissa, was being punished for surviving. On June 4, 2012, Judge Daniel Moreno sentenced CeCe to forty-one months and gave credit for the 245 days already served; she also had to pay restitution for Schmitz's funeral expenses.[153] For defending herself against a brutal, transphobic assault, CeCe was imprisoned in a men's facility for her entire nineteen months behind bars.[154] After her release, which included supervision by the state for the remainder of her sentence, she became a prominent trans activist.[155] She told and continues to tell her powerful story in hopes that it will shed light on the epidemic of violence against Black trans women. At the crossroads of antiBlackness, transphobia, and misogyny, victimized Black trans women routinely experience unjust outcomes in the criminal punishment system.[156] Black trans women are among the most vulnerable group of women to violent crimes, yet CeCe's act of self-defense was criminalized.[157] If she had not defended herself, she may have been one of too many Black trans women murdered in the past decade.[158] She fought back to avoid becoming another fatal and too easily forgotten statistic. She fought back for her life, and too few fought for the value of hers.

For Black women and girls, the inaccessibility of legalized "self-defense" produces two harrowing options: (1) do not fight back and either continue being brutalized and or risk being killed; (2) fight back and risk being incarcerated for surviving. These are not viable, just, or humane options. These options do not create space for Black women and girls to protect themselves from a range of violent acts. A legal system refusing to account for mitigating circumstances for Black women and girls charged with violent crimes will continue to convict and harshly sentence them for defending themselves. Cyntoia, Marissa, Bresha, and CeCe feared for their lives, whether in the long or short term, and defended themselves. The criminal punishment system severely punishes Black women and girls for being victims of violence, especially those who defend themselves. A system grounded in antiBlack racism and sexism routinely neglects Black women and girls as victims. The incarceration of Black women and girls for defending themselves against potentially fatal threats sends a powerful and distinct message: survival is a racialized, gendered, and class-based privilege overdetermined by white supremacy, patriarchy, capitalism, transphobia, and misogyny. Striking similarities exist among some of these higher-profile cases of "survived and punished" Black girls and women. These parallels expose the depths of misogynoir in criminalizing systems.

Whether in police custody for allegedly committing minor offenses or being incarcerated for acts of self-defense, Black women and girls' stories within the criminal punishment system are harrowing. Scholars such as Beth Richie, Monique Morris, and Emily Thuma powerfully document the specific ways policing and prisons directly impact Black women and girls. The screams from those who died in police custody and who fought back to survive, however, remain largely unheard. More often, we talk about the effects of antiBlackness in this system by noting how deeply impactful the incarceration of Black men and boys is on Black women and girls, who are mothers, aunts, sisters, nieces, god-daughters, grandmothers, and cousins. Black women and girls directly feel the loss in their families and communities when Black men and boys are incarcerated. Often it is us putting money on the books, sustaining our families, and visiting and doing our best to support our loved ones on lockdown. The ripple effects of mass incarceration of Black women and girls are simply in overabundance.

It's equally important, however, to chronicle the direct experiences Black women and girls have with prisons, jails, juvenile detention centers, and policing. We are also behind the wall. Our deaths in police custody and our incarceration for acts of self-defense must be railed against and stopped. Every year the list of Black women's and girls' deaths in police custody and those convicted for responding to violent victimization grows. This list conveys the extent to which we are criminalized and at the mercy of a purposefully unjust criminal punishment system. Our victimization within a criminalizing system is a huge part of the violence we face, but it's certainly not the only perpetrator of note. Violence against us often occurs in the spaces where we love and make love. Harm at the hands of those closest to us is a huge part of the story of violence against Black women and girls. It's much more challenging for me and a lot of us to tell that part of our story because it requires calling out the same Black men and boys with whom we build community and family and with whom we rage against white supremacy. The violence that I find most difficult to talk about is that which occurs within Black communities—and, too often, in our homes. The names of those harmed or killed in intracommunal contexts may not become hashtags, but their lives and livelihoods matter too.

3 *Up against the Wind*

Intracommunal Violence

I traveled home to the D.C. area in June 2020 to celebrate my mom's seventieth birthday and our first Father's Day since my dad passed. I quarantined and social distanced for months just so I could drive from Columbus to see my mother for these festive and mournful occasions. Hugging her was my first form of human contact since the arrival of the COVID-19 global pandemic. I lingered in the hug, knowing it would be one of few moments of touch I would experience for the rest of 2020. I'm not a hugger by any stretch, but a global pandemic brought to light a basic need for touch—the feel of care. I soaked up every second with my mom, as it fortified me for the ensuing months of uncertainty, collective despair, and loneliness.

On a drive to southeast Washington, D.C., to do a curbside pickup of my mom's favorite hair cream, we pulled behind a white van. We instantly noticed something disturbing. From the car's sideview mirrors, we saw a young, Black couple arguing. The driver, a young Black man probably in his twenties, pushed the young Black woman in the passenger seat. Traffic, at this point, had briefly come to a stop at a red light. The young man got out of the van, walked around it, opened the passenger door, and grabbed the young woman. *My heart stopped.* Time seemed to simultaneously speed up and slow down as I watched him assault her. It happened in a matter of seconds, but each second after he exited the van filled me with wrathful indignation. He violently tossed her out of the car and threw her belongings onto the street next to her spindly body. As he called her a "fucking bitch" and a "stupid ass ho," she begged him not to leave. He left.

When he grabbed her out of the car, my mom and I pulled over, as did a couple of cars in front of us. In my mask, I quickly went over to her right before he pulled off. Tears streamed down her face as she kept calling for him to come back. The van was already at the next light, nearly out of sight. She couldn't get up off the ground. One of the couples from a car that pulled over noticed her inability to move as well. Our concern intensified. In between asking each other how this man could just assault this young woman and leave her on the damn street, someone watching this unfold called the police.

Her cries deepened. Her breathing became labored. As I sat down next to her shaking and frail body, I saw a medical wristband on her right arm, a bandage over her jugular I assumed was from a recent intubation, and medical discharge papers on the ground next to her. She'd just been released from the hospital. After gently telling her, I wasn't going to leave her side, I asked her, "What's your name sista?" She struggled to reply, "Montana."[1] Her next words nearly broke my heart, "I can't breathe." Just a few weeks prior to this incident, the world witnessed the last nine minutes and twenty-nine seconds of George Floyd's life, as Minneapolis police officer Derek Chauvin pressed his knee against Floyd's neck despite Floyd's repeated professions of "I can't breathe." Six years prior, the viral video of the police killing of Eric Garner in Staten

Island, New York, showed Garner pleading with an officer choking him. Garner told the officer again and again, "I can't breathe." Looking at Montana's frightened face as she uttered those words, I feared what might happen next.

Within seconds of informing me of her name and inability to breathe, Montana began seizing. Her dark brown arms and legs hit the pavement with such force with each convulsion. Her eyes rolled back into her head. Her spasms were visible to onlookers passing by in their cars, as we were still in the middle of a very busy street. One of the people who stopped ran to get a blanket from their car while I and another person turned Montana on her side. We didn't want her to choke. By the time the person ran back with a blanket and placed it under her head and neck, Montana began vomiting a yellowish-brown viscous fluid. The bandage on her neck gradually became brownish red. I laid down next to her on the pavement, reassuring her more help was on the way and that WE wouldn't leave her.

As I lay there, hot tears of anger and sadness poured down my face. Someone picked up her discharge papers to get some insight into what might be happening. He leaned over to me and said, "She's epileptic." I immediately began internally timing the seizure, so I could inform the paramedics about the length of it. Every few seconds, her seizing appeared to get more and more erratic. *Where was this damn ambulance? Is the young Black woman going to die in the middle of the street after being assaulted by someone she knew and perhaps loved?* I couldn't help but also hope that the police wouldn't come. In addition to being in the middle of one of the largest national uprisings against racist policing and police brutality in U.S. history, I knew all too well how cops tended to handle Black women in distress. As I detailed in my first chapter, cops' responses to Black women in distress too often result in carceral or fatal outcomes. I also had concerns about how the paramedics would handle this seizing Black girl who'd just been assaulted and left on the street by her companion. I didn't trust that who was coming would care about her the way those of us who stopped to help did. I didn't trust any of the people charged with aiding Montana. But in this moment, I couldn't wait for more help to arrive.

As I lay on the ground, out of the corner of my eye, I saw a young Black man in a Black T-shirt crossing the median from the other side of the street. He headed toward us. It was him, the guy who assaulted Montana and threw her out of that white van. He ran over to her and knelt beside her still seizing body commanding her to "get up." My fear of what would happen when "help" arrived quickly transformed into fury as I lay next to Montana. He then started asking those of us who pulled over, "What happened?" More incredulously, he posed an even more absurd question: "Did she get hit by a car or something?" Before I could even say, "Shut the fuck up. You know you did this," an ambulance and two cop cars arrived.

The young man, clearly under the influence of something, literally attempted to lift Montana's writhing body off the ground. One of the helpful bystanders interjected, just as the paramedics walked over to me and asked what happened. I wanted to yell, "Do you not see a whole ass person seizing and vomiting?" But I knew that would only negatively affect the level of care Montana might receive. Two paramedics began assessing and assisting her. Another paramedic asked me again what happened and how long she'd been seizing. He seemed caring enough. I wiped a few remaining tears away and began telling him what I witnessed. While I conversed with the paramedics, two of the police officers began asking my mother and one of the other bystanders about what had transpired. All of us took turns reluctantly and sparsely informing the police about the events leading up to Montana's seizing. Our reluctance stemmed from our shared and unsaid understanding that by even engaging the cops, this awful situation could become more violent. It's not that we didn't want accountability for what this man did to Montana; we just knew that what accountability looked like for the cops might include a deadly escalation.

Another cop car arrived, and three of the cops already on the scene began questioning the young Black man. Paramedics got a still-seizing Montana onto a stretcher and put her into the ambulance. Two bystanders left at this point, relieved that medical assistance had arrived. Around five of us stayed, as we now felt compelled to ensure that the young man who just assaulted Montana would not be harmed. The cops surrounded him. His gestures became more and more fitful as he denied any wrongdoing. Someone began filming the encounter on their iPhone. My mother and I stood close to each other and used witnessing as our passive intervention into what could've been a violent escalation. After several minutes of questioning and taking our statements, the officers let the young man go. I felt conflicted and momentarily relieved that this didn't turn into yet another fatal police encounter. That brief respite, however, subsided as soon as I got back in the car, sanitized my hands, and cried again. I didn't know Montana's fate. What I did know is that in the middle of a pandemic, her companion assaulted her and left her in the middle of the street. My concern for her outweighed my concern for her assailant, and I still couldn't turn away from my instinctive impulse to protect him as well. Nothing about my politics allowed me to divest from caring about this young Black man, even as I worried about the harm he may inflict on Montana in the future. I didn't sleep well that night or the following for that matter.

Just a couple of months after bearing witness and withness to Montana's assault, one of my favorite new rappers, Megan Thee Stallion, went on Instagram Live to share details about an allegation of a violent encounter she had had with fellow rapper Tory Lanez. Prior to this very public disclosure, Meg's statements about being shot in her foot were scrutinized, derided, and dismissed by a considerable number of people. Her decision to share her truth, the same week she celebrated reaching #1 on the Billboard Hot 100 alongside rapper Cardi B, was prompted by a barrage of jokes, silence from many within the popular music industry, and a palpable lack of sympathy. Someone she cared about allegedly shot her. People laughed, searched for reasons not to believe her, and even dabbled in transmisogynoir to justify the violence that had befallen the young star.[2] Her pain didn't matter.

In the IG Live she unequivocally identified her attacker as Tory Lanez, explained why she didn't cooperate with police, and defended her decision to protect everyone in the car with her on the night of her violent assault, including the alleged perpetrator. Megan noted that "even though he shot me, I tried to spare him. And y'all aren't sparing me." Meg's inclination to protect the person who harmed her felt eerily like my decision to ensure that the young man who assaulted Montana didn't incur harm from the police. Meg knew the police could escalate the situation and potentially harm her and him. She couldn't trust the police, even at a moment when she needed someone to care for her. She received backlash for protecting him and for her sharing truth. Numerous people found a way to villainize the victim of a shooting. Her pain was either illegible or unimportant. Too few of her rap industry peers—especially Black men who had collaborated with her or previously publicly professed their love and respect for her—offered any semblance of public support for her in the aftermath of the violent encounter. Even after Lanez was charged in the incident, people continued to aggressively denounce Meg for speaking out and, worse, for "lying." Megan's choice to protect those involved in the incident follows a troubling pattern across centuries of history in which many Black women and girls navigate patriarchal, gender, and sexual violence within our communities. *Silently endure, unequivocally protect.*

The impulse to protect those who harm us emerges out of a desire to care for ourselves without relying on the state to intervene or further criminalize and pathologize Black people. Admittedly, at times this feels incompatible because of the pervasiveness of violence against us perpetrated by loved ones and those in our own communities. I don't want to give any more lives to the criminal punishment system to devour *AND* I want us to be cared for and unharmed in our intimate relationships, homes, institutions, and communities. Both can be true. The learned compulsion to protect those who harm us from the criminal punishment system, however, often leaves us silent, bruised, battered, or, worse, dead.

This chapter looks at intracommunal violence against women and girls. I strongly resist the pathological framing of "Black-on-Black" crime. I also recognize that this problematic framing tends to solely refer to violence perpetrated and experienced by cisgender Black men and boys. Of the 2,925 homicides where the victim was Black/African American in 2018, almost 90 percent of the perpetrators in those cases were also Black/African American.[3] Irrespective of race, however, men and boys are more likely to perpetrate violent crimes, the majority of which are against other men and boys.[4] Most people also harm those with whom they share proximity, which means most violent crimes happen intraracially and intracommunally.[5] The racist framing of "Black-on-Black violent crime" relies on a deliberate omission of how and why crimes happen within specific communities. We never talk about "white-on-white crime," even though the majority of violence against white people is caused by other white people. Racial segregation, redlining, and other forms of structural racism, but particularly antiBlack racism, construct racial, ethnic, and class enclaves where Black folks, people of color, and poor people of all races and ethnicities endure systemic neglect, criminalization, and overpolicing.[6]

Contextualizing intracommunal violence through exploring how antiBlack racism operates at structural, systemic, and institutional levels, however, doesn't sufficiently address what happens to Black women and girls. Our victimization within Black communities requires both more nuance and attention. As the late, great poet and activist Pat Parker said:

> Brother
> I don't want to hear
> about
> how my real enemy
> is the system.
> I'm no genius,
> but I do know
> that system
> you hit me with
> is called
> a fist.[7]

Patriarchy, misogynoir, sexism, capitalism, and white supremacy combine into an interdependent superstructure, as well as a dangerous intracommunal force in our lives. The fear of feeding into pathologizing narratives coupled with warranted trepidation about investing in existing carceral responses to violence make it difficult for me to talk about Black intracommunal violence honestly and without deep contextualization. I don't want to contribute to injurious ideas about Black people. The hypercriminalization of Blackness is an ongoing, venomous, and dehumanizing facet of the U.S. criminal punishment system. Yet ignoring the reality of intimate and intracommunal violence puts Black women such as myself at a demoralizing crossroads.

By the age of thirty-five I personally knew too many Black women who were killed by their current or ex-partners. In 2016, a Black woman in the United States was killed by a man every seventeen hours.[8] More than 90 percent of these murders happened intracommunally. While slightly more than 90 percent of Black women victims of homicide knew their killers, 58 percent of those who knew their killers were the wives, ex-wives, partners, or ex-partners of those who killed them. Black women are killed by men at more than twice the rate of white women. One of the key conclusions proffered by the Violence Policy Center in its September 2018 report, *When Men Murder Women: An Analysis of 2016 Homicide Data* is that "the disproportionate burden of fatal and nonfatal violence borne by black females has almost always been overshadowed by the toll violence has taken on black males." The report also acknowledges unnamed societal factors contributing to these alarming statistics. Without contextualization and radical honesty, however, the report feeds into existing antiBlack stereotypes about Black men and boys as inherently and uncontrollably violent. The data is just a starting point. It's the unnamed "societal factors" that unveil important truths about intracommunal violence against us.

Accurately documenting and contextualizing the frequency with which Black men harm Black women and girls poses distinct challenges. Although I want the aforementioned statistics to be false, the story behind them is far too important to dismiss as a white supremacist plot to "denigrate" Black men and boys. Even as I typed this, I feared the weaponization of my words against Black men and boys. The desire to protect, coupled with my efforts to wholly reject pathologizing explications for intracommunal violence against Black women and girls, informs every carefully chosen word in this chapter. What fuels this chapter is also the reality that physical assaults and sexual violence also happen primarily in intracommunal contexts.[9] According to a study conducted by Black Women's Blueprint in 2012, between 40 and 60 percent of Black girls experience some form of sexual violence before turning eighteen.[10] Slightly more than 40 percent of Black women will experience domestic violence in their lifetime; the national average for all women in the U.S. is 33 percent.[11]

One of the most pressing examples of intracommunal violence is the crisis of Black trans women and girls being murdered. Six Black trans women and girls were found dead over the course of just nine days in late June / early July 2020.[12] By mid-July 2020, twenty-two trans women and girls had already been killed in 2020, most of them Black. The year 2020 was one of the deadliest years yet for Black trans women. The perpetrators of these underreported and underinvestigated murders are often Black men and boys. At the cruel intersection of transmisogynoir and antiBlackness are the unsolved and largely unknown murders of more than one hundred

Black trans women in the twenty-first century. In 2016, *Mic* released a database tracking the deaths of transgender homicide victims. Between 2010 and 2016, 75 percent of the transgender and gender nonconforming people killed were Black trans women. This means that between 2010 and 2016, a Black trans woman was killed every month.[13] Eighty-two trans people, most of whom were Black women and girls, were killed between 2017 and 2019.[14] In the first seven months of 2020, the number Black trans homicide victims surpassed the total number for 2019.[15] This is what violence against Black women looks like in the twenty-first century.

What's the story behind these statistics? Is it possible to resist the weaponizing of these statistics against Black men and boys without decentering Black women and girls? What's at stake when we are not honest about how misogynoir, patriarchy, queerphobia, ableism, and transphobia show up within Black communities? How do we fully and justly contextualize what is happening without replicating harmful and criminalizing narratives and tropes about Black people more broadly? Do we always have to foreground our attempts to not pathologize before diving into the reality of intracommunal violence? These questions remind us that violence against Black women and girls is also a form of antiBlack violence. Not all Black people are cisgender Black men and boys. Their experiences can't be the sole focus when we discuss and organize around antiBlack violence. Black girls' and women's well-being and lives depend on a reckoning that includes holding our communities and loved ones accountable.

A Sordid History

In activist and scholar Angela Davis's germinal 1971 article "Reflections on the Black Woman's Role in the Community of

Slaves," Davis attempted to recover the lived experiences of enslaved women. Chattel slavery produced a context in which enslaved people of all genders faced the daily threat of white supremacist violence. It is nearly impossible to understand the violence of chattel slavery without talking about sexual violence against enslaved people. One of the most common forms of violence Black women and girls endured was rape and sexual assault.[16] Understanding rape as being a form of institutional terrorism designed to subjugate women rather than as individualized spontaneous acts of violence is one of the most significant interventions Davis made with her 1971 article on enslaved Black women.[17] Similar to when Ida B. Wells called out the frequency with which white men sexually assaulted African American women in the late nineteenth century,[18] Davis illuminated rape as a prominent facet of white supremacist, patriarchal violence.

A tool of both social control and forced reproductive labor, the commonness of white men raping Black women and girls during slavery is foundational to grasping gender-specific experiences of enslaved people. Without question, Black men and boys experienced rape and sexual assaults as well, particularly in the context of forced breeding, compulsory intimacies, and castration.[19] As Emily West argues, "because rape and sexual assault have been defined in the past as non-consensual sexual acts supported by surviving legal evidence (generally testimony from court trials), it is hard for historians to research rape and sexual violence under slavery."[20] The difficulty, however, has not stopped scholars like Davis or Black women's historians from digging into the archive for the meaningful silences and "hidden in plain sight" truths about slavery-era sexual violence.

After the abolishing of the transatlantic slave trade by the U.S. government in 1808, systematic practices of white supremacist violence intensified. "Rape and forced breeding became common experiences for the enslaved" in the aftermath of the abolition of the slave trade.[21] Beyond forced breeding, sexual abuse took on multiple forms including quotidian sexual assaults, as well as psychological and emotional abuse. Widespread sexual violence against enslaved people as a preferred disciplining apparatus affected Black women disproportionately. Enslaved women who participated in fugitive acts, such as the Southampton Rebellion, were raped, brutally assaulted, and even hanged.[22] White supremacy and patriarchy normalized sexual violence as a fixture in the lives of enslaved women. From the master's house to slave cabins, it was nearly impossible for enslaved women to escape violence.

One of the more difficult parts of the history of slavery in the U.S. to recover are enslaved women's experiences with intimate partner violence—specifically, intracommunal sexual violence.[23] There was no legal standing for the rape of enslaved women or the rape of any woman within marriage.[24] For enslaved women, perpetrators could be slave owners and, in some cases, enslaved men. Violence against enslaved women and girls isn't only a story about white supremacy or racial capitalism; it's also about more intimate harmful interactions occurring within a marginalized, exploited, and violated community. Until I read historian Deborah Gray White's pioneering book on Black women and slavery, *Ar'n't I a Woman? Female Slaves in the Plantation South,* I hadn't fully considered the extent to which violence occurred among enslaved people. I only really thought about the violence of slave owners and white people more broadly against my ancestors. What White drives home is that "while there were slave women raped by black men, this abuse is overshadowed by white male exploitation of black women, and it is overlooked because it hardly ever turned up in court since there was no legal injunction against it."[25] I dug deeper into the work of Black women's historians and found that they were asking the difficult but important questions about gender and sexual violence among enslaved people. When historian Sasha Turner asked, "to what extent were enslaved men collaborators in the subordination and sexual abuse of enslaved women," I braced myself for what the archives might say.[26] While the fear of slave owners predominated, some enslaved women and girls suffered harm at the hands of those with whom they shared the nonperson status of chattel.

It is obvious that enslaved Black men were victims of white supremacist violence during slavery. Concurrently, some of them also harmed enslaved Black women and girls. The placing of enslaved women into households where enslaved men were positioned as head of household reproduced "Euro-patriarchal standards that granted household heads unrestricted sexual access to their dependents."[27] This imposed organization of enslaved households ushered in Black patriarchal power over Black women, even as these enslaved men were victimized by "their owners' expectations and machinations."[28] The combined force of white supremacy and patriarchy in enslaved people's lives produced a distinct context in which violence against Black women and girls flourished. The afterlives of this convergence of racial and gender oppression show up in those statistics about contemporary violence against Black women and girls. The silence about intracommunal violence against us also mirrors the muzzling of enslaved women who endured violence at the hands of white men and women and, sometimes, Black men. Dredging through this ignoble and complicated history allows for a critical consideration of how and why intracommunal violence remains challenging to examine and to mobilize around in more impassioned ways.

From Jim Crow to the Present

Postslavery, many formerly enslaved men and women sought to forge new relationships not tied to their reproductive capacities and forced intimacies. Formerly enslaved people, as well as free people of color, began building communities. Although the Reconstruction Amendments and other federally initiated policies and bureaus put in place after the Civil War offered a semblance of possibility for equality, progress proved ephemeral.[29] White supremacy reconstituted itself via new laws, policies, and extralegal means of maintaining an antiBlack status quo.[30] Jim Crow America ushered in a violently enforced racial order premised on white supremacy and antiBlackness. AntiBlack violence thrived at the hands of the state, organized white vigilantes, and even parts of the white laity.[31] Black communities largely fended for themselves and, in many ways, opted to fight racial violence without confronting the reality of intracommunal patriarchal, gender, and sexual violence against Black women and girls.

The harsh realities of white supremacist violence, coupled with the proliferation of racist stereotypes about the inherent criminality of Black people and the "innate" sexually predatory nature of Black men, had specific consequences for Black women and girls. Given the frequency and intensity of white supremacist violence, how would one come forward about physical harm caused by those also victimized by antiBlack violence without adding fuel to the fire of white supremacy? Since Jim Crow–era white supremacist and patriarchal logics also rendered Black women and girls unrapeable and unassailable and cast Black men as uncontrollable rapists and perpetually violent offenders, our foremothers had few outlets to detail the range of violent acts they experienced. The choice for many to remain silent about the harm they experienced under white supremacy at the hands of Black men reflected a desire not to further criminalize their own communities. With white supremacy always surveilling and in search of justifications for its antiBlack core, calling out violence at the hands of the men being lynched by the same people raping and lynching you was unfathomable for many Black women and girls. *Silently endure; unequivocally protect.*

The penchant for protection comes at a high cost. Bruises untended, care unafforded, and pain ignored. In efforts to reject framings of Black men as hyperviolent, Black women and girls in the Jim Crow era made strategic choices regarding intracommunal violence. To be clear, some Black women and girls called out gender and sexual violence within their communities. Although the archive is limited, it seems plausible that some who called out intracommunal harm found ways outside the U.S. criminal punishment system to hold those who caused harm accountable. Airing this "dirty laundry," however, meant risking being labeled a race traitor or a henchwoman for white supremacy. Even worse, allegations could alienate you from the very community you needed to help you survive in an intractably antiBlack world. Under the watchful eye of white supremacy, Black women and girls made difficult choices about their vulnerability and well-being at both interpersonal and systemic levels.

At the societal level, many Black women and girls engaged in a "culture of dissemblance" to navigate racial, gender, and sexual violence. Dissemblance, the act of disguising and masquerading, afforded Black women a way to traverse the ever-violent terrain etched out by white supremacist and patriarchal violence.[32] When people tend to think about or reference the "culture of dissemblance," it's common to identify the oppressors from which Black women "shielded the truth of their inner lives," as primarily white men.[33] When trailblazing Black women's historian Darlene Clark Hine defined the "culture of dissemblance," she carefully noted how Black women shielded their truths "from their oppressors." Without question, violence at the hands of white men and white women during the antebellum and Jim Crow eras was a driving force to shape a culture of dissemblance. Black women's truths, however, also included what happened in slave cabins, in tenements, in their houses, or in alleys and backroads in their neighborhoods at the hands of the men and boys with whom they were in community.

When discussing the culture of dissemblance, it is common for folks to erase or not engage a significant assertion levied in Hine's groundbreaking article "Rape and the Inner Lives of Black Women in the Middle West." Hine unambiguously acknowledges the desire of Black women to escape from "sexual exploitation from inside and outside of their families and from rape and the threat of rape by white as well as Black males."[34] Chronicling why Black women migrated out of the South to the Midwest in particular, she uncovered that "the most common, and certainly the most compelling, motive for running, fleeing, migrating was a desire to retain or claim some control and ownership of their own sexual beings and the children they bore."[35] Hine is pointed in naming white men and women, and to a lesser extent Black men, as opposing forces for Black women "involved in a multifaceted struggle to determine who would control their productive and reproductive capacities and their sexuality."[36] The Black men part of this "multifaceted struggle" is most often where Black women and girls historically and contemporarily *silently endure, unequivocally protect.*

The archives of gender and sexual violence against Black women and girls are limited because Black women have chosen to hide their experiences as a mode of protection for themselves and, sometimes, their families and communities. In the late 1960s and the 1970s, at the height of the civil rights, Black Power, women's liberation, and queer liberation movements, Black women became more explicit in their calling out of Black men for violence against them. Through poetry, fiction, nonfiction, speeches, plays, choreopoems, and debates, Black women refused silence regarding intracommunal violence. Many opted out of a politics that saw the discussion of their victimization at the hands of Black men as divisive. Black feminists and womanists brought the fire to those who thought that violence against Black women and girls was secondary to Black freedom struggles.

In poet Pat Parker's aforementioned 1972 poem titled, "Brother," the activist, poet, and Black lesbian feminist made it plain. The poem refused to excuse Black men from their role in harming Black women and girls. Black fists battered their faces and bodies. For Parker, the system was a real enemy, but so were those Black fists. Parker's body of work shows that she was undaunted in her willingness to explore violence against Black women perpetrated by Black men. Her 1978 poem "Womanslaughter" chronicled the murder of her sister, Shirley Jones, by Jones's husband.

One of the most striking lines of the poem reads "Her things were his/including her life." Jones's husband possessed her, and he could therefore treat her as disposable. Her sister's killer spent one year in a work-release program. The rather lenient response from the criminal punishment system to this heinous act of violence compelled Parker to bring her sister's murder to the International Tribunal on Crimes against Women in Brussels in 1976.[37] She knew her sister's life mattered and that patriarchy, misogyny, and white supremacy stole Jones's life and barely held anyone accountable.

Critically acclaimed and revered poet and playwright Ntozake Shange's first theatrical work, *For Colored Girls Who Have Considered Suicide/When the Rainbow Is Enuf,* used poetic verses, music, and dance to tell the fictional stories of interconnected, unnamed Black women living at the intersection of antiBlackness and sexism. I discovered this groundbreaking work during my junior year at Oberlin College, as I struggled with confronting my own experiences with violence perpetrated by Black men and boys. As a dancer with a background in theater, I knew I wanted to bring this play to life on my storied campus. It wouldn't be the first time a Black woman at Oberlin read Shange's words in *For Colored Girls* and fought to put on a production of the choreopoem on our campus. We connected to the experiences of rape, domestic violence, poverty, and emotional neglect highlighted in Shange's work. It seemed to resonate with Black Oberlin women in almost every decade since it was published.

What struck me as my codirector and I moved forward with casting our production was how many Black women on my campus who auditioned connected intimately with the experiences of these fictional women. Some of us were survivors of gender and sexual violence, and nearly all of us survivors knew those who harmed us. None of us reported the harm against us to police. Some of us simply didn't believe in the criminal "justice" system. Others didn't want to be reviolated by not being believed or by being dismissed as race traitors by identifying the Black men and boys who harmed us. Although written almost thirty years before our performance, *For Colored Girls* spoke directly to our experiences and our trepidations about truth-telling. It left me and my codirector to ponder how little had changed. Would our production of this work bring about calls of divisiveness? Would we still feel compelled to preface our production with a note about not pathologizing Black men and boys? In the end, there wasn't backlash to our production, and we felt no need to explain ourselves or the stories presented in our production of the choreopoem. Perhaps there was some progress from the era in which Shange wrote and staged the debut of this groundbreaking text.

The backlash from Black men against writers like Shange, Parker, Michele Wallace, Alice Walker, and other Black feminists and womanists who shed light on intracommunal violence caused by Black men and boys was remarkably vicious. In a 1979 article, "The Myth of the Black Macho: A Response to Angry Black Feminists," Robert Staples disparaged the work of Shange and Michelle Wallace's *Black Macho and the Myth of the Superwoman* by weaponizing their "middle-class" backgrounds to discredit their analyses. Furthermore, Staples claimed that sexism wasn't as pernicious within Black communities as in white communities.[38] He was not alone in his attempts to dismiss the gravity of intracommunal violence against Black women and girls. A 1986 article in the *New York Times* reported on the debates within Black communities about Steven Spielberg's latest film, *The Color Purple,* which was based on Alice Walker's novel. The article featured opinions from

Black men and women praising and disparaging the depiction of intracommunal violence within Black communities.[39] Positioning the work of Black feminists and womanists such as Shange and Walker as contributing to a further pathologizing and criminalizing of Black men and boys gained traction among Black people of all genders. It also magnified the uphill battle for the struggle against gender and sexual violence within Black communities. Those who saw Black women's truth-telling as "anti-Black men" viewed Black feminists and womanists as inimical to Black liberation.[40]

Tensions continue to bubble to the surface with how we confront intracommunal violence against Black women and girls in the twenty-first century. Black women are still viewed as divisive when they talk about these experiences. We still contend with demands from many within our communities to focus on the "shared enemy" of white supremacy. To address the acts of harm we endure within our communities requires a radical honesty, one not preoccupied with the concern regarding the strong possibility that this discussion will feed into harmful stereotypes. The risk for further criminalizing and pathologizing of Black people of all genders looms large when we get to the details beyond the data. A greater risk exists, however, if we refuse to confront intracommunal violence against Black women and girls.

Sexual Violence

In early 2012, *XXL Magazine* posted a video on its website, xxl.com, featuring rapper Too Short providing "fatherly advice" to young boys about how to "turn out their female classmates."[41] His advice included instructing teenage boys to push girls up against the wall and digitally penetrate them. Too Short stated that by stimulating or possibly arousing young girls, tween and teenage boys could get "whatever they want." He identified these coercive and violent acts as mind manipulation. Although Too Short is known for his sexually explicit lyrics and affinity for pimp culture, his attempt to advise teenage boys on how to sexually assault teenage girls still shocked me.

Almost immediately after the video went semiviral, activist Rosa Clemente mobilized a group of women of color to coauthor and sign a statement denouncing the video, calling for *XXL* to feature anti-sexual violence content and demanding the firing of then-*XXL* editor-in-chief, Vanessa Satten.[42] The signatories, of which I was one, became formally, though temporarily, known as the We Are the 44% Coalition. Comprising activists, scholars, writers, and artists, this coalition brought attention to a harrowing statistic reported at the time by the Rape, Abuse, & Incest National Network: 44% of rape victims are under eighteen years old in the United States. Many of us who signed identified as victims and or survivors of sexual assault or rape. The joking matter-of-fact nature with which Too Short delivered his advice was a painful reminder of the ubiquity of rape culture and the ease with which people can make light of acts of harm against girls and women. Our warranted outrage spoke not only to Too Short's reprehensible comments but to a pointed concern about sexual violence against girls of color.

According to a report compiled by the National Center on Violence against Women in the Black Community, one in four Black girls will be sexually abused before they turn eighteen.[43] Anywhere from 40 to 60 percent of Black girls under eighteen report being subjected to coercive sexual contact, not unlike what Too Short discussed in his "fatherly advice" video.[44] Among high-school-age Black girls, 11 percent report having been raped.[45] These statistics only convey data retrieved from those who report. While sexual violence remains underreported by people of all genders, age groups, races, ethnicities, and sexualities, it is estimated that for every fifteen Black women and girls raped, only one reports. Numerous obstacles exist for adults reporting sexual assaults; for youth, we perhaps have only scratched the surface of their sexual victimization. Most of the sexual violence that Black girls endure occurs intracommunally. Often, the perpetrators aren't strangers. So not only do Black girls combat antiBlack violence from teachers, police officers, and other "authority" figures, but they withstand violent treatment from loved ones, those entrusted with their care and protection, and those who live and work in proximity to their homes, schools, religious institutions, and leisure spaces. When folks within the community promote such harmful ideas about sex and consent, it creates a context void of protection for Black girls.

Black girls receive victim-blaming and slut-shaming messages about the risk of speaking out about intracommunal sexual violence.[46] Perhaps nowhere is the messaging stronger to *silently endure, unequivocally protect,* than popular culture. It took a searing docuseries helmed by dream hampton featuring numerous allegations of sexual and physical violence, a book, and a social media campaign just for the needle to move somewhat in the case against singer, songwriter, and producer R. Kelly.[47] It literally took more than twenty years of allegations of sexual and physical violence, news coverage, a social media campaign (#MuteRKelly), and a powerful book from the journalist who first brought attention to a rape tape allegedly featuring Kelly with a Black teenage girl for there to be collective outrage. Through coverage of the allegations for almost twenty years, investigative journalist Jim DeRogatis concluded, "Nobody matters less in our society than young black girls."[48]

When I interviewed DeRogatis after the release of his book *Soulless: The Case against R. Kelly,* I revisited those painful words about mattering. AntiBlack racism, misogynoir, and other oppressive forces render Black girls disproportionately vulnerable to sexual violence. When they speak out about sexual violence against them, they often encounter distrust and blame. In late fall 2013, Black feminist writers Mikki Kendall and Jamie Nesbitt Golden launched a twitter conversation and hashtag, #FastTailedGirls. The online chat focused on a prevailing racist and misogynistic stereotype about Black girls being fast or "fass." The "gender-specific pejorative term," as writer Goldie Taylor notes, "is nothing more than a synonym for a whore."[49] In a society that both devalues sex work and punishes women for being perceived as "too sexual," the word *whore* carries violently negative connotations. Calling a Black girl a "whore" within this context not only makes her more vulnerable to sexual violence but also swiftly and plainly blames her for her own victimization.

Black girls contend with antiBlack and sexist stereotypes derived from white supremacist notions of Black girlhood.[50] They also come up against a profound internalization within Black communities of damaging labels such as hypersexual, lascivious, promiscuous, prematurely mature, aggressive, and resilient to the point of being impervious to pain. The weight of white supremacy and misogynoir leaves Black girls with little to no recourse for sexual violence against them or for the maligning they experience when they identify as victims or survivors of sexual violence. Being "fass" means you wanted it and that you willingly and enthusiastically consented. *Fass* assigns Black girls culpability for being sexually violated. In her piece about #FastTailedGirls, Taylor stresses that "in the most horrific incidences, this intra-cultural 'red-lining' has been historically used to malign and silence victims of molestation and rape. Its usage is designed to assuage any notion of guilt for the person who commits these acts, reassigning the blame to the young girl that he has victimized. Sadly, fass is an epithet most frequently weaponized and hurled by older women—women who have an emotional and/or physical stake in the outcome."[51] If you search the hashtag #FastTailedGirls, you will see an abundance of tweets of Black women sharing their stories about being labeled fass. Even more disturbing, Black women using the hashtag talked openly about how their experiences with childhood and adolescent sexual violence led to intracommunal and familial victim-blaming and slut-shaming. I saw myself and my experiences with sexual violence in those tweets but still feared what would happen if I publicly shared my story.

The hashtag resurfaced in a substantive way when *Surviving R. Kelly* aired. Since the release and widespread circulation of a tape allegedly featuring R. Kelly raping a young Black teenage girl in 2002, I can't begin to count the number of times I have heard people refer to the victim on the tape and other Black girls who came forward accusing Kelly of sexual and physical assaults as fass or as fast-tailed girls. The refusal to see these girls and young women as victims wasn't just about our love for R. Kelly, though that played a large role. To identify what Kelly serially did as violent and predatory would mean holding a mirror up to ourselves, our families, and our communities and seeing the truth about how rampant sexual violence against Black girls is. We'd have to acknowledge that we didn't care and that we, too, dismissed allegations under the comfortably antiBlack and misogynistic guise of describing Black girls as fass. Intimately connected to the sexually brutalizing conditions under which our captive and enslaved foremothers lived, resisted, and died, contemporary misogynoir and antiBlack racism create a context in which Black girls remain "unrapeable" in the eyes of far too many people, institutions, and systems.

One in five Black women in the United States will be raped in their lifetime.[52] Of Black women and girls in the U.S., 35 percent experience some form of sexual violence in their lifetimes.[53] Black women and girls constitute at least 40 percent of the confirmed sex trafficking victims in the nation as well.[54] Based on my friends and family alone, I suspect a high percentage of Black women and girls suffered at least one form of sexual violence in their lifetimes. At least a third of those in my life have told me about their sexual victimization. I assume some folks in my life haven't told me or perhaps anyone else. Nearly all the Black women in my life who identify as survivors or victims of sexual violence relayed that their perpetrator was someone they knew. About half of us had said "I love you" at some point to the person or persons who sexually violated us. Only one of us reported what happened to the police. She regrets it to this day, not only because of the way police handled her but because it costs her loving relationships with family members. I think of her often as I wonder if she wishes she would have silently endured and unequivocally protected the perpetrator. I would never ask, though I believe I know the answer.

Domestic and Intimate Partner Violence

Unfortunately, sexual violence is only one form of intracommunal violence Black women and girls endure. The aforementioned stories of Montana and Megan Thee Stallion are among millions of similar stories that emerge every year.[55] Parents, partners, and ex-lovers wield their hands, knives, guns, and other injurious and sometimes fatal objects against us at a higher rate than almost every racialized group in the U.S. with the exception of Indigenous women and girls.[56] The ones we love, who we believe love us, and, in some cases, do love us are too frequently harmful. The worst of these millions of stories end at funeral services for the dearly departed.

More than 40 percent of Black women and girls experience physical violence caused by intimate partners in their lifetime. When including psychological abuse, the percentage rises to above 50.[57] One of my favorite shows, *A Different World,* enlivened the reality of intimate partner violence for me as a child. It stuck with me as I began working on issues of gender and sexual violence against us. In the season 5 episode "Love Taps," sophomore Gina is being physically and verbally abused by her boyfriend, Deon. Once made aware of the abuse, the campus community rallies around Gina. From advice to storytelling, Gina receives the kind of support many Black women never receive when trapped in cycles of abuse. People believe her, offer her assistance, and affirm her worth. Mr. Gaines tells her a story about a woman whose abusive husband beat her to death. This story appears to be the final straw for Gina. She ends her relationship with Deon and files a police report. She survives and thrives after this relationship, a fate too often not afforded to Black women in abusive intimate partnerships.

In Gina's case, she ends the relationship and does not return at any point. Thankfully, she also survives. It is significant that the possibility of death is written into the episode as it sheds light on a reality of then and now: Black women in the U.S. are more than 2.5 times more likely to be killed by an intimate partner than white women.[58] The mention of death sounds the alarm, while Gina's survival and ability to leave an abusive relationship are an ideal outcome for those of us in abusive relationships and those in a community with someone being abused. I wish more stories of Black women in abusive relationships ended like Gina's did. While I will always be grateful for an episode about domestic violence, I can't help but see a gaping distance between how the Hillman community showed up for Gina and how folks tend not to show up for the Ginas in our own lives. Gina had friends who believed her and intervened to stop the abuse. I didn't see interventions into abusive relationships I've witnessed and still don't see it. The stories I've personally encountered about intimate partner violence against Black women too often ended in murder.

On an eerily cold March day back in 2009, my father's mournful voice asked me if I'd heard about a brutal triple homicide in my hometown, Washington, D.C. I was in the depths and recesses of working on my dissertation on a history of Black women in the nation's capital and had tuned out the news. I felt his grief from miles away and reluctantly asked why he was asking if I knew about the murders. He simply and somberly stated, "It's Erika and the kids." I sat quietly as he asked if I remembered my slightly older childhood friend from around the old neighborhood. Of course, I did. Although no longer as close as we had been, she was a part of my childhood and someone for whom I always had a place in my heart. I quickly got off the phone and began searching for any information about my childhood friend.

A quick internet search provided horrifying details about the murder of Erika and two of her children, Erik Harper (11) and Dakota Peters (10). They were repeatedly and fatally stabbed in their apartment. Almost immediately after news broke of the homicides, police charged Peters's forty-four-year-old boyfriend, Joseph Randolph Mays, with these horrendous murders.[59] The police stated that a "domestic dispute" preceded the killings. Within a few days of this brutal crime, all signs pointed toward a domestic violence homicide. The day of the murders, Erik called his grandmother and told her "the sky is blue." This statement was a coded attempt to alert his grandmother about the threat or presence of violence by Mays.[60] The family contacted police. Hours later, police arrived at the apartment and broke down the door to find Erika, Erik, and Dakota riddled with stab wounds.[61] Erika and Dakota were pronounced dead at the scene, Erik perished shortly after. A two-year-old girl, the only child biologically connected to both Mays and Erika, was found unharmed at the apartment. The police also found Mays in the apartment with self-inflicted wounds.

According to police reports, after the argument between Erika and Mays began, Dakota ran into the bathroom to hide.[62] Mays followed him into the bathroom and viciously attacked him. Erik ran toward the front door of the unit but was unable to unlatch the safety bar before Mays stabbed him multiple times. Three people bled out as police took more than an hour to forcefully enter the home.[63] Mays was still inside when police finally entered the home. I remember wondering: What if there were no delay in police response? What if they could've prevented all of the murders or at least gotten to Erik in time to save his young life? These questions, along with so many others, haunted me for days, if not weeks. Although devastated, her family had long suspected that this abusive relationship would have a tragic ending. I didn't know the extent of the abuse Erika or her kids endured, but the streets were talking. Nothing in me blamed her for not leaving the city because I knew that many women are killed by partners after they leave.[64]

Realistically speaking, where could she have gone and not fear being violated by her ex-partner? I knew people reading news stories about the triple homicide and possibly even some folks in her life would blame her for her death and the deaths of her children.

But I knew this story all too well. It is easier to blame women victims in domestic violence situations than it is to wrestle with the prevalence of domestic and intimate partner violence. We would rather scream at women for being in abusive and violent relationships than scream at those perpetrating abuse and harm. We prefer screaming about all the things she should've done instead of hearing the screams of women brutalized by their loved ones. Erika's screams, figuratively and literally, haunted me. They still do. I think of her every time a new story breaks about a domestic violence homicide. It hurts that Erika's story isn't singular by any stretch. It's the story of Aisha Fraser of Shaker Heights, Ohio. Aisha was murdered by her ex-husband, Lance Mason, in 2018. Prior to killing his ex-wife, the former Cuyahoga common pleas judge was convicted of assaulting her in front of her kids in 2014.[65] As a result of punching his then-wife twenty times, smashing her head against the dashboard, and breaking her orbital bone, Mason was disbarred, prohibited from ever being a judge again, fined $250,000, and sentenced to two years (of which he served nine months).[66] Just four years after his conviction, Mason stabbed Aisha to death in her own home. Aisha had gone to the criminal punishment system for support and still ended up being killed by Mason.

The story of Shanta Singleton even more eerily reminded me of Erika and her children. Upon returning from a trip to Myrtle Beach with a man and her children on Tuesday, May 20, 2020, thirty-seven-year-old Shanta was followed by her ex-boyfriend, Gabriel

Jordan. When she arrived at her residence in St. Matthews, South Carolina, Jordan confronted Shanta in what police described as a jealous rage.[67] Almost immediately, he began strangling her. Twelve-year-old Tre'vay Stroman, Shanta's youngest daughter, attempted to intervene in the violence by jumping on Jordan's back. Jordan fatally shot Tre'vay. After shooting the youngest daughter, he turned around and shot Shanta's eighteen-year-old daughter, Shantasia Stroman. Injured, though not fatally, Shantasia fled the scene but not before witnessing Jordan chasing her fifteen-year-old sister, Essence Stroman, into the house. When police arrived at Shanta's home, they found Shanta's body and Tre'vay's outside and Essence's lifeless body inside a bedroom. Police also found Jordan deceased from a self-inflicted gun wound not too far from Shanta's home.[68] Mays had also allegedly attempted to die by suicide after killing Erika, Erik, and Dakota. Jordan executed a multiple murder-suicide. Like Erika and Mays, Shanta and Jordan were in an on-again, off-again relationship for many years. The volatility and abuse apparently prompted Singleton to end the relationship. Sadly, her fate proved once more how deadly it can be for battered women who leave abusive partners, particularly Black women. The deaths of her and two of her children exemplify the terror of domestic violence homicide for Black women.

Domestic violence extends beyond intimate partner interactions; it includes all violent and aggressive behavior in the home. While partner and child abuse are perhaps the most recognizable forms, an understudied occurrence is violence perpetrated within the home to regulate or punish individuals for their gender and sexual identities. One of the most harrowing examples of this in recent years was the murders of Britney Cosby and Crystal Jackson by Britney's father, Larry James Cosby.[69] Police found Crystal and

Britney's bodies in a dumpster behind a convenience store in Bolivar, Texas. On the morning of March 6, 2014, inside the home of Britney's great-grandmother, Annie Lee Cosby, where Britney and Larry Cosby and Crystal Jackson resided, an altercation ensued. Crystal's five-year-old daughter was left alone in a car as she awaited Britney and Crystal's exit from the home to take her on a school field trip to the Houston Livestock Show and Rodeo. Her mom and mom's girlfriend didn't make it out of the house alive. Larry Cosby strangled and bludgeoned his daughter to death. He also strangled Crystal. The fatal moment occurred when he shot her in her right temple. Sometime between the murders and the next morning, Cosby disposed of the bodies in the dumpster.

The motive remained "unclear" throughout the investigation and the trial. Family members, especially Britney's mother, however, believed Larry Cosby killed her daughter and her girlfriend because they were lesbians.[70] On numerous occasions Larry spoke about not liking his daughter being gay.[71] While we may never know the exact reason behind such a brutal murder, his homophobia is documented and viewed as virulent and potentially violent. He killed his own daughter and the person she loved and then left their bodies in the trash. They were literally disposable to him. The politics of disposability don't just operate at the level of the public sphere; they enter and structure family and community dynamics in violent and, at times, fatal ways. Black queer and trans folks of all sexualities are distinctly vulnerable in homes, communities, and a larger society in which homophobia and transphobia thrive.

At the community level, we see this kind of violence play egregiously in the victimization of Black trans women. In May 2020, in Minneapolis, amid the uprising in the aftermath of the murder of George Floyd, a mob of primarily Black people brutalized Iyanna

Dior, a Black trans woman. After a car accident in which Iyanna hit a few other cars, she was followed into a convenience store by a man whose car she hit.[72] Within minutes of seeking refuge in the store Iyanna was attacked by multiple people. A group of what appeared to be no less than ten people mercilessly assaulted a twenty-year-old woman with almost no one intervening to stop the brutality. Even the owner of the store declined to assist in any way, including calling any first responders to the scene.

Thankfully, Iyanna survived the vicious attack. It was harrowing, nevertheless, to note how little had changed regarding violence against Black trans women in the same city where CeCe McDonald had been attacked almost ten years prior. Caught on video that subsequently went viral, the attack was horrific. I could barely stomach watching it. Given how ferocious the beating was, it's miraculous that Iyanna didn't become one of the hundred plus Black trans women killed thus far in the early twenty-first century. She couldn't defend herself from the onslaught of punches. She was at the mercy of a few bystanders who dared to intervene. She survived but not because the conditions of transphobia, misogyny, and antiBlackness didn't converge to attempt to kill her.

An antitrans assault in August 2020 went viral in which a Black man robbed and assaulted a group of trans women of color on Hollywood Boulevard in Los Angeles.[73] Bystanders filmed and encouraged the attack while many yelled transphobic slurs. The three women—Joslyn Allen, Jaslene Busanet, and Eden Estrada—survived being forcefully grabbed, hit on the head with a bottle, and knocked to the ground. Not one person stepped in to help. The crowd egged on the cruel attack of these three vulnerable women. Notably, the attacks on Iyanna, Joslyn, Jaslene, and Eden happened during a summer in which more people talked about and rallied around violence against trans people, particularly Black trans women, than ever before.[74] The majority of that antitrans violence occurred at the hands of other Black people.[75] Even in a summer characterized by protest affirming the value of Black life and rejecting a violent politics of disposability, intracommunal violence against Black trans folks intensified.

Who Fights for Us?

The mobilization of protestors across the country in response to Minneapolis police officer Derek Chauvin killing George Floyd was a dynamic moment in modern social movement history. Footage from all over the nation and eventually the world featured impassioned speeches from people angered and exhausted by the incessant reality of antiBlack police violence. Even during a global pandemic, police maintained "business as usual," as it pertained to Black people. Although many of the voices calling out police brutality, racial injustice, and systemic antiBlack racism struck a chord with me in the early days of the 2020 Black Uprising, there was a young Black woman whose words and delivery stayed with me long after I watched a video of her speech.

A video circulating on Twitter featured nineteen-year-old Oluwatoyin (Toyin) Salau speaking at a protest in Tallahassee, Florida. Her words moved me, although it was how she said them that resounded. Salau proclaimed:

> Right now, our lives matter. Black lives matter. Black trans lives matter. Trans lives matter. Because guess what? We all [are] minorities. But right now, let's focus on the person who got killed. Tony McDade was a Black trans man. We do this for him. We [are]

doing this for our brothers and sisters who got shot but we [are] doing this for every Black person. Because at the end of the day, I can't take my fucking skin color off.[76]

The tremble in Toyin's voice, coupled with her demand that we amplify the story of a Black trans man, Tony McDade, who police killed in Tallahassee just two days after the killing of Floyd, struck me. The uprising largely pivoted around the killing of Floyd and to a lesser extent, the police killing of Breonna Taylor and the killing of Ahmaud Arbery by white vigilantes.[77] Her impassioned insistence in this moment to center Tony and Black trans lives was cogent. Too few protests uplifted the name of Tony McDade, contributing further to a pattern of erasing Black trans people as victims from our conversations about and mobilizations around police brutality.[78] Toyin's profession of "Black lives matter" was inclusive and accountable to multiply marginalized Black lives and communities.

Only a few days after her speech went viral, she posted a tweet about being sexually violated. She described a violent encounter with an older man who offered her a ride and a place to stay. He sexually assaulted her. Toyin's tweet rattled those in community with her and sparked outrage on social media. Without mincing words, she posted: "Anyways I was molested in Tallahassee, Florida by a black man this morning at 5:30 on Richview and Park Ave. The man offered to give me a ride to find someplace to sleep and recollect my belongings from a church I refuged to a couple days back to escape unjust living conditions."[79] Toyin even contacted police about the sexual assault. Of note, she was in search of "just living conditions." She wasn't protected in her own home and needed to find shelter. She posted the tweet on June 6, the last day anyone who knew Toyin saw her alive. Just days after electrifying protestors in her community with her insightful words, friends and fellow activists reported Toyin missing. She became one of more than sixty thousand missing Black girls and women in the United States.[80]

Just a week after her disappearance and tweet about being sexually assaulted, police found the body of Toyin along with the body of a seventy-five-year-old woman, Victoria Sims, on a road in southeastern Tallahassee. On the same day police found their bodies, Aaron Glee Jr. confessed to raping and murdering Toyin. He was the man Toyin had tweeted about just days earlier. Her and Victoria's bodies were found near his rental property. The discovery of her body sent shockwaves through her community, as well as those of us who only became familiar with her a few days before her rape and murder. I cried, my tears filled with anger and sadness. She was fighting for us. Her death came at the hands of a person she thought would help her. This Black woman literally put her life on the line for Black people, and intracommunal violence took her life. She sought protection in the "care" of someone she thought wanted to support her. Instead, Glee raped and killed her. She ran away from a home situation in which she was vulnerable to a man who preyed on that very vulnerability. Toyin died in search of a nontoxic place and fighting for Black lives, including her own.

Who fights for Oluwatoyin Salau? Fighting for her requires acknowledging and holding coextant truths about the inescapability of police violence against Black women and girls, as well as intracommunal gender and sexual violence against us. Her story illustrates that even when we seek solace, protection, and care from the very folks we fight for and alongside, we risk violation. We can't escape the violence of white supremacist patriarchy. It's part of our experiences that often get written off as distractions to the "more important" project of racial justice. *We are not a distraction.* White supremacy should not dictate how we hold those in our communities accountable for harm. Fear of proving "white supremacy" right regarding racist stereotypes about Black men and boys can't continuously underpin our reluctance to declare that violence against Black women and girls is antiBlack violence too.

Violence against us manifests in multiple forms, some not as easily identified as gender and sexual violence at the hands of loved ones or brutality at the hands of police. The risk of violation occurs in less spectacular ways that compromise our well-being. When we expand how we think about violence to encompass the range of systemic harm too many of us encounter, we get a better understanding of our forced intimate relationship with premature death. In the next two chapters, I look at medical violence and unlivable living to grapple with forms of Black violability that aren't typically centered in discussions about antiBlack violence. Many of us do survive the violence of antiBlackness, misogynoir, and multiple jeopardy but not without enduring irreparable harm. This kind of harm can be a global health pandemic or the crisis of houselessness.

4 *Violability Is a Preexisting Condition*

Dying in the Medical Industrial Complex

One in one thousand. My mouth dropped as I watched the first presidential debate in September 2020. Yes, it was a shit show. There were numerous moments in which I wanted to scream at the television. But when then–former vice president Joseph Biden said that "one in one thousand African Americans has been killed because of the coronavirus," my mouth dropped in utter shock. It's not that I didn't know that Black USians made up a disproportionate number of COVID-related deaths. I just couldn't wrap my mind or heart around that number. Had Biden misspoken? I did some research. Sadly, he hadn't. According to APM Research Lab, by mid-October 2020, 1 in 920 Black USians had died a COVID-19-related death. As the death toll climbed throughout 2020, Black and Indigenous People in the U.S. suffered the greatest losses.[1] The disparate impact was gallingly predictable. By February 2021, one in 645 Black USians had died as a result of the coronavirus.[2] As the old saying goes, "If white folks get a cold, Black folks get pneumonia."

When the disproportionate mortality rates of the novel coronavirus became blaringly evident, we were bombarded by explanations for such high death tolls in Black communities. Over and over again we heard "preexisting conditions" and "comorbidities" as the reasons for the devastating impact of this virus.[3] While organizations such as the Centers for Disease Control and Prevention reported on which medical conditions increased risk of severe illness from the virus that causes COVID-19, I couldn't help but become exhausted by this uncritical framing.[4] It felt like an incessant loop of patient-blaming those with "underlying medical conditions." Furthermore, few of any of these national health organizations interrogated why certain communities overindex with preexisting conditions. The predominating focus of public medical discourse is on "unhealthy people," not unhealthy and untenable systems, structures, and institutions. A preexisting condition too few seem to care about is antiBlackness.[5] A comorbidity for Black women and girls not being discussed ad nauseum is misogynoir.

What we heard throughout the pandemic was that Black folks are obese and hypertensive.[6] Fatphobia and fat-shaming became default responses to a virus that affected millions of people worldwide of varying sizes.[7] Our disproportionate rates of asthma, autoimmune disorders, heart disease, and other chronic illnesses were highlighted not only as conditions that made us more vulnerable but as conditions we created through "unhealthy" behaviors.[8] On April 10, 2020, during the height of the first wave of COVID-19, U.S. Surgeon General Jerome Adams stated during a press briefing that while no evidence existed indicating Black and Brown people are more biologically or genetically susceptible to COVID-19, we are "socially predisposed to coronavirus exposure, and have a higher incidence of the very diseases that put you at risk for severe complications of coronavirus."[9] *Socially predisposed?* I wasn't entirely sure what that meant, but it rubbed me the wrong way.

Although Adams's statement appeared to delegitimize a problematic eugenics-like explication for the disproportionate number of Black people dying from or severely harmed by the novel coronavirus, I couldn't help but feel the sting of *socially predisposed*. It teetered on the line of victim-blaming, with a strong hint of admonishment. Adams went on to strongly "encourage" African American and Latinx communities to adhere to established guidelines. I sensed a tinge of condescension as Adams directed his comments straightforwardly at us and stated "we need you to do this, if not for yourself, then for your abuela. Do it for your granddaddy, do it for your Big Mama, do it for your pop-pop."[10] Even if Adams intended to connect to communities being ravaged by a virus that we still didn't know enough about, the lack of naming at the very least racism as a reason for these disparate outcomes was glaring.

Less than a week after the Adams press briefing, Edna Bonhomme published a piece for *Al Jazeera* titled "Racism: The Most Dangerous 'Pre-Existing Condition.'" Bonhomme called out a long history of racist inequalities and disparities in health outcomes. More pointedly, Bonhomme acknowledged that the U.S. government "put the responsibility entirely on minority communities to protect themselves against health inequities they are not responsible for."[11] Without equivocation, she centered racism as a primary reason for the spread of COVID-19 in Black communities in the United States. COVID-19 was new, but antiBlack racism, extant in every major system in the U.S., was not.

Exactly a week after the press conference and after seeing a tweet from Madonna calling COVID "the great equalizer," my anger fueled me to publish a piece for *Women's Media Center* about why COVID-19 hit Black folks, and more specifically Black women, so hard.[12] What was clear from the data and stories emerging in the first several weeks of the pandemic was that this virus magnified the preexisting conditions of antiBlackness and misogynoir. COVID became yet another fatal force causing the premature deaths of tens of thousands of Black people. It was and is horrifying yet wholly expectable. AntiBlack politics of disposability and vulnerability had once again taken center stage.[13] COVID-19 was horrifyingly just a new manifestation of endemic antiBlackness.

Black people of all genders can and do experience harm when seeking healthcare.[14] For Black women and girls, specifically, the U.S. medical industrial complex has exploited, demonized, and underserved us from its inception.[15] We have been among the most victimized by medical violence. Medical violence encompasses direct violence to the body, structural violence, rhetorical violence, and demeaning interactions between healthcare practitioners and patients.[16] COVID-19's disparate impact is infuriatingly one of the more recent examples of how medical violence manifests against us. Many of the deaths of Black women and girls because of the novel coronavirus illuminate how antiBlackness and misogynoir function as preexisting conditions contributing to poor health outcomes.

Unfortunately, there's no shortage of contemporary examples of medical violence causing significant harm or worse, killing Black women and girls. From maternal morbidity to disproportionately higher rates of death from breast cancer to wholly inadequate and inaccessible care for Black trans women and nonbinary people, healthcare in the U.S. routinely fails us. Our "health profile" is used to explain why we encounter such dismal outcomes with barely a mention of the structural, systemic, and institutional factors that *actually* amalgamate to harm or kill us. The convergence of damaging antiBlack and sexist stereotypes, transphobia, queerphobia, poverty, ableism, fatphobia, and systemic misogynoir and anti-Blackness render us distinctively exposed to careless care.

The U.S. healthcare system is rife with recklessness toward and derision of us. It shields itself from blame by deeming us irresponsible and as wholly accountable for the harm we endure. The refusal to wrestle with a wretched history of medical violence against Black people and its enduring legacy make it easy to downplay disparate outcomes. Even though there's greater consensus around the reality that once upon a time, medical practitioners engaged in egregious treatment of Black patients, too many people see this as part of a distant past. What's happening to Black women and girls in the twenty-first century thus far, however, shows us how present that ignoble history is. Our health outcomes are historically bound and socially constructed by medical violence. It's not about social predisposition; it's about a nation's medical system being built on violence against, exploitation of, and contempt for Black feminized flesh and bodies.

They Need Us to Be Disposable

Unsurprisingly, medical/health-related violence against Black women and girls in the United States commenced during the transatlantic slave trade.[17] Historian Sowande' Mustakeem describes the oceans and seas that slave ships traversed as a "zone of death" for captive Africans.[18] During the perilous and disease-filled transporting of bondspeople on ships bound for the Americas, captors heinously balanced a need to maximize their profits by transporting "healthy" Africans and a desire to render them as subhuman and undeserving of care.[19] Diseased, maimed, and infirm captive Africans were less valuable, but shipmasters "preferred slaves whose bodies displayed optimal health."[20] Nevertheless, those transporting and trafficking often extended little to no care to enslaved people as illness and disease ran rampant aboard ships.[21] The desire for healthy and "ideal slaves" coexisted with the infliction of unimaginable suffering on the bodies and flesh of those who became enslaved in the Americas.[22]

For women and girls enslaved at sea, the Middle Passage took direct aim at their womanhood and girlhood. Historian Jessica M. Johnson argues that slave traders, "operated under the assumption that African women's and girls' bodies existed to be used, exploited, and ultimately sold for profit." "The captives' size, musculature, and reproductive capacity" were the primary concerns of those engaged in profiting from the Atlantic slave trade.[23] It is not health and wellness that slave captains desired for women and girls enslaved at sea but bodies that could be deemed productive, reproductive, and "able."[24] For prospective slave owners, the processes of evacuating personhood of captive Africans aboard ships was valuable for the creation of the subordinate status of enslaved person as well.[25] Compulsory productive and reproductive exploitation and, eventually, experimentation contributed to the antiBlack, partial or nonperson designation of the enslaved person.

In this long history of exploitation, systemic denigration, and experimentation on Black people, we can see the foundational scaffolding for a medical industrial complex that would directly and indirectly harm Black women and girls. It was the job of many physicians in the antebellum era to attest to the soundness of enslaved people.[26] In fact, physicians in this era were "dependent upon slavery both for economic security and for the enslaved 'clinical material' that fed the American medical research and medical training that bolstered physicians' professional advancement."[27]

The health and wellness of captive African women or enslaved Black girls only mattered to medical practitioners to the extent of their productive and reproductive capacity for slave owners or for the purpose of advancing scientific racism and hierarchized racial difference.[28] Enslaved Black people were the victims of what medical ethicist Harriet Washington identified as "southern medicine of the eighteenth and early nineteenth centuries."[29] Keeping enslaved Black people sound for productive labor, sustaining profitable reproductivity from those with gestational capacity, and rudimentary and daily experimentation on enslaved people were par for the course for doctors in the U.S.[30] The exploitation of their Black patients and subjects was simply, and horrifically, "the job."

The history of experimentation on Black people extends far back into our history. U.S. medical journals from the South in the nineteenth century contained numerous articles by physicians and medical practitioners documenting how they "purged, puked, and bled their Black patients, often to unconsciousness."[31] We typically, however, boil this ghastly history down to the notorious Tuskegee Syphilis Experiment of the early to mid-twentieth century.[32] When we view this experiment, which is widely known as one of the prime examples of the convergence of "experimental monstrosities and racial injustices," as exceptional, we erase the larger pattern of medical abuse via experimentation on Black folks.[33] In short, "the Tuskegee Syphilis Experiment hyperfunctions as a metaphor for anti-Black racism in medical research."[34] Like so many comparatively well-known examples of antiBlack violence, this exemplar centers the experiences of Black men. The Tuskegee study should never have happened. It reverberates in such profound ways with regard to Black men's formidable and

more than reasonable distrust and hatred for the medical industrial complex.[35] Black people of all genders reference this experiment as a primary source of contempt for and fear of the medical
industrial complex. The study is significant in revealing a history of
antiBlackness in the U.S. healthcare system, but sadly, it is not singular. There are numerous examples, many of which include
experimenting on Black women and girls.

I first heard of James Marion Sims when a textbook I had identified him as the "father of modern gynecology." I was a first-year
student at Oberlin College. Something in my gut told me to inquire
about this moniker. So I went to see my biology professor during
his office hours. When I asked about Sims, he quickly noted that the
physician and researcher was a somewhat controversial figure. We
briefly discussed the history of racism and medicine. Only minutes
into the conversation, my professor conceded that while Sims was
innovative, his methods were, at the least, unethical. He didn't call
him racist outright. He did concede that Sims's legacy is more complicated than simply being a pioneer in the field of modern medicine. I pushed for him to tell me more because it felt like he was
avoiding something crucial. I could feel his discomfort with my
questions about what "complicated" meant.

Eventually, another student arrived for a meeting. My professor invited me to continue this "difficult" conversation at another
time. I sensed he hoped I wouldn't come back with more questions
about this though—and I didn't. I inferred that he wasn't prepared
to truly grapple with Sims beyond a conversation of medical ethics.
His unease signaled that there was so much more to say. Looking
back, I believe he was either ill-equipped or unwilling to dive into
a more honest conversation with an eager young Black woman. I
should've done my own research as soon as I got back to my dorm

after dance practice. I didn't. By the next day, I was on to new curiosities.

Sims reentered my orbit while I was in graduate school at Duke. I read Harriet A. Washington's book, *Medical Apartheid: The Dark History of Medical Experimentation on Black Americans from Colonial Times to the Present.* As I read her book, Sims's "controversial" status came into sharp focus. I learned about the "nightmarishly painful and degrading experiments" Sims conducted on enslaved women without consent. He was also a plantation doctor. In that role, he both (mis)treated and experimented on Black infants.[36] The receipts of egregiousness piled up as I read. I could feel my blood boiling. Up until that point in my life, I had never had a white doctor. My parents were deliberate. They may not have intimately known this history, but they knew something that led them to make that decision. Their choices seemingly reflected an informed distrust and skepticism about the treatment I might receive in the care of a white doctor.

While Sims did a lot of harmful things to enslaved people throughout his inhumanely prolific career, what stuck with me the most were his experiments on twelve enslaved women. He "acquired" these women, who had vesicovaginal fistula, and performed numerous, painful procedures and surgeries on them without their consent.[37] To be clear, as enslaved women, they could not freely refuse; therefore, all experiments on these women "given" to Sims by slave owners were nonconsensual. He advanced gynecological medicine through exploiting the pain and anguish of these enslaved women. This is what my professor hadn't wanted to share with me. He didn't mention racism, let alone antiBlackness, as a complicating factor in Sims's legacy. He reduced this atrocious violence against these enslaved women to "being unethical." This wasn't simply a matter of ethics. Reducing Sims's legacy to bad ethics was one of the most uncritical takes one could surmise from all that Sims did.

Sims operated from the widely held belief that Black people don't feel pain in the same way as their white counterparts.[38] He also misrepresented his research when engaging audiences in nonslaveholding areas by concealing "the ethnicity of his subjects, portraying them as white in the illustrations that accompanied his accounts of the surgery."[39] His lies and his acts certainly make him more than a controversial figure. He can be both the father of modern gynecology and someone who committed atrocities against Black people. It's the latter truth about him, however, that my professor and others in medicine and the biological sciences need to confront more boldly. Leading with his innovations allows for the harm he caused more than a dozen enslaved women to be secondary, if mentioned at all. The truth of the matter is that Sims invested in antiBlackness and experimented on enslaved people who could not consent, which made it possible for him to innovate modern gynecology. His research intended to improve the lives of white women at the expense of Black women.

Medical practice more broadly in his era relied on surgical experimentation on enslaved people, but Sims wasn't the only practitioner. The reality that Harriet Washington illuminated for me was that "for black women, forced experimentation was the standard of care."[40] Dr. Francois Marie Prévost experimented on enslaved Black women in his quest to improve cesarean sections in the 1820s and 1830s; Dr. Ephraim McDowell used enslaved women to test and eventually "perfect" a then-radical surgical procedure to remove an ovary.[41] Washington's book shook me to my core, as it chronicled numerous examples of medical abuse of Black people, specifically Black women. I hadn't learned anything about this prior to reading her book. A palpable disappointment sank in as I realized how many people like me would probably never know this history but would have experiences in healthcare that tapped into this abusive legacy of experimentation.

It was also around this time in my studies that I learned about Henrietta Lacks and the HeLa cell line.[42] Lacks went to Johns Hopkins University Hospital in January 1951—the only medical facility in her area in Maryland that treated Black patients at the time—with pain and knottiness in her womb.[43] Doctors discovered she was pregnant, which her family had suspected. She gave birth and suffered a severe hemorrhage. After extensive testing and a misdiagnosis, she was accurately diagnosed with adenocarcinoma.[44] During her treatments, two samples from her cervix—one with healthy tissue and the other with cancerous cells—were taken without her permission. Those who collected the samples gave them to cancer researcher and physician George Otto Gey. The cancerous sample produced the world's first known immortal human cells. Named the HeLa immortal cell line, the cells scraped from her cervix just months before she died became one of the most important cell lines in medical research.[45]

The cancerous cells that killed Henrietta Lacks breathed life into others via the development of the polio vaccine, the study of leukemia, and groundbreaking research on HIV/AIDS and numerous forms of cancer.[46] The cells taken from her without her consent continue to provide essential medical data for researchers.[47] The cells of a dying Black woman saved lives, but no one was able to save her. Her life is an excruciating metaphor for what it means to be a Black woman here: we demand that Black women save others with no interest or plan for saving Black women. Researchers continue to experiment with her cell line. We benefit from it, though she was never even asked to be our savior. While it may be easy to dismiss ethical concerns given what's been made possible by her cells, it is shameful to ignore how experimentation on Black women like her and the enslaved women Prévost, Sims, and McDowell used was, at best, disturbingly exploitative and, at worst, downright violent. Henrietta was only thirty-one years old when she perished, and in the 2020s and the foreseeable future, her non-consensually attained cells will continue to advance medical research.[48]

It would be impossible for this legacy of experimentation not to seep into our current medical industrial complex. So how do we reconcile, as historian Deidre Cooper Owens clarifies, that "Black lives mattered medically because they made white lives healthier and better?"[49] This abusive and exploitative history offers more credence to the assertion that "Black women save America," even when this nation continually fails and discards us. Not that we needed any more proof of this remarkably uneven relationship of Black women and girls to the nation. Sadly, the history of experimentation on us isn't the only ignominious part of our past within the U.S. medical industrial complex. Those of us who had or have gestational capacity confront a vast history of reproductive violence that stretches into our current moment as well.

Our Uteruses as Battlegrounds

Uterus Collector. I first saw those words on my Twitter timeline in late September 2020. I was afraid to click on the link in the tweet because I knew I would be horrified. To what in the world could this be referring? I don't regret hitting the link, but I wish I'd better prepared myself for what I read. Dawn Wooten, a nurse at a U.S. Immigration and Customs Enforcement jail operated by the private for-profit prison company LaSalle Corrections, sent a complaint to the Homeland Security inspector general detailing "horrifying conditions" at the Irwin County Detention Center in rural Ocilla, Georgia. Dawn described bug-infested food and filthy conditions.[50] The most shocking part of her whistleblowing, however, was reports of immigrant women detained at the facility being sterilized via hysterectomies and other procedures by a gynecologist without their consent. Dawn herself referred to what was happening as a "silent pandemic."[51] This mass reproductive atrocity occurred during the COVID-19 pandemic, alongside those being detained and even those working at ICE facilities being at extremely high risk for contracting the virus owing to the unsanitary and overcrowded conditions at ICE facilities.[52] She simply could not wrap her head around how so many women who were sent to Dr. Mahendra Amin ended up undergoing a hysterectomy or sterilizing procedure.[53] That's why she identified Dr. Amin as the "uterus collector."

I thought about the women who underwent those procedures for months after I read article after article about what transpired. We didn't get many individual details about their experiences or the demographic breakdown of the victims of this "silent pandemic." What I did know was that in September 2020, Haitian families made up 44 percent of all families detained by ICE.[54] Immediately, I wondered what percentage of those sterilized were Black immigrants, refugees, and asylum seekers. In November 2020, news broke of the Trump administration trying to deport several of the women who alleged mistreatment by Dr. Amin; the administration had already deported six former patients who lodged complaints against him. One of the women now facing deportation, thirty-seven-year-old Mbeti Ndonga from Kenya, had spoken with government investigators twice about being "abused, tortured, and dehumanized" by Dr. Amin.[55] Just hours after her first interview with investigators, Mbeti learned from her lawyers that ICE had just lifted the hold on her deportation back to Kenya. Ndonga could now be sent back to Kenya any day. Additionally, after the procedures she underwent in Dr. Amin's care, she believes she will never be able to reproduce. She continues to experience uncontrolled bleeding and pain as well, a daily reminder of the "care" she received while being detained for seeking a new life for herself.

The story of the "uterus collector" made me think about the long, injurious history of Black women being forcibly sterilized. I knew, from having read *Medical Apartheid* while in graduate school, that "African Americans have always been staggeringly overrepresented in the ranks of the sterilized."[56] It was logical to infer that at least some of the folks with gestational capacity at the Irwin County Detention Center were Black. After all, the U.S. has long been a front-runner in the race for eugenic and punitive sterilization, and Black women endured a disproportionate share of this violent infringement on reproductive freedom.[57] Mbeti's experience fits within a long multicenturies history of reproductive violence against Black women.

Substantive reasons exist for therapeutic and "medically necessary" sterilizations—specifically, hysterectomies. For more than a century though, doctors motivated by eugenics discourse performed the procedure on those deemed unfit and reproductively disposable.[58] Systemic involuntary and coerced sterilization of African American women coincided with the global rise of eugenics, a racist, pseudoscientific movement fixated on creating a superior white race.[59] AntiBlack, sexist, ableist, and antipoor stereotypes abounded. Concerted efforts were made throughout the Jim Crow era to designate Black people in the U.S. as a permanent underclass. This meant that Black women were primary targets for efforts to regulate and control their reproductive lives.[60] Laws and accepted medical practices provided a legal-medical context in which compulsory sterilization could occur with the explicit intent to stop those deemed "unfit." The nation sought to stop African American, Jewish, Mexican, Native American, Puerto Rican, mentally ill, and criminalized and incarcerated people from reproducing.[61]

So, what did and does this mean for Black persons with gestational capacity? It meant that by 1983, 43 percent of all women sterilized through federally funded family planning programs were African Americans. This percentage just reflects those conducted in legal, medical settings. As Washington expounds, "most sterilizations of poor black women have been performed outside of the law and in violation of medical mores."[62] I cringe at the thought of what those numbers may be. When sitting with this history, I also think of one of my favorite freedom fighters, Fannie Lou Hamer. She endured an involuntary hysterectomy and became one of the most outspoken critics of this racial-sexual form of violence, which was so commonly used against Black women in her home state that people called it the "Mississippi Appendectomy."[63] This renowned freedom fighter went to the hospital to have a stomach cyst removed and awakened without a uterus.[64] She used her story to amplify those of numerous poor southern Black women. She fought alongside Black women in the state of Mississippi who understood this statewide effort to sterilize them as an infringement on their reproductive and civil rights. They also recognized the eugenic underpinnings of the widespread practice of sterilization of Black women: the powers that be didn't want women like her reproducing.

By 1965, one-third of Puerto Rican women of child-bearing age (twenty to forty-nine) had been sterilized—voluntarily and involuntarily. A sizable percentage of these women identified as Black/ of African descent.[65] It was so common, Puerto Rican women called it "La Operación."[66] This rampant sterilization of Puerto Rican women was a form of colonial violence that relied on anti-Black, antiIndigenous, misogynistic, and antipoor ideologies to justify the remorseless assault on Puerto Rican women's reproductive futures. Dating back to the 1990s and extending through 2010, more than two hundred inmates were coercively sterilized in two California prisons, many of whom were Black as well.[67] It's hard not to think about these recent histories of sexualized and gendered antiBlack violence when my friends and other Black women share their stories about sterilization. Forced sterilization was and is, as scholar of race, gender, and law Dorothy Roberts contends, "an extension of brutality inflicted on black Americans."[68]

Personally, I know quite a few Black women under forty-five who've undergone some form of sterilization. Most were voluntary and therapeutic, but a few of my friends shared with me how pressured they felt to take such aggressive measures to address comparatively minor gynecological issues. While I shudder to think that too many doctors continue to hold retrograde, antiBlack, antipoor, fatphobic, ableist, and misogynistic views about Black women's reproductive capacity and rights, history emboldens my trepidation. Here's what I know: none of my white friends under forty-five have disclosed to me that they underwent any form of sterilization. This is a nation that actively, coercively, and forcibly sterilized Black women well into the 2010s, using everything from welfare policies to downright deception.[69] This isn't some distant history. Going to see a gynecologist in the 2020s as a Black person with presumptive gestational capacity can and does still lead to heartrending outcomes. These stories and histories, coupled with the more recently publicized crisis of Black maternal mortality and morbidity in the United States, make the severity of reproductive violence against us undeniable.

Dying to Give Birth

Serena Williams is one of my favorite athletes. Although I played a little tennis before she and her amazing older sister, Venus Williams, changed professional women's tennis as we know it, my love for the game reached a new level with their dominance. Despite the misogynoir and rampant antiBlackness the Williams sisters faced throughout their careers, they excelled.[70] With twenty-three grand slams and numerous Olympic medals under her belt, Serena emerged as (arguably, though indisputably to me) the greatest women's tennis player of all time. And though it may be pointless to compare athletes across sports, Serena also belongs in the conversation of greatest athletes of all time. Just ask Nike.[71]

When she formally announced her pregnancy with her first child, I was elated. Previously, she had expressed a desire for a family. Although competing at a remarkable level, she embraced a new chapter in her life, which many thought might derail her career.[72] In true GOAT fashion, she won the Australian Open in 2017 while pregnant—effectively and brilliantly silencing her detractors. HBO cameras followed her and her husband, Alexis Ohanian, in the months leading up to the birth of their first child.

The five-part docuseries aired in May 2018. A very pregnant Serena allowed viewers into very intimate parts of her life as she prepared to give birth. Unlike many celebrity-centered reality shows, this series felt sincere in its efforts to show the day-to-day life of one of the most famous athletes on the planet. With her consent, we got to see a little more of her off-the-court life. I enjoyed being invited into these more intimate parts of her world, especially after reading about her nightmarish childbirth experience.[73]

Prior to the docuseries's debut, Serena shared her harrowing experience during and immediately after childbirth with *Vogue* magazine. She explained that even though her daughter's heart rate dropped to dangerously low levels during contractions, Olympia was born via a standard, emergency C-section. As she held her newborn to her chest, she recounted that her bundle of joy fell quiet. The next day, however, things took a turn for the worse. According to *Vogue* reporter Rob Haskell, Serena recalled the following:

> Serena suddenly felt short of breath. Because of her history of blood clots, and because she was off her daily anticoagulant regimen due to the recent surgery, she immediately assumed she was having another pulmonary embolism. (Serena lives in fear of blood clots.) She walked out of the hospital room so her mother wouldn't worry and told the nearest nurse, between gasps, that she needed a CT scan with contrast and IV heparin (a blood thinner) right away. The nurse thought her pain medicine might be making her confused. But Serena insisted.[74]

Initially, Serena's insistence only led to a doctor performing an ultrasound of her legs. Knowing her own body and preexisting health conditions, she once again asked for a CT and heparin drip, as the ultrasound revealed nothing. The doctor finally ordered a CT, and, unsurprisingly, they discovered several small blood clots in her lungs. They placed her on the drip she had requested earlier. They should've listened to "Dr. Williams" about her own health and body, but thankfully she survived this potentially fatal medical condition.

As I read her story, I couldn't help but think of the popular refrain "Listen to Black women." If one of the most famous Black women in the world was almost dismissed at a critical moment in her care, one can only imagine what a poor Black woman endures when she attempts to advocate for herself in a system in which she is anywhere from two to five times more likely than a white woman to die as a result of childbirth.[75] There's "maternal death," which the World Health Organization defines as the "death of a woman while pregnant or within 42 days of termination of pregnancy or its management but not from accidental or incidental causes."[76] But maternal death is only one form of pregnancy-related death. "Pregnancy-related death" is defined as "the death of a woman during pregnancy or within a year of the end of a pregnancy from pregnancy complication, a chain of events initiated by pregnancy or the aggravation of an unrelated condition by the physiologic effects of pregnancy."[77] Sadly, there's no shortage of recent examples of Black women dying from pregnancy-related causes. Across class, sexuality, disability, body size, and educational background, Black folks with gestational capacity are dying to give birth.

For the past few years, I'd heard more and more about the Black maternal health crisis. Generally speaking, research and reports regurgitated that same phrase we heard when talking about COVID-19's disparate impact on Black communities: preexisting conditions.[78] Even the reports that extended beyond preexisting conditions and the lack of access to prenatal care as reasons for notable disparities would only go so far as to identify "racial bias" as a potential contributing factor.[79] What many of those looking at the data seemed to miss, however, were the roles of antiBlackness and misogynoir. Racial bias isn't specific or capacious enough to capture what's happening to those succumbing to pregnancy-related deaths. Recognizing the role of oppressive systems in health outcomes for Black folks with gestational capacity should be the entry point for those of us invested in addressing this crisis.

For me, that entry point could be the story of Dr. Chaniece Wallace, a pediatric chief resident at the Indiana University School of Medicine who died from preeclampsia just days after giving birth via a premature C-section.[80] Chaniece accessed prenatal care and fit the "general profile" of someone who would survive labor and delivery and even a pregnancy-related illness, except for the fact that she was a Black woman. Although most women and people with gestational capacity with preeclampsia survive, it can be and too often is death-dealing for Black women in the U.S.[81] Pregnant Black women's rate of preeclampsia and eclampsia is 60 percent higher than the rate for pregnant white women.[82] Preexisting conditions simply don't account for this potentially fatal disparity. Differential access, which is also rooted in anti-Blackness and, often, multiple jeopardy and misogynoir as well, doesn't fully explain why Black women like Wallace or global pop star Beyoncé encounter this sudden increase in blood pressure while pregnant or in or soon after labor and delivery.[83] And race, "the mélange of physical features and social clues" that organize how we categorize people, isn't sufficient either.[84] Antiquated race science isn't the path we need to journey further down to explain how we got here.[85] We have to say it with our chests: antiBlackness and misogynoir significantly contribute to the Black maternal mortality and morbidity crisis.

Whenever one of my Black friends gives birth, it's hard for me not to think about how frequently pregnancy-related deaths occur. That these deaths occur "even up to a year afterward" compounds my anxiety as I attempt to celebrate new life in the world.[86] I think my fears around Black people giving birth hit a new level with the tragic pregnancy-related death of twenty-seven-year-old racial justice activist Erica Garner, the daughter of Eric Garner. She exemplified a cadre of Black women dying months after giving birth. Although the cause of death for the mother of two was attributed to an enlarged heart and major brain damage suffered during a heart attack, that's not the entire story.[87] Anthropologist Christen Smith astutely pointed out that "in the wake of the deaths of black people at the hands of the state—from the police to the prison system—the living are often weighted with a sadness that is too heavy to bear, and in the weeks and months following the initial death of a loved one, they become sick and many die prematurely."[88] Smith studies police violence in Brazil and the United States. One of her most significant findings in both geopolitical contexts is "the ways that police violence kills Black women slowly through trauma, pain and loss."[89] The loss of Erica Garner's father to antiBlack police violence, the incalculable weight of living life as a Black woman in the U.S., and the intensive and soul-crushing labor of racial justice activism were all preexisting conditions that didn't show up on Erica's autopsy.

According to the National Center for Health Statistics, of the 658 women who died of maternal causes in 2018, Black women fared the worst. In 2018, Black women's maternal mortality rate was 2.5 times higher than white women's.[90] From 2007 to 2016, the CDC's Pregnancy Mortality Surveillance System found that Black mothers died at 3.2 times the rate of white mothers.[91] Alas, the difference between the rates doesn't mark an improvement. There's simply a qualitative difference between what each study identified as a maternal death.[92] The 2018 study only accounted for deaths within forty-two days of giving birth. The study covering 2007 to 2016 included maternal deaths within a year of giving birth. Regardless of which data set we use, these rates only scratch the surface of documenting the reality of Black people with gestational capacity dying as a result of pregnancy or giving birth.

Consider the story of thirty-nine-year-old Kira Johnson, who, after giving birth via a planned Cesarean section, died from internal bleeding and cardiac arrest.[93] Kira gave birth at 2:33 p.m. on April 12, 2016, and died just twelve hours later. After her C-section, her husband noticed blood flowing into her catheter and informed doctors of his concern. She wasn't taken back into surgery until after midnight, at which point doctors discovered three and a half liters of blood in her abdomen. She had bled internally for ten hours before doctors attempted to save her life, but it was too late. No matter how we look at it, Kira got careless care. This is also the story of Sha-Asia Washington. Sha-Asia went into cardiac arrest during an emergency C-section and died on the operating table.[94] While some details remain unclear, what we know is that she went to Woodhull Medical Center for a routine stress test a few days past her due date.[95] Doctors decided to keep Sha-Asia for observation because of her abnormally high blood pressure and eventually convinced her to take Pitocin to induce contractions. Within hours of arriving, she died, her baby was born, and her loved ones were left with so many unanswered questions and concerns about the care this young Black woman received. No answers, just the cloud of *careless care*.

The stress of delivering a child in an antiBlack world can't be underestimated as we search for more solutions to the Black maternal mortality and morbidity crisis. For those considering pregnancy, it's hard to ignore story after story of Black women dying during or soon after pregnancy. The new "attention" to this crisis is healthful only if more of us are willing to reckon with antiBlackness and white supremacy as opposed to race as a driving factor of these deaths. A social construct created to assign an "inescapable status" to nonwhite persons isn't killing Black women; the systems built around this construct are.[96] They—both the systems and those who wield power within them—must be held accountable for our premature deaths. I don't want to hear another word about "race" killing us. That framing belies how multiple forms of oppression coalesced to leave thousands of us in the twenty-first century dying to give birth.

Careless Care

Reproductive injustice is only one of the many ways antiBlackness and misogynoir show up in the U.S. medical industrial complex. From higher fatality rates for breast cancer, despite having lower incidence rates for it than white women, to being "disproportionately burdened by lupus," a debilitating and complex autoimmune disease, Black women and girls are often deprived of quality care.[97] And while it's too oversimplifying to say antiBlack racism and sexism cause such disparate outcomes, they are preexisting conditions negatively affecting our health outcomes and well-being. Explaining these disparities through the lens of our "unhealthiness" lets the medical industrial complex, as well as systemic anti-Blackness and misogynoir more broadly, off the hook for their roles in creating such unequal outcomes. It's easier to tell individual people to do better than it is to demand that entire systems such as healthcare actually work to do better by us.

Too much is at stake for there not to be a large-scale callout of what has been and is happening. Take, for example, the story of Amira Lewally. In an October 2020 story for the *Los Angeles Times* titled "As a Black Woman, I Had to Beg Doctors to Take Me Seriously When My Brain Was Leaking," Amira shared her painful story of seeking care in a system that refused to care for her. After losing hearing in her left ear and searching for a doctor with whom she felt comfortable and who she thought would listen to her, she got a prognosis that seemed inadequate: allergies. Although skeptical, she listened to the doctor. Months later, Amira wrote that "a clear fluid started to drain out of my left nostril," and she knew it wasn't just a runny nose.[98] Even after she told her doctor about a prior diagnosis of pseudotumor cerebri, a pressure buildup in the brain that causes headaches and eyesight issues, the doctor insisted that she simply had allergies.

With no one listening to her, Amira went to social media, which can and does lead to folks misdiagnosing themselves. Nevertheless, she saw a link on Twitter for an article titled "Man's Runny Nose Turns Out to Be Leaking Brain Fluid," read it, and shared it with her doctor. Unconvinced, her doctor dismissed the possibility and stuck with the allergies prognosis. Over the next year she sought out ear, nose, and throat specialists until she finally found one willing to, in the least, provide her with some "instant relief" by draining a small amount of fluid from her ear.[99] After the procedure, the doctor confirmed that she did in fact have a cerebrospinal fluid leak—the same thing she had seen earlier in the article she showed the first doctor, who had insisted it was allergies. Thankfully, Amira was insistent, believed in herself, and had healthcare coverage and the ability to travel to different locations in search of quality care. Otherwise, her story would've ended quite differently.

For three years, fluid leaked out of Amira's brain, and doctor after doctor ignored her cries for help. Amira framed what happened to her as either "neglect or indifference or bias." As I read her distressing story, however, antiBlackness and misogynoir immediately came to mind. In the article, she acknowledged, "I think about all of my sisters who don't have the healthcare coverage or the job flexibility to chase a dozen doctors down. I think about all my sisters whose birthing experiences quickly shifted from the happiest moment of their lives to the deadliest. I think about all my sisters who avoid physicians because of the horror stories. Sadly, I am not the first Black woman to be ignored by doctors, and unless we make a swift change, I won't be the last."[100]

Gallingly, her assessment is spot-on. In the U.S. medical industrial complex, deadly or life-altering outcomes are par for the course. She concluded her piece by averring that "many doctors do not care about cries from Black women."[101] Those cries don't get a humane response from those doctors because of long-standing myths and harmful stereotypes that identify Black women and girls as being impervious to pain because of their race and "overly hysterical about pain because of their gender."[102] The convergence of both racist and sexist stereotypes render us vulnerable to being dismissed, misdiagnosed, under- and untreated, and misunderstood. The consequences of all of this? Unlivable living and premature death.

For Black trans and nonbinary people, the additional burdens of transphobia and adherence to rigid gender binaries in healthcare situate them in an even more precarious situation. On June 12, 2020, the Trump administration finalized a rewrite of section 1557 of the Affordable Care Act, which prohibits discrimination based on race, color, national origin, sex, age, or disability.[103] Under the Obama administration, this prohibition of discrimination included gender identity.[104] In a profoundly, but unsurprisingly, transphobic and trans-antagonistic move, Trump's rewrite of this section reaffirmed an interpretation of sex discrimination according to the plain meaning of the word *sex* as male or female and as determined by biology.[105] In effect, this new rule made trans people even more vulnerable to discrimination in "accessing health services, receiving care consistent with their gender identity, and getting coverage for gender transition service."[106] The rewrite put trans people in danger of not receiving the same quality or access to healthcare as their nontrans counterparts. At the height of a pandemic disparately affecting marginalized communities, discarding gender identity as a protected status was frankly a heartless and antilife move.

Even prior to the pandemic, a poll conducted by the Robert Wood Johnson Foundation, NPR, and the Harvard T.H. Chan School of Public Health found that 31 percent of transgender USians lacked regular access to healthcare.[107] And Black trans women and nonbinary people represent a significant number of those without access to care.[108] While arguably the most commonly cited pandemic affecting Black trans women is direct violence, and specifically fatal violence against them, healthcare or lack thereof is a leading cause of premature death for those living at the intersection of antiBlackness, transphobia, and transmisogynoir. Their health outcomes reflect the worst of multiple jeopardy because Black trans and nonbinary people enter a medical industrial complex predominated by white, nontrans men as both health practitioners and as the pinnacle of healthiness.[109] The potential for multiple forms of harm exists when Black trans women and nonbinary people seek healthcare.

A 2018 study published in the February edition of the *Annals of Emergency Medicine* found that the majority of transgender adults who visited the emergency room reported that healthcare providers lacked competency in issues specific to the transgender community. Discrimination and harassment were also part of some of the respondents' experiences in the emergency room.[110] When you add in antiBlackness and misogynoir, where does that leave Black trans women and nonbinary people in terms of care? It leaves them uncared for, creating their own networks for health and wellness, and distinctly vulnerable for multiple, coextant medical conditions. If you fear the treatment you may receive from healthcare providers more than you fear whatever illness or affliction you may have, the system is failing.

What happens when the existing healthcare infrastructure fails Black trans women? It leads to nearly 20 percent of Black trans women living with HIV.[111] To put this percentage in perspective, 0.3 percent of the U.S. population lives with HIV. Once again, it's easy and misguided to look at the percentage of Black trans women and assign blame for high infection rates to risky behaviors. That explanation is rooted in HIV stigma first and foremost. Additionally, it ignores how antiBlackness, misogynoir, and transphobia shape the daily lives and choices of those living at the margins of the margins. Ultimately, "poverty, stigma, addiction, high rates of violence, unemployment, untreated mental health concerns and limited social support create an environment that increases one's vulnerability and risk for HIV."[112] While preventative measures and early treatment can reduce HIV transmission, access to these measures and treatment necessitate that Black trans women seek support and care from a system rife with antiBlackness, misogynoir, and transphobia.

According to a report from the National Institutes of Health, Black trans women confront barriers such as "refusal of care by providers and harassment and violence in medical settings."[113] These barriers create a context in which Black trans women over-index for attempted suicide and substance abuse.[114] Careless care for Black trans women means they are predisposed to being mistreated or untreated by a healthcare professional. And when discrimination and threats of criminalization and violence loom ever-present on a daily basis, that stress takes a toll. It renders one more susceptible to a range of chronic illnesses. These oppressive forces also make you less likely to seek care from systems that could further harm you. It's a vicious cycle that can't be broken without a large-scale undoing. A destruction of the gender binary, dismantling of white supremacy, divesting from antiBlackness, unlearning misogynoir, eliminating ableism, unequivocally rejecting transphobia, and meeting of the basic needs of the most vulnerable—these are foundational requirements for stopping medical violence and neglect of Black trans women in the United States. Without all these steps of undoing, there's no possibility for Black trans women to be unviolated and cared for within our healthcare systems.

Dying to Live

Healthcare should be a place where we will feel cared for, but it hasn't been and can't be within the existing medical industrial complex. Instead, Black women get second-class treatment.[115] While we've always found ways to treat, heal, and repair ourselves within our communities and amid our traditions, it's severely unjust that seeking care can put us at greater risk for premature death. Not only do many of us fear getting sick; we fear the very people and institutions that supposedly exist to help us. It's an impossible conundrum shrouded in a history so reprehensible and, in many ways, so ever-present that we seem to be stuck in an incessant loop of careless care.

For the last several years, I had been almost certain that I did not want to have children. It wasn't until I took some time during the "mandated" and my self-imposed lockdown of 2020 that I even contemplated what role fear played in my decision not to have children. I feared what it would mean to bring a Black child into a world where they would be perpetually criminalized, targeted, and disparately impacted by damn near everything terrible. I also confronted my own internalization of all these stories about pregnancy-related deaths. If I did decide to try and reproduce, would I die trying? Since I was pretty certain I didn't want kids, I was shocked by what I discovered as I got to sit with all of my thoughts. I realized that although I was still pretty sure about my reproductive future, fear and anxiety shaped my resolve around childbearing.

My personal experiences in the medical industrial complex have been a mixed bag. I've had doctors ignore my pain and dismiss my concerns. Others have taken me more seriously and done deep dives to provide quality care. When a significant portion of my hair began falling out in 2017 and my energy levels dropped in wholly unfamiliar ways, I went in search of answers. My gut told me to find Black specialists, but I was also impatient. My hair was falling out in clumps. I was so deenergized that on some days

I couldn't even make it out of my bed. All the Black specialists, especially the Black women, were booked for months. So I went to white specialists who had availability. While I wasn't wholly dismissed by these doctors, probably because of my highly educated, professional, and upper-middle-class socioeconomic status, they didn't take my concerns seriously. They saw a woman dealing with "routine hair loss" and sent me off to the dermatologist. It wasn't until I got an appointment with a Black female hematologist and a Black female oncologist that I got any answers that made sense. Within days of meeting with both of them, I had a diagnosis and a treatment plan. The simple act of them believing me changed the quality of my life.

My symptoms weren't indicative of anything fatal at the time, but it was clear that stress played an important role in my overall health. As a bi-queer, Black woman in the U.S., I didn't have the best plan for minimizing stresses beyond my control. I was thankful, however, for doctors who believed and advocated for me. If I hadn't had them, I don't know where I would be right now. Looking at the history of Black women and medical violence, as well as examining current examples of this violence, makes me think that my relatively positive experiences with doctors are exceptional. In so many arenas, Black women and girls are expected to accept the bare minimum or nothing at all. Consequently, for millions of us, our health is inscribed by the conditions of unlivable living.

Medical violence against us is both a historical fact and a contemporary reality. For those of us who don't perish from illnesses, medical neglect, or direct violence at the hands of the medical industrial complex, our daily lives still tend to situate us as the barely surviving. AntiBlackness, misogynoir, and oftentimes poverty join together as a death-dealing, preexisting condition. We may not die immediately, but we die prematurely and painfully. And while dying or being killed, we must combat all the other forms of harm and violation that affect us disproportionately. We fight to close a Black-white death gap *and* numerous disparities that produce unlivable conditions. We struggle to not disappear.

5 *Unlivable*

The Deadly Consequences of Poverty

I dedicated my first book, *Colored No More: Reinventing Black Womanhood in Washington, D.C.*, to Relisha Rudd. At the time, she was an eight-year-old Black girl who disappeared in Washington, D.C. on March 1, 2014. Relisha's tragic and unfinished story stuck with me as I revised my dissertation into a book about Black women who made the nation's capital the country's first major chocolate city. I began my love letter to my hometown by Saying Her Name. It felt like the least I could do. I wanted her name alongside her D.C. foremothers, who would've fought for her and did fight to create a world in which Black girls didn't go missing. Against all odds, I hoped one day Relisha would be found. Honestly, I still do. I fantasized about this little Black girl seeing her name in a book and knowing someone cared. I also thought that folks picking up my book would see her name and perhaps google her story. In the best-case scenario, the dedication would compel readers to Say Her Name too, even if for only a brief moment.

Every time I saw a picture of Relisha, tears would well in my eyes. She looked like she could be my kin. She lived close to my childhood home, too. When I was growing up, the shelter in which she resided didn't exist. The building was a part of D.C. General

Hospital, which was founded as the Washington infirmary in 1806.[1] The storied hospital, which was controversially shut down by former D.C. mayor Anthony Williams in 2001, provided "de facto universal healthcare" to uninsured, unhoused,[2] impoverished, and marginalized D.C. residents.[3] Founded as the city's poorhouse, it is unsurprising that D.C. General Hospital evolved into a healthcare site serving primarily those with no other options for care. Growing up, I knew it as the hospital folks went to if they got shot or stabbed or had overdosed. It was triage for a community relegated to unlivable living.

After it closed in 2001, the city reappropriated the facility, located in the shadows of the crumbling RFK Stadium and the D.C. Armory, for usage as a homeless shelter for families. Relisha, her mother, and younger brothers were among the families housed there.[4] According to multiple sources, Relisha's mother struggled with drug addiction.[5] D.C. General Shelter was also notoriously "filthy, chaotic, crime-ridden, [and] infested with vermin."[6] People can and do survive environments like this, but they're not fit for living. They're a setup for something terrible to happen to almost anyone navigating these conditions, but especially for a poor Black girl who sits at the intersection of multiple forms of oppression.

The first time the Children and Family Services Agency (CFSA) in D.C. had contact with Relisha and her mother, she was only one year old.[7] CFSA workers discovered that Relisha wasn't being housed or fed adequately.[8] There were also signs of physical abuse.[9] It's worth noting that Relisha's mother, Shamika Young, had grown up primarily in the foster care system, with an absent father and a mother with a drug addiction, who was also in the foster care system.[10] As a teenager, Shamika was diagnosed with a mental disability and hospitalized in a psychiatric residential treatment facility.[11] I don't bring up these details to pathologize Shamika and her family or even "excuse" the harm she may have inflicted on her children. I do, however, want to contextualize the intergenerational ecosystem of unlivability in which both Relisha and Shamika lived. Understanding these details about Shamika helps me to put into perspective each of the decisions she made before and after the disappearance of her daughter. Her decisions, however disheartening, emerge out of a shredded social safety net.

To this day, conflicting reports abound with regard to what happened in the weeks leading up to and immediately after Relisha's disappearance. What is clear is that a series of failures occurred. Prior to Relisha's disappearance, Shamika befriended a man working as a janitor at the shelter, Khalil Tatum.[12] Although Shamika disputes allegations that she let Relisha stay with Tatum on various occasions in the weeks prior to her disappearance, D.C. General had a "no-fraternization" policy between staff and residents that Tatum failed to follow and the shelter didn't enforce.[13] He regularly interacted with Relisha both inside and outside the shelter.[14] Relisha's aunt, Ashley Young, recalled Shamika informing her that Relisha knew Tatum as her godfather after he called Ashley's house to tell her he was coming to pick her niece up from there.[15]

Relisha's grandmother, Melissa Young, immediately became suspicious of Tatum after meeting him and learning about him taking Relisha shopping, on tours around the city, and other outings.[16] Although Melissa raised concerns about this man's relationship with her granddaughter, she understood her daughter's decision to let Tatum spend so much time with Relisha as a way to get the young girl out of the caustic life at the shelter.[17] The morning of March 1, 2014, Relisha spent time at Ashley's house. Relisha wasn't feeling well and stayed home from school that day. Ashley put "pink and white bows" in Relisha's hair.[18] This was the last time anyone in her family saw her. She was now in Tatum's "care."

There's footage of Tatum with Relisha on February 26, 2014, in a hallway at a Holiday Inn Express in D.C. and of the two walking into a room at a Days Inn in D.C. on March 1, 2014—the last time Relisha was seen before disappearing.[19] Prior to Relisha's disappearance, she'd already missed more than thirty days of school at Payne Elementary.[20] Despite the school being required to report "ten or more excused absences to social services within two days," the school delayed reporting because Shamika told them she had documentation to explain the absences.[21] According to school officials, Shamika told them that Relisha was under the care of "Dr. Tatum."[22] After more absences, the school eventually reached out to Tatum on March 10, 2014, and asked him to provide documentation for Relisha's continued absences; he responded that he was "treating her for neurological problems" and that she would be discharged by the end of the following week.[23] Following Relisha's tenth consecutive, unexcused absence in March, the school reported her family to CFSA.[24] Unfortunately, her case was not prioritized until March 19, 2014, when a CFSA social worker arranged a meeting with Tatum.[25] He didn't show. It was only at this point that the social worker and school learned that Tatum was not a doctor.

During the period between Relisha's disappearance and authorities approaching this case as a missing person and then a "recovery operation," a few key things happened that in addition to the numerous absences should've raised concern. On March 2, 2014, Tatum purchased "a carton of black 42-gallon contractor trash bags, a shovel, and lime."[26] According to police, lime can be used to speed up the process of decomposition of bodies.[27] When people at Payne Elementary asked about her daughter's absences throughout March, Shamika said her daughter was attending a conference with Dr. Tatum, a story that differed from what Tatum had shared with school officials.[28] After missing a meeting with the CFSA social worker on March 19, authorities finally got involved with the case and considered Relisha a "missing person." On that same day, police discovered Tatum's wife, Andrea, fatally shot in the head at a Maryland motel.[29] Less than two weeks later, after the FBI issued a warrant for Tatum's arrest, his body was found in a shed in Kenilworth Park in Northeast Washington, D.C.[30] He died from a self-inflicted gunshot wound caused by the same gun used to kill his wife.[31] All evidence pointed toward a murder-suicide. But where was Relisha?

The trash bags, shovel, and lime pointed toward a grave end for this young Black girl, but her body wasn't recovered in that park or anywhere else near either crime scene. There remains speculation about her possibly being trafficked since her body was never found.[32] This is why I refuse to speak about Relisha in the past tense. I don't hope that she was trafficked. It's just that every fiber of my body wants her to be alive. I want her to know that people—especially those of us connected to Black D.C.—have never forgotten her. In March 2021, seven years after Relisha's disappearance, Howard University graduate Jonquilyn Hill debuted a new podcast on WAMU 88.5 in Washington, D.C., titled *Through the Cracks*. In the podcast, Hill reexamines Relisha's disappearance and the failures of multiple social safety nets in the life of this young Black girl.[33] I am heartened by the continued investment of folks like Jonquilyn in unpacking the many truths of this vexing story. I write these words with the same conviction and yearning with which I wrote the dedication for *Colored No More*. I still await the day when we can fully answer the question: what happened to Relisha Rudd?

Words fail to capture the closeness I still feel to Relisha. Her story wasn't exceptional per se in D.C. or in the U.S. more broadly, but it hit me exceptionally hard as I read detail after detail. Even as the worst-case scenario becomes more and more likely as years fly by, I can't help but circle back to her as a propelling force for this book. Because of such paltry coverage of her disappearance outside the "DMV" (shorthand for the metropolitan area including D.C., Maryland, and Virginia) or media outlets geared toward Black audiences and social media posts, I try and tell her story whenever I can. For me, her life and story illustrate a death-dealing set of compounding failures to care for both Black girls and Black women. What I glean from recounting her story is all of the ways nonspectacular, everyday injustices and inequities slowly but surely erase or kill us. What is spectacular about this reality, nevertheless, is the frequency and consistency with which quotidian experiences with antiBlackness, misogynoir, and multiple jeopardy manifest in lives of Black women and girls. We disappear without a trace because of several systemic failures, as we struggle to survive. This is unlivable living.

This chapter explores the multiple forms of harm that poor Black women and girls experience day in, day out. Much of this harm is quotidian—not having stable housing, clean water, or food to eat. Relisha's story underlines the ways that her mother's daily frustrations and desperation led her to living with addiction and to houselessness—two threats to Black women—which, in turn, created a vulnerable situation in which a horrific, spectacular event took place—Relisha's abduction. The disappearance of Relisha was the result of pervasive failures in our safety net that leave poor

Black women struggling every day to survive in unlivable situations and in which the welfare of poor children isn't prioritized. Poor Black women are forced to navigate the unlivable.

While the previous chapters explored more easily identifiable forms of violence, this book would be incomplete without addressing the range of ways systemic oppression wears down Black women and girls. Quite often, these day-to-day experiences set the stage for more explicitly violent encounters, such as kidnapping or intimate partner violence. When you wear someone down, they become more susceptible to other forms of harm. Poor Black women and girls are unhoused, unfed, hypersurveilled, under- and unemployed, and viewed as expendable or valueless by those with the power to marginalize and criminalize. It is thus unsurprising that these same people struggle to survive, let alone live. I use *unlivable* to describe this kind of living because far too many of us are relegated to a life predisposed toward premature death. If that's not violent, I'm not sure what is.

Trying to Make a Dollar Out of Fifteen Cents

The stark effects of poverty on Black women and girls are immense. We pathologize those impoverished by capitalism's merciless cycle of exploitation and prioritization of profits over people—especially us. African American women in the U.S. are poorer than any other racial/ethnic group, irrespective of gender.[34] Despite the fact that the slight majority of poor women do not have dependent children, "Black single mothers are more likely to be poor than any other demographic."[35] This also means Black children in the care of Black women and girls are more likely to live in poverty than non-Black youth. And while there's been exhaustive scholarship on the "feminization of poverty," which primarily occurred in the late twentieth century, there's considerably less work that frames the "dramatic change in the composition of the poverty population" as a form of indirect violence against Black women and girls.[36]

Considering the overrepresentation of Black women and girls categorized as poor in the U.S., it's unsurprising how easily we shame and blame those living in poverty. Antipoor discourse in the United States is fueled by antiBlack and sexist stereotypes that deem us unfit, unworthy, and disposable.[37] Whenever I hear the phrase *welfare queen,* I shudder at the damage it's done to Black women. It's merely shorthand for a lazy, cheating, hypersexual, and mendacious Black woman who "abuses" public assistance to support her and her children.[38] Despite the fact that millions of the 21.4 million women who live in poverty and seek some form of government assistance are white, Black women bear the brunt of collective, national ire for being poor.[39] More than half of the U.S. populace still believe that African Americans account for the majority of people receiving government assistance in any form, when in reality white people have been and are the predominant recipients of assistance ranging from Medicaid to food stamps.[40] Furthermore, a lot of people only associate welfare with programs that specifically assist poor people and not with a range of government programs that financially support businesses and nonpoor people as well.[41] One of the greatest tricks capitalism ever played was convincing a whole lot of people that rich folks aren't wholly reliant on government intervention and subsidizing.

The durability of racist and sexist ideas about welfare from the 1980s and 1990s to the present means that poor Black women remain the metaphorical punching bags for a nation promoting a myth of scarcity amid unprecedented prosperity. The ease with which we see poverty as a failure of the individual to work hard enough or as the result of a series of bad choices stems from antipoor discourse entrenched in misogynoir. It allows us to see Shamika Young, Relisha's mother, as wholly culpable for her daughter's disappearance without even mentioning the paucity of choices afforded to her. It's more comfortable to write her off as a "bad mother," a label too often assigned to Black women and nonbinary people who mother, especially poor ones.[42] We more readily ask why Shamika would leave her daughter in the care of a stranger as opposed to why Shamika may have felt Relisha would be less vulnerable and better cared for by this stranger.

A House Is Not a Home

Houselessness is one of the most visible examples of what poverty can look like. It plays a huge role in putting Black women and girls on the path to barely surviving. The Homelessness Research Institute found that Black USians have the highest rate of houselessness compared to other U.S. racial and ethnic groups and that Black USians made up 40 percent of the U.S. unhoused population in 2018.[43] Additionally, half of unhoused families in the United States are Black families, like Relisha, her mother, and siblings. Black houselessness, according to researchers on poverty and housing insecurity, "are the result of centuries of discrimination in housing, criminal justice, child welfare and education."[44] Add to that the more recent, devastating effects of the woeful stigmatization and criminalization of drug addiction and the underfunding of mental health services, particularly for people of color, and rampant houselessness for Black USians in the twenty-first century was systemically inevitable.

One area of the houselessness crisis in the U.S. that distinctively and disparately affects Black women is eviction. In a comprehensive quantitative and ethnographic study of the effects of eviction on poor people in urban areas, sociologist Matthew Desmond found that Black women are exposed to the hardship of eviction at a higher rate than white men and women, white Latinx men and women, and Black men. Desmond found that a dire combination of economic insecurity, fewer well-resourced social networks, and existing discriminatory practices left Black women scrambling to remain housed.[45] One of the most profound conclusions Desmond drew from his research pertained to the gender-specific ways Black people experience unlivable living.[46] Desmond stated that, "black men are *locked up* while black women are *locked out*."[47]

We don't talk about mass houselessness with nearly the same fervor or urgency with which we talk about mass incarceration, yet both contribute directly and indirectly to unlivable living for Black women and girls. Because ultimately, as Desmond's research has shown, "women from poor black neighborhoods are overrepresented in the eviction records because men from these neighborhoods are overrepresented in the criminal justice system and on the unemployment rolls."[48] Consequently, formerly incarcerated Black men can't get leases, and the Black women in their lives become the leaseholders, making these mostly poor Black women the only ones accountable for all the consequences of unpaid rent.

The connection Desmond's study made between high incarceration rates for Black men and the alarming rate of eviction for Black women was unsurprising to me, yet seeing it laid out so plainly gave what I personally witnessed growing up some data-based heft. What I saw during my coming-of-age in Northeast D.C.

and Prince George's County, Maryland, was Black women in my neighborhoods and those in the hoods nearby burdened with the stain of past evictions and the shame of new ones. I can't begin to count the number of times I saw everything from Cabbage Patch Kid dolls to curling irons piled up outside in front of apartment buildings, duplexes, and townhomes in the aftermath of an eviction. When I was around six, I asked my parents why people just left their stuff on the street. All my parents could say was that the people who owned the building put the stuff there and that it was not a nice practice. The toys and beauty tools always stood out to me when I was younger, perhaps because I connected those items to kids like me and to my mom and aunties, respectively. Those items told me a story about eviction that centered on Black women and kids.

In a similar way to a Black person with a criminal record having trouble with finding adequate housing, a Black woman with an eviction on her record endures many challenges in her attempts to secure housing. Evictions are a form of displacement. They disconnect Black women from their communities and formal and informal networks of support. Evictions also heighten the probability for houselessness at some point.[49] Economic insecurity fuels evictions. It often leaves Black women and their loved ones without any options except for houselessness or life in shelters like D.C. General.

According to the U.S. Department of Housing and Urban Development, women-headed families make up more than 80 percent of all unhoused families in the United States, but economic insecurity isn't the only driving factor.[50] Gender and sexual violence play a significant, catalyzing role in houselessness among Black women and girls as well. A study conducted by the National

Center on Family Homelessness found that "92% of homeless mothers experienced some form of severe physical or sexual abuse by a family member or intimate partner."[51] Sociologist Anne Roschelle, in her study of "violent victimization as an antecedent" to houselessness for women of color, found that the overwhelming majority of unhoused mothers of color reported some form of physical violence and sexual abuse in either or both their childhood and adulthood.[52] To put this into more stark perspective: in order to attempt to free themselves and their children from abuse, Black women often must *choose* to be unhoused.[53] That's not a choice anyone should have to make—to not be violated by a loved one or to be housed. Yet thousands of Black women every year make the choice between pervasive violence or houselessness.

Unlivable living in the context of houselessness for Black women and girls means a set of unthinkable choices. Do you sign a lease for a place to ensure that your formerly incarcerated loved one can be housed, even while knowing that he and you lack economic security? Do you stay in an abusive relationship with a partner because the alternative is a shelter that could be violent and unfit for you and your children? These choices exist within the confines of multiple jeopardy, antiBlackness, and misogynoir. As Roschelle explains, "finding stable housing and a living wage job might mitigate their class oppression, but it would still leave women vulnerable to the violence of patriarchy and racism," as well as to the burden of living with the untreated trauma caused by antiBlack, gender, and sexual violence.[54] Additionally, the structures and systems of racial and gender inequity that uphold economic inequality encase Black women and girls in a sadistic cycle of struggling for basic necessities. It's a cycle that without question would wear anyone down.

In November of 2019, Dominique Walker, an unhoused Black mother and community activist, and her kids moved into a vacant home in West Oakland. After moving into the unoccupied home without the owner's permission, Walker and her family "pressure-washed the outside; did construction on the roof; installed a water heater, a fridge, and a stove."[55] Community members brought over items such as cookware and flowers and plants to make the space feel more like a home fit for a family. Shortly after moving in, Walker and her family were joined in the house by four other unhoused/marginally housed Black mothers and their children: Misty Cross, Sameerah Karim, Tolani King, and Sharena Thomas.[56] The Black mothers living in the home eventually became the Moms 4 Housing, "a collective of homeless and marginally housed mothers . . . coming together with the ultimate goal of reclaiming housing for the community from speculators and profiteers."[57] Each of them had her own story of how she ended up unhoused. Sameerah worked three jobs but still couldn't afford rent in one of the most expensive cities in the nation.[58] Misty had repeatedly attempted and failed to get housing information and assistance from 211, an Alameda County, California, hotline for "linking people and resources," including housing.[59] Dominique moved back to the Bay Area after fleeing domestic violence while living in Mississippi.[60] These women, to varying extents, were each directly impacted by the shortage of affordable housing, widespread foreclosures, and displacement by investors and other corporate entities that helped make decent housing inaccessible to poor Black mothers in the Bay Area.[61]

Prior to moving into the West Oakland home, Misty and Dominique became acquainted through their involvement in community-based activism pivoting around issues such as houselessness. By the fall of 2019, neither woman was able to find adequate housing for her family. So when someone in the community informed Dominique that a two-story home in the neighborhood had been vacant for two years, she and her newborn and young daughter moved in and created a home. Misty and her four children soon followed, as she could no longer bear life in the shelter, which she deemed unfit for her children's well-being and development. Misty, like Shamika Young, didn't see the shelter as a healthy place for her children. In a May 2020 interview with *Vogue,* Misty expressed the pain of being unhoused by comparing it to her previous experience with being shot: "Even after I couldn't talk and walk after being shot . . . when I felt that I could not provide for my kids and find a place for them to sleep, that was my breaking point."[62] The move to the house on Magnolia Street gave Misty new life and a sense of possibility. She was now in a coliving space with another Black mother who understood the unlivability of houselessness and who believed in taking a stand against the growing crisis.

Within three weeks of these women occupying this vacant home, the company that owned it, Catamount Properties (a subsidiary of Wedgewood, a speculative real estate company) sent the moms living at 2928 Magnolia Street a notice of eviction.[63] A spokesperson for Wedgewood, Sam Singer, identified what these women did as a "straightforward case of illegal entry and occupation." In a graceless and inconsiderate statement to *Vogue* regarding Wedgewood's move to evict these unhoused Black mothers, Singer went on to say that the company "is sympathetic to the plight of the homeless and is a major contributor to shelter programs, inner-city youth, and the disadvantaged."[64] In reality, what Wedgewood truly contributed to was the rapid gentrification and rising rents and home prices that directly and indirectly displaced Black mothers like those they sought to evict.[65]

The Moms 4 Housing, armed only with community support, growing media attention on a national debate about the houselessness crisis, and an unwavering belief in housing being a human right, went through the court system seeking to stop their eviction from this home.[66] The civil side of the U.S. legal system, much like its criminal counterpart, however, failed to dole out justice for Black women. With no legal standing, in January 2020, Alameda County Superior Court judge Patrick McKinney effectively ruled that "housing is not a human right" and that the eviction could proceed.[67] Furthermore, Judge McKinney stated that if the women refused to vacate, a sheriff would escort them off of the property.[68]

Within just a few days of the ruling in favor of Wedgewood, in the wee hours of the morning and as Dominique was giving an interview on *Democracy Now,* the Alameda County sheriff's department accompanied by officers in military fatigues, riot helmets, and an armored vehicle arrived to forcibly evict these Black mothers.[69] On Twitter, I saw a video of the officers busting down the front door with a battering ram, handcuffing these Black mothers, and transporting them to jail.[70] It was harrowing and infuriating to watch these women being treated as criminals because they took proactive steps to be housed in a world where too many barriers exist to accessing adequate and affordable housing. They were criminalized for embracing wholeheartedly the belief that housing is a human right. Their occupation of 2928 Magnolia Street exposed the cruel absurdity of the coexistence of vacant houses and unhoused people. For that they were treated as criminals. Unsurprisingly, houselessness put these Black mothers at greater risk for encountering the criminal punishment system. That they did go quietly created a powerful moment of resistance to injustice and criminalization. These Black mothers understood the power of showing the world the unjustness of criminalizing the unhoused seeking housing.

Houselessness also compounds criminalization for Black queer and trans unhoused youth.[71] It is "the greatest predictor of involvement" in the juvenile criminal punishment system.[72] According to the Prison Policy Initiative, "LGBTQ youth usually face homelessness after fleeing abuse and lack of acceptance at home because of their sexual orientation or gender identity. Once homeless and with few resources at hand, LGBTQ youth are pushed towards criminalized behaviors such as drug sales, theft, or survival sex, which increase their risk of arrest and detainment."[73] Greater than 30 percent of LGBTQ unhoused youth who come into contact with youth service providers identify as Black/African American despite Black youth constituting only about 14 percent of the U.S. youth population.[74] The criminalization of houselessness, queerness and transness, and Blackness makes Black trans, nonbinary, and queer youth uniquely exposed to unlivable living. Criminalization as children and teenagers often leads to juvenile delinquency records that then make it even more challenging for them to secure housing or employment on their release.[75]

For Black trans people, specifically, the houselessness crisis is even more dire. In a survey conducted by the National LGBTQ Task Force, greater than 40 percent of Black trans respondents stated that they had experienced houselessness at some point during their lives.[76] Without question transphobia and antiBlackness create a context for such an alarming number of Black trans folks to be unhoused. Extreme poverty also plays an integral role in this distressing reality. More than 30 percent of Black trans respondents to that same survey reported an annual household income of less than $10,000.[77] Consequently, a disproportionate number of Black trans people live at the criminalizing nexus of anti-Blackness, antitransness, poverty, and houselessness. Protection and a decriminalized existence become mirages for those living at the margins of the margins. For Black trans women, even the mirage can be damn near impossible to ascertain. The dream of basic needs being met can be hard to conjure.

Bread and Water

It seems almost unfathomable that access to clean water and decent food would be among the things for which we must fight. Yet the fight for food and water is routinely waged by poor Black women and girls in the twenty-first century. The U.S. Department of Agriculture (USDA) defines food insecurity as "a household-level economic and social condition of limited or uncertain access to adequate food." The department identifies hunger as "an individual-level physiological condition that may result from food insecurity."[78] Poor Black USians are also more than twice as likely as white USians to live in residences with substandard plumbing and in rural areas are three times as likely as their white counterparts to lack plumbing altogether.[79] Substandard plumbing, paired with discriminatory land-use patterns, the water-related effects of urbanization on Black communities, and a long history of toxins being dumped in predominantly Black areas, makes clean water access a pressing, livability issue.[80] An 1899 study done by pioneering sociologist and Black studies scholar, W. E. B. Du Bois found that access to clean water among Black residents of Philadelphia was paltry.[81] Du Bois's study of Black Philadelphians remains foundational to our understanding of the still-unfolding history of Black people's unequal access to clean water and food security. Without question, depriving us of basic necessities for survival is a recipe for a compromised quality of life and is a direct path toward premature death.

Although there continues to be very limited publicly accessible data about Black women in the U.S. and food insecurity and clean water access, we do know the following:

1. Nearly 94 percent of the U.S.'s majority Black counties are food insecure.[82]
2. Almost 25 percent of Black households are food insecure.[83]
3. Slightly more than 30 percent of all female-headed households are food insecure.[84]
4. More than seventy-seven million people are served by water systems that violate health-based standards established in the Safe Drinking Water Act, a federal law that requires the EPA to identify and regulate drinking water contaminants.[85]
5. Black households account for nearly 17 percent of plumbing-incomplete households in the U.S.[86]
6. AntiBlack zoning ordinances dating back to early twentieth century, white supremacist city and suburban planning, redlining, residential segregation, and the decimation of development in Black communities led to the deterioration and underdevelopment of water systems serving Black people.[87]

These are the conditions under which Black women seek food security and access to clean water. Bread for the World, a national organization working to end hunger and food insecurity, argued that "since poverty rates are much higher and income levels are much lower in African American female-headed households compared to the general population, we expect that food-insecurity levels are also much higher among African American female-headed households."[88] It's also fair to presume, based on known disparities, that Black women comprise disproportionate numbers of those living in residences with underdeveloped or deteriorating water systems. Environmental racism, antiBlackness in housing and community development, and an overarching antipoor national political discourse come together to put these most basic needs out of reach for millions of Black women and children, especially those living in poverty.

The water crisis in Flint, Michigan, in the 2010s—which, in effect, showed "an entire city collectively punished with lead-poisoned water for the crime of being poor, Black, and politically disempowered"—became the most visible example of the U.S.'s problem with unclean water.[89] Over the course of a number of years, residents of Flint, a predominantly poor/low-income Black city, imbibed and used toxic water that effectively poisoned them and significantly compromised the health of thousands of Black people.[90] For me, the crisis really hit home when then-eight-year-old Amariyanna "Mari" Copeny, now more widely known as Little Miss Flint, wrote a letter to then-president Obama, asking him to come meet with her and other Flint residents about the crisis that in 2014 had already poisoned many in her community and killed at least twelve people.[91] Mari became an activist because people around her were suffering and dying and too few with power to do anything seemed to care.

The Flint Water Crisis grabbed national and even global head-lines. People rallied around clean water justice for this underserved community, while connecting it to a chronic global crisis of unclean water.[92] The problem with some of the coverage, however, was that it rendered Flint as an outlier in the U.S., as opposed to an exemplar of a national crisis that had particularly stark consequences for Black communities. Flint is a singular story insofar as nearly every predominantly Black community in the U.S. has a place-specific history with systemic antiBlackness and white supremacy. We can both center Flint in our discussions of access to clean water and look beyond it to see a macrolevel problem incongruently impact-ing poor Black communities across the country.

When some of the illnesses and health conditions associated with lack of access to clean water in Flint came to light, I immedi-ately pondered the gender-specific implications for drinking, using, and playing in poisoned water.[93] What became clear as I dug in was that a "serious consequence of contaminated drinking water is harm[ful] to reproductive health."[94] A coalition of organizations focused on reproductive justice found that the reproductive health of women of color is disproportionately affected by lack of access to clean water.[95] In their report, they pointed to an exposure to lead, one of the leading water contaminants, as a causal factor for "permanent damage to the nervous system, behavior and learning disabilities, impaired hearing and impaired function of blood cells" among babies born to the people with gestational capacity.[96] A similar report by the March of Dimes also found that because Black women in particular were at a high risk for lead exposure, they were also at risk for "fertility problems, premature birth, and miscarriage."[97]

In Flint, for example, researchers found that

the water poisoning in Flint caused undeniable harm to residents' reproductive health. Analyzing health records from 2008 to 2015, researchers found that fertility rates in Flint dropped by 12 percent and fetal deaths rose by 58 percent after the water was switched to the Flint River in 2014. Additionally, babies who were born at full-term during the water crisis had lower birth weights. The lead exposure also increased the risk of hypertension for pregnant women and may have interfered with their choice of whether or not to breastfeed. Moreover, the health effects of lead exposure in children in Flint increased the risk of impaired cognition, behavioral disorders, hearing problems and delayed puberty.[98]

In that same report, the authors noted similar trends and reproductive health outcomes related to unclean water in cities such as my hometown, Newark, New Jersey, and Pittsburgh, Pennsylvania.[99] These outcomes impede Black people with gestational capability to both birth and raise children without preventable chronic or even terminal illnesses. Unclean water blocks the reproductive futures of Black mothers, especially poor Black mothers and, by extension, Black communities. Consequently, contaminated water prevails as a poisonous example of how misogynoir, anti-Blackness, and poverty unite as a death-dealing force devouring the reproductive capacities of Black women and the overall well-being of Black children.

As a Black child in a working-class family in what was then firmly Chocolate City, I never went hungry. While there wasn't always an abundance of food in our modest, two-bedroom apartment, I never wanted for food. I do remember, however, going grocery shopping with my mom at stores located relatively far from my childhood home. The grocery store closest to us was at best subpar.

The produce never looked fresh, everything seemed to be in low-stock, and it often smelled like rotting meat and spoiled milk. I hated our infrequent trips to this store located just a few driving minutes away from our apartment. But for most of my neighbors, this was the only place they could access owing to limited transportation and a general lack of knowledge about not-so-nearby options.

I also recollect going to a pretty nice farmers market not too far from my home almost every Saturday. That's where we got our greens, some good roasted nuts, and the best slab of bacon I've ever had. The prices weren't too bad, the market accepted food stamps, and most of the sellers were Black farmers. The farmers market was probably the only thing that kept my community from being in full-blown food apartheid. In an interview with *The Guardian,* food justice activist Karen Washington proclaimed that food apartheid, as opposed to the more commonly used term *food desert,* better describes "the root cause of some of the problems around the food system. It brings in hunger and poverty."[100] What Washington's comment brings into sharp focus is how *food desert* denotes the absence of or limited access to food. *Food apartheid* captures the multiple systemic forces, including but not limited to redlining, the eroding social safety net, and economic divestment from predominantly Black communities.[101] Black people in neighborhoods like the ones I grew up in are starving and suffering from malnutrition. They are up against intractable systems that produce and reproduce food insecurity and hunger.

Hunger and food insecurity intensify in times of spectacular crises and disasters. For several months in 2020, during the COVID-19 pandemic, 20 percent of Black women reported that they didn't have enough to eat.[102] Pictures from around the nation of cars lined up for miles at food banks throughout 2020 confirmed this reality before I knew anything about these numbers.[103] It's not like there weren't millions of Black people hungry and food insecure prior to the pandemic that left tens of millions of people spiraling into or further into poverty and unlivable conditions. COVID-19 appallingly increased the numbers of those existing at the margins and threw poor Black women an even worse set of circumstances to navigate.

Poor Black women were among the hardest hit by COVID-19 in 2020. As political scientist Evelyn Simien contended in "COVID-19 and 'The Strong Black Woman'," "the stage was set long before the pandemic hit the United States."[104] Prior to the pandemic, food-insecure Black women were already slowly dying, as anthropologist Ashanté Reese explains, because of "a lack of access to healthy, affordable foods, the continuous expansion of multinational food corporations that control not only access but also wages of folks who produce food, and the cutting (and erasure) of social services." What Reese points to with regard to food inequities is indeed the "everydayness of anti-Blackness."[105] For poor Black women, it's also the everydayness of misogynoir and racial capitalism that locks them into food insecurity. Impoverished and unhoused Black mothers make difficult choices day in and day out as they attempt to care for their children and themselves. The norm for them is what millions came to experience because of the COVID pandemic. They already knew what it meant to go to bed hungry night after night, while trying to ensure that their children wouldn't. Poor Black mothers were already overdetermined as "bad mothers" and "blamed for structural inequities" before COVID-19 hit.[106] In its wake, however, these structural inequities have become even more pervasive.

Being a poor, Black, unhoused, food-insecure mother who doesn't have access to clean water more often than not is seen as evidence of deviance, recklessness, and immorality. The death-dealing forces that created an underclass comprising millions of Black women and girls are rarely viewed as the "monstrous" systems predicated on antiBlack, patriarchal, and antipoor subjugation.[107] While it's encouraging to see mainstream media coverage of the disparate impact of COVID-19 on Black communities, not enough coverage grapples with history, systemic failures, or Black people's prepandemic predisposal toward premature death. It is within those histories and systems that poor Black women find themselves with so few options to survive. Accounting for history and multiple systemic failures that leave Black girls without the basic needs of housing, food, and clean water helped me refocus on how and why Relisha disappeared.

I suppose the lessening of any of the death-dealing forces in the lives of Black women and girls could have helped Relisha. There were just too many of these forces extant in her life. From the day she was born, she became a prime candidate for unlivable living. A Black girl born into poverty and a complicated family situation, including untreated mental illness and addiction, had few chances from her first breaths to not be unjustly worn down by the interconnected realities of antiBlackness, misogynoir, and multiple jeopardy. What we ask girls like Relisha to survive is impossible. AntiBlackness, poverty, and girlhood situated this bright-eyed, gap-toothed brown-skinned girl on the margins of the margins. She and her mother lived the unlivable. It was only when something spectacular occurred—Relisha's disappearance—that the world even came to know all the ways we failed her and her mother.

Just because we don't die immediately from houselessness, poverty, a lack of clean water, or food insecurity doesn't mean these systems don't operate with murderous intent and effect. This world demands that Black women and girls in the U.S. move through a world hell-bent on making the mere act of survival grueling. When we can't do it, the blame is placed squarely on us, with little or no mention of the politics of disposability that authored our wearing down.[108] That's why we blame Shamika more than our disintegrated social safety net for her daughter's disappearance. These systems count on being imperceptible and so deeply ingrained that we don't indict them when unhoused eight-year-old Black girls go missing without a trace. The systems operate knowing how little noise people other than us will make about the disproportionate number of unhoused Black trans women. These systems also rely on our silence and feed on our internalization of the worst ideas and stereotypes about us.

6 *They Say I'm Hopeless*

They say I'm hopeless as a penny with a hole in it.

—DIONNE FARRIS

Doing research for and writing this book brought up a lot for me. Tapping into violence I've experienced, histories of violence, and deep explorations of more recent examples of direct violence and unlivable living was emotionally exhausting. I reached my capacity for grappling with injury and death on numerous occasions as I wrote. Resisting hopelessness became one of my biggest challenges as I learned about and chronicled story after story of violence against Black women and girls. It was just so unrelenting. That particular hopelessness, however, paled in comparison to what emerges among many of us enduring the onslaught of both experiencing and witnessing the weight of antiBlackness, misogynoir, and multiple jeopardy. Because of the ubiquity of a politics of disposability in our lives, it's not hard to imagine that we would absorb some of the more painful ideas and ideologies used to justify our criminalization and premature deaths. It's also not difficult to understand why the struggle for justice can seem damn near impossible.

In psychologist Tameka L. Gillum's study of the effects of houselessness and poverty on Black women, Gillum documented a sense of hopelessness among impoverished and abused Black women.[1] The inability to access permanent reprieves from abusive partners or security in a carnivorous economy that underpays and hyperexploits Black women fuels an overwhelming sense of futility. Fighting a powerful current of multiple systemic and institutional failures, it's not hard to understand why a poor Black mother like Shamika Young might seek the assistance of a stranger to provide her daughter with opportunities she couldn't or why a group of unhoused Black women might occupy a vacant home with their children. It's also foreseeable that at least some poor Black women would internalize that they are architects of "self-inflicted chaos" instead of faulting multiple systems warring against them.[2] It's not just that society as a whole blames and shames poor Black women for being poor Black women; it's also that some of these women digest and invest in negative and soul-crushing narratives about themselves.

Internalizing antiBlackness, misogynoir, and antipoor sentiments has demoralizing consequences for those attempting to imagine themselves beyond the threat of violence and the boundaries of unlivable living. Consequently, the systemic failures get to hide behind what anthropologist Savannah Shange identifies as a "ritual practice of internalizing the necessity to do the impossible."[3] That ritual has a powerful history among Black women. In 1909, Nannie Helen Burroughs adopted the motto "We specialize in the wholly impossible" for the National Trade and Professional School for Women and Girls, a school she founded in my hometown.[4] Burroughs knew what Black women and girls were up against in the early twentieth century. She embraced a mantra that in just a few words identified the unbearable weight of white supremacy, Jim Crow laws, patriarchy, capitalism, and other systems of domination. "The wholly impossible" were the subjugating conditions to which Black women and girls were subjected.

For generations, poor Black women tried to navigate the land mines of unlivable living and numerous forms of violence. They found strategies to uplift, overcome, disprove, and debunk. All along, they carried the weight of what Saidiya Hartman calls "burdened individuality," a perpetual state of being held responsible for the systemic harm inflicted on them.[5] The "suffering and striving" of poor Black women, nevertheless, doesn't resound as loudly or affect policy as pointedly as all of the injurious discourses about them do.[6] We tend to revert back to demonizing poor Black women and girls. This rhetorical violence inculcates a collective lack of care or empathy. Across socioeconomic statuses, stereotypes, tropes, and recurring narratives can deeply affect how we see ourselves. How we internalize these messages can also shape how we respond to our own experiences with violence and unlivable living.

Unlearning toxic and harmful ideas about Black womanhood and girlhood has been an ongoing process for me. I can't recall the first time I realized how antipoor, antiBlack, and antiwoman this country is. I know that at my all-Black neighborhood elementary school in Northeast Washington, D.C., kids who came to school in what appeared to be dirty clothes and with "un-styled" hair were the butt of jokes. Even though the majority of us qualified for free or reduced lunch, even five-year-old kids knew that being visibly poor had consequences. For kids, those consequences ranged from being made fun of to being friendless. Even if most of us were poor and working class, the performance of not being poor saved you from this particular form of playground ridicule. At five I knew there was almost nothing worse in the world than *looking poor*.

For those who came to school without looking or smelling "clean," more often than not you could expect vicious jokes about you and your mother. It was always your mama; daddies were nowhere to be found in the jokes about how poor you were, even when they were present in your lives. I didn't really find "Yo Mama" jokes funny, though I always laughed. I just assumed making fun of and deriding Black women, even when not maliciously intended, was part of the culture. They/we were the butt of the joke. It's something I imbibed as ordinary. It wasn't until I got to graduate school that I realized that this was an introduction to the normalization of misogynoir. I was being primed to see Black women and girls as less than, as flattened caricatures, and as beings deserving of whatever harm befell us.

This brief chapter looks at discourses that can foster a sense of hopelessness and a tendency to blame and shame ourselves for both the violence we face and the unlivable living many of us endure. By looking at my own experiences with violence and the rhetoric I heard growing up about Black women and girls, I want to take a moment to explore how and why it's so easy for other USians, including us, to devalue, mythologize, and ignore us. Even as someone who studies and writes about historical and contemporary violence against us, I am still divesting from problematic labels and ideas that operate to justify harm against us. I find myself still railing against ensconced impulses to blame, shame, or dismiss Black women like me who speak out about our experiences with violence and unlivable living. A sense of hopelessness floats around this wretched internalization. When we don't even believe us, it's hard to fathom that anyone else will.

There's a long history of using antiBlack and sexist stereotypes of us to justify the violence and unlivable living to which many of us are subjected. As sociologist Patricia Hill Collins argues in her groundbreaking book, *Black Feminist Thought*, "maintaining images of U.S. Black women as the Other provides ideological justification for race, gender, and class oppression."[7] Our Othering has taken on many forms throughout our history in the U.S. During slavery, the mammy image emerged to "hide the cruelty of slavery" by depicting a loving and paternalistic relationship between enslaved women and slave owners. The image also depicted enslaved Black women as willingly submissive and "smiling caretakers."[8] The key to the mammy trope was Black women's nurturing of white people, especially white children. There wasn't room in this one-dimensional stereotype's life for the mothering of her own child(ren). The mammy caricature could at once be the primary child-rearing figure in white children's lives and a negligent and unfit mother for her own children.

Good Black mammies, bad Black mothers. I could go on a book-length rant about all the ways Black women and girls get depicted as bad mothers. Black mothers have been accused of "failing to discipline their children, of emasculating their sons, of defeminizing their daughters, and retarding their children's academic achievement."[9] In sum, Black mothers were to blame for the deterioration of Black families and, by extension, Black communities. It's a hell of a load to carry, while also being viewed as ideal for the work of caring for and rearing white children. I struggled to wrap my mind around how both of these vilifying stereotypes could coexist as such potent tropes. I eventually resolved for myself that those perpetuating both of these myths/controlling images found yet another way to evacuate full personhood from Black women and girls.[10] We are being used to serve what is needed, whether that be unpaid or underpaid care work for white families or to be the cause of "Black economic disadvantage," their children's "failures" in school, and their kids' entry into the criminal punishment system.[11]

The depiction of Black mothers as "dangerous" and "deviant" matriarchs affected how my mom and many of her friends parented. I knew not to do anything that would "embarrass" her or make her look like she hadn't taught me how to comport myself. My mom didn't even need to mention white people as who this comportment was for in certain ways. She forcefully though lovingly instilled in me, however, that I was a reflection of her. And she wasn't about to be the butt of "yo mama" jokes. She wanted her little Black girl to be the epitome of burgeoning femininity—poised, not too loud, and always put together. She knew I was spirited, talkative, precocious, creative, and very expressive. My mom loved all these things about me but knew that I could be read as having an attitude, as misbehaving, and as uncontrollable. If I were assessed as such by teachers or administrators, she would be blamed. My dad and my mom shared the intense work of parenting in a pretty balanced way, yet she knew, and I came to know, that only my mother would be blamed if I transgressed in any way. She strove to defy all of the stereotypes she knew existed about Black mothers. While I am certain she has critiques of those stereotypes and the power they hold, she also knew the reality of how her mothering would be assessed. She was a Black mother of a Black child growing up in poor and working-class Black neighborhoods. She knew what was at stake in a world that devoured women like her and girls like me. In due course, I would come to know too.

Other racist/sexist stereotypes emerged in the aftermath of slavery to validate the existence of intersecting oppressions in

Black women's and girls' lives.[12] In the mid-twentieth century, the "angry Black woman"/Sapphire trope surfaced.[13] Depicting Black women as "aggressive, loud, obnoxious, and capable of taking down any man," this stereotype is still used to rationalize both the imposition of "heavy work" and violence on Black women.[14] The angry Black woman is, as Black feminist scholar Brittney Cooper says, "an entity to be contained" and an "inconvenient citizen."[15] This particular trope infuriates me to no end because it renders us irrationally emotional and unhinged in our righteous and eloquent rage. Thankfully, Audre Lorde taught me, as well as Cooper and many others, that rage is indeed a legitimate and necessary political emotion.[16] I own my anger, my rage, and resent when I'm told to calm down or not be so angry. If violence and unlivable living are at your doorstep on a regular basis, being enraged is quite befitting.

The trope that stands out to me the most as I think about unlivable living and the ways we fail Black women is the "crack whore." This came into sharp focus for me in the 2010s when I first encountered the phrase "opioid patients." While reading it in a headline in a piece I can't recall, I asked myself: *What the fuck is an opioid patient?* Of course, I'd heard about the opioid crisis. There were stories everywhere. Profiles of white folks whose lives and or loved ones were destroyed by drug addiction were inescapable in mainstream media. I came to know that from 1999 to 2018, nearly 450,000 people died from an overdose involving an opioid.[17] As I dug in, both perturbed and fascinated by this more humane approach to drug addiction, I learned that because of that tenacious antiBlack racist stereotype that says we have an innate threshold for pain, African American patients received fewer opioid prescriptions.[18] As a result, fewer Black folks in the U.S. died during the escalation of the opioid crisis in the late 1990s through the 2010s.[19] This myth about pain tolerance, in conjunction with the strong possibility that doctors with the power to prescribe pain-killers believed that Black people were more likely to become addicted to the drugs and would be more likely to sell the drugs, may have led to fewer initial deaths in the crisis.[20] This finding also proved once more how deep-rooted antiBlackness is in the medical industrial complex.

What the opioid crisis also revealed to me and many others was the tremendous gap between how the media and the criminal punishment system treat a predominantly white drug epidemic and how they engage Black folks depicted as the primary users in the crack epidemic of the 1980s and 1990s.[21] It wasn't hard to decipher that "during the crack epidemic, there was a greater emphasis on punishment and incarceration. With the opioid crisis primarily affecting white people, there has been more emphasis on empathy and rehabilitation."[22] The director of opioid policy research at Brandeis University, Dr. Andrew Kolodny, confirmed in a 2019 interview with the *New York Times* that "race played an obvious role in the policy response" and that those responding to these respective epidemics shifted from "'arrest our way out of it' to 'It's a disease,'" when the racial demographics of the patients changed.[23] Dr. Kolodny is absolutely right in acknowledging the blatant shift that happened when those most directly affected were white. But the doctor failed to call a spade a spade. It's not race that changed how elected officials and the criminal punishment system responded to a drug epidemic; it's antiBlackness. To name race as a contributing factor to the push toward decriminalizing drug addiction is to tiptoe around the fact that we waged a war on Black and Brown people for decades that left our communities ravaged and forever changed.[24] My Black neighborhoods were targeted in the 1980s and 1990s.

I saw countless arrests of people living with addiction. We got the criminalizing response. Now white folks get compassion.

Black women were called "crack whores." The colloquial term intimated that Black women addicted to crack cocaine would "do anything to get their drugs, especially trading sex."[25] Black mothers-to-be addicted to crack cocaine were also maligned as whores and criminals because of their usage of drugs during their pregnancies, which could result in poorer birth outcomes.[26] A whore warrants no respect in a patriarchal society that devalues sex workers and the labor of sex work. A crack whore, however, is multiply maligned by antiBlackness, misogynoir, and our disdain for women working in sex economies. The "crack whore" stereotype brings together the Jezebel trope and the image of the bad mother into a singular devalued status.

I've never heard the term *opioid whore* casually thrown about to describe white women living with drug abuse addiction. I rarely read stories about white women engaging in sex work in connection to their addiction that aren't told with compassion or context. I haven't heard many jokes about white women addicted to opioids either. I still haven't heard a song mocking and viciously deriding mothers addicted to painkillers.[27] They get to be patients, a category indicating a medical condition. I don't wish anything different for those affected by the opioid abuse epidemic. I just can't help being infuriated by the folks in my communities not being afforded an ounce of the empathy these more affluent white suburban women addicted to opioids received. Imagine if we had been cocaine patients and the entire crack cocaine epidemic treated as a public health issue. We'd have to envision a world in which Black folks in the U.S. weren't criminalized, which isn't a world that's ever existed in this nation.

Crack whore stuck with me because I knew Black women who were living with addiction to crack cocaine. I won't pretend that I never uttered the words "crack ho." Usually in a joking manner but clearly at the expense of a Black woman, my friends and I deployed the word with stunning regularity in the 1990s. It did a lot of work without having to say much. Without question, it was a harmful and dismissive way of negating the personhood of Black women living with addiction. These women were many things in my neighborhood: some were mothers, some were infrequently employed in low-wage jobs, some went to my church, and some told the best stories about growing up in my neighborhood. Almost all of them knew me as Treva and Anthony's baby. They were a part of our community. I remember thinking I just wanted them to be well, whatever that means. I saw the cops harass them and men from inside and outside of the neighborhood seek them out for sexual acts in exchange for money or drugs. Both the cops' incessant patrolling of the neighborhood and these men desiring sexual interactions often put these women around my way in danger of encountering the criminal punishment system. There was no care or empathy, just jokes and the reality of being harassed, violated, or locked up for living with addiction.

What they experienced in both their addiction and in the criminal punishment system's response to it was unlivable living. Black women living with addiction to crack cocaine were criminalized because they were sick, even when they sought help. Their pain didn't register enough to change policy on the criminalization of drug use. So, they remained trapped in a cycle of living to feed an addiction that in so many ways made their lives uninhabitable. Arbiters of criminalization in the U.S. knew that Black women in urban areas using drugs designated as illicit were more likely to use and be dependent on crack cocaine than any other drug.[28] Yet studies weren't launched to understand this as a public health crisis. The lack of investment in decriminalizing approaches for Black people meant that Black women living with addiction were relegated to teetering on the brink of premature death with each usage.

My heart breaks when I think about how many lives could've been saved had these systems been even a little less antiBlack, misogynoiristic, and antipoor. I think about all those Black women in my neighborhood who were written off as crack whores and the authors of their own pitiful demise. They heard our words, which were unkind and unhelpful. For those who survived this debilitating addiction, I wonder what they think when they hear "opioid patient." Does it resound as a reminder of how easily they were derided and disposed of because they were Black, women, and in many cases poor? Our words hurt, not just on a personal level but at a policy level at which we criminalized and disposed of Black women living with crack cocaine addiction.

More recently, there's a different kind of mothering-based stereotyping that's occurred with Black women being centered as caretakers for the nation. It's the supposedly celebratory narrative of Black women saving America. It pops up frequently around electoral politics. For example, in 2017 there was a special election for a U.S. Senate seat in Alabama. In the race was GOP candidate Roy Moore and Democratic candidate Doug Jones. In a reliably Republican-led state, Moore was the obvious front-runner. His path to victory, however, became rockier when credible allegations surfaced accusing Moore of sexually assaulting at least two minors while he was in his thirties. In total, eight women accused Moore of sexual misconduct or impropriety.[29] Moore vehemently denied all of the allegations and subsequently filed defamation suits against all of his accusers.[30] These suits, among others pertaining to Moore's alleged misconduct, remain in litigation. The credibility of his accusers and believability of their stories undeniably impacted the outcome of this election. Jones won in a very tight race.

In the aftermath of the race, exit polls showed that 98 percent of Black women voted for Jones.[31] Of white women, 63 percent voted for Moore, a candidate convincingly accused of sexually violating multiple white women and girls. I was in Kruger National Park in South Africa when I read the news about Jones's narrow victory and how white women voted. I knew immediately that there would be an abundance of think pieces and news segments about the outcomes of the election, specifically the vast difference between how Black and white women voted. I also knew that there would be several people proclaiming that "Black women saved the day." In fact, I was one of them. I wrote a piece for *The Grio* titled "Just a Reminder: Black Women Saved Alabama but Not for the Reasons You Think." I was in good company with Black women writers such as Renée Graham and Doreen St. Felix, who offered a richer contextualization of what occurred. Each of us pushed back in different ways against the desire to frame Black women's votes as driven by a desire to save America and, by extension, white people. We responded to an uncritical deification of Black women and a contemporary call to mothering white people.

My pushback wasn't about whether what Black women did actually "saved" America or if what happened exemplified Black women's political power as voters.[32] I balked at the exhausting premise that relies on the fallacy that Black women gleefully went to the polls thinking about everyone else and not our own survival. The "savior" narrative erases how Black women strategically participated in a political process that rarely if ever yields tangible gains for us. It was so clear to me that we saw the greater harm Moore's election to the U.S. Senate could cause to our families and communities. I was infuriated by the "Black Women Save America" takes because I knew that "damn near everyone benefits from our 'voting' except" us.[33] Like Graham, I didn't want white women walking up to me, hugging me, and saying "thank you for saving us."[34] I affirmed, as Graham did, that "Black women are not here to save America. We are not a safety net designed to catch this nation when it willingly plunges off the cliff. When black women go to the polls—we are our own saviors."[35] We did not sign up to be Captain Save America.

In the aftermath of the 2020 Election Cycle, I saw tweets once again championing the overwhelming number of Black women who voted against Trump and those who fought against voter suppression. While Black women once again reviled then-president Trump as they did in 2016, the tendency to water down the efforts of Black women through headlines suggesting that "we saved America" felt off. Apparently, it wasn't our attempt at perhaps surviving in a world that shows us time and time again that we are disposable; it was our desire to save a "democracy" that's literally built on systems operating to deny our personhood. Stacey Abrams, the political force who worked tirelessly on voting rights in the aftermath of voter suppression stopping her from winning the 2018 Georgia gubernatorial race, became the "Captain Save America" du jour. Not that she, Black women organizers such as LaTosha Brown of Black Voters Matter, Kayla Reed of Action St. Louis, or many organizers and organizations led by Black women don't deserve tremendous credit for their work around electoral organizing, but to reduce those efforts to saving U.S. democracy is a woeful misread of the political stakes powering Black women to the polls. And to be clear, if we had not shown up in expected ways, we would've been blamed for the outcome.

We are expected time and time again to care for, protect, and nurture those who refuse to do an ounce of the work required to actualize a democracy. The expectation that we become "smiling caretakers" of a nation while hiding the cruelty of what this nation unleashes on us is blood-boiling. More directly, it's straight out of the historical playbook of expectations of how Black women should engage the nation. While some of us might want the gratitude and the praise for being the force propelling the U.S. toward becoming "a more perfect union," I could care less about empty calls to listen to, trust, or follow Black women. Those calls ring hollow when you take into account the long record of harm against us. Historical ideas about Black women mothering white people merges with the trope of the "strong Black woman"[36] to form this fictive superbeing who keeps going despite being worn down by both systems and expectations. Our needs remain decentered and unmet. Just because we *can* specialize in the wholly impossible doesn't mean we should have to do it over and over again.

The ease with which people put extraordinary demands on me and the Black women and girls in my life without once genuinely considering our capacity never ceases to amaze me. People resent when Black women say "no." They feel entitled to our time, resources, energy, and expertise. When I listen to the to-do lists of the Black women in my life, I get exhausted. It's wholly impossible for us to care for others at the level being demanded *and* healthily care for ourselves. Often, however, many of us choose to care for others at the expense of our own well-being. Whether we articulate it or not, most of the Black women in my life feel compelled to specialize in the wholly impossible. We willingly take on the burden of sacrifice, and in the process, we deprioritize or, worse, ignore our own needs. We feel inadequate when we don't show up as the extraordinary strong Black women superbeings who should be listened to, trusted, and followed. The demand for selflessness is all too familiar and debilitating.

To want Black women to be selfless is such a peculiar and harmful proscription. For a group that's been historically denied the basic protections of personhood, it's telling how easy it is for people to ask us to leave the self behind. So while I don't vote to save folks who don't say a word about violence against us or the conditions of unlivable living, I recognize how easily my survival tactics are romanticized and used to stall the project of dismantling multiple oppressive systems. I can't and don't want to speak for all Black women, but I know that the conflation of strength with how we necessarily navigate oppression is injurious and potentially death-dealing. As Black feminist scholar bell hooks notes in *Ain't I a Woman,* "to be strong in the face of oppression is not the same as overcoming oppression."[37] In fact, our strength gives everyone else cover for their inaction in the struggle for justice.

I want to say "no" so much more than I do. But I often feel as though I can't. I worry about what will happen if a panel or a committee doesn't have a vocal Black woman on it. I hate that because I practice specializing in the wholly impossible that my hard work can easily go overlooked as normal output. I am concerned that like so many Black women before me and that I know, my health will decline because I keep doing the most. I always wonder if the stress of showing up repeatedly factored into me developing an autoimmune disorder. I internalize my inability at times to do the impossible as failing. It took my mom, multiple friends, my literary agent, and my editor pleading with me to take a breath from work after I was in a serious car accident in November 2020. I had deadlines and people who needed things from me. The number of texts and calls ensuring I wasn't working or doing any mildly strenuous activity revealed to me the love in my life. Those check-ins from my loved ones pleaded with me to stop specializing in the wholly impossible, if only for a little while. I pumped the brakes a little bit and realized how tired and sore I was. I wish it hadn't taken an accident where I could've been more seriously injured or even killed for me to reject buying into doing the impossible. An expectation grounded in a harmful trope pushed me toward harming myself by not resting and not resisting absurd expectations.

The trope of Black womanhood that's played perhaps the most harmful role in my life is the Jezebel. The white supremacist and patriarchal myth of the "unrapeable" Black woman/girl emerged during slavery and continued through the Jim Crow era.[38] This controlling image of Black womanhood became, as Black feminist scholar Tamura Lomax explains, "indispensable to white Western and global dominion."[39] For more than two centuries, the Jezebel trope and its present-day iterations, such as the T.H.O.T. (that ho over there), have relied on "the myth of Black women's and girls' hypersexuality."[40] Do you know how hard it is to tell anyone you've been raped when far too many people continue to invest in the ridiculous idea that we are unrapeable? Most folks coming forward about sexual violence are met with skepticism and disbelief. But for Black women and girls, this distrust stems from both antiBlackness and misogynoir. As aforementioned, there were actual U.S. laws that said we were unrapeable. Just because laws changed doesn't mean perceptions, norms, ideologies, or beliefs changed, too.

Sexual violence played a role in both my childhood and teenage years. I am still hesitant to talk about all that has happened. Earlier, I detailed my experience with police sexual violence. I never shared that story with anyone before writing this book. I wish that what happened that night in 2001 was my sole encounter with sexual violence. Unfortunately, it wasn't. I kept most of my experiences with sexual violence to myself. Even now I still don't feel comfortable sharing all of my experiences, especially not in a book anyone could pick up and read. Once upon a time I was concerned with people calling me a "fass-tailed girl" or victim-blaming me for what happened. Although I know many victims and survivors of rape and sexual assault confront slut-shaming when they come forward about being sexually violated, the trope of the Jezebel and the "fass-tailed girl" loom large for Black women and girls who share our stories of sexual violence. Without question, I know I internalized these harmful stereotypes and feared how my loved ones, friends, and others would respond if I told them what happened to me.

I don't have those concerns anymore per se. As I figured out my life after multiple experiences with sexual violence and learned more about the normalization of viewing Black girls as adults and therefore culpable for bad things that happen to them, I let go of a lot of shame I had around being sexually violated.[41] I stopped blaming myself. I began undoing the damage those stereotypes had done to me. I still remind myself, though less frequently as time marches on, that what happened to me wasn't my fault. I must confess, however, that I still get a lump in my throat whenever I identify as a sexual violence victim/survivor. It still unnerves me how much sexual violence, the internalization of racist and sexist stereotypes, and misogynoir shape my daily life.

The first time I ever spoke publicly about what happened to me in my early teenage years occurred during my second year of graduate school at Duke University in Durham, NC. I was on campus when a Black woman who attended North Carolina Central University in Durham accused three white male Duke students of raping her.[42] The allegations and the case became national news as it magnified issues of race, class, sexual violence, and long-standing tensions between the community and the university. The convergence of discussions and the eventual outcome of the case—the dismissal of all charges against those accused—was a shit storm. It was a distinctively tough time to be a Black woman and rape survivor at Duke. Because of the work I was doing at the time on violence against Black women in the late nineteenth century and early twentieth, local and national news outlets reached out to me for commentary regarding the allegations and the broader context of sexual violence against Black women. I didn't know what to expect from these interviews, but I knew that as an emerging scholar and a survivor of multiple forms of sexual violence, I had something to say.

During an interview for NPR, something unexpected happened. As I spoke about the pervasiveness of sexual violence against Black women and the vulnerability of Black women working in sexual economies, I identified myself as a survivor. I hadn't planned on doing that. These outlets contacted me because of the work I was doing. That's what I intended to talk about in the interview. Much to my surprise, the word *survivor* fell out of my mouth and onto the airwaves. On a national platform, I spoke my truth in a public forum for the very first time. I wasn't relieved or ashamed, although I immediately knew I needed to call my parents to tell them this truth. They listened to every interview I did. They weren't listening live on that day, so I had an opportunity for them to not learn about their daughter's rape alongside hundreds of thousands of strangers. As soon as the interview ended, I prepared myself to retell my story and to answer their questions. My parents and I had such an open and honest relationship that I figured one of their many responses to my story would be sadness that I didn't share with them when it happened or soon after this life-altering event. I knew they would think they failed me.

I took several deep breaths. I called within an hour of the interview's ending. My dad answered his cell phone and greeted me with the usual, "Hey baby girl." This normally felt endearing and loving, but on this call his affectionate greeting felt weighted by what I was about to tell him. I told him to put me on speaker so my mom could hear. I could feel their worry mounting from hundreds of miles away. I took another deep breath and began telling them what happened, although I excluded the more graphic details that I could remember. Being violently pushed up against the wall. Having his hands wrapped tightly around my neck to the point where I almost lost consciousness. Feeling his dirty fingers and then penis forcibly enter my vagina. I told them what I could. I knew even that would be too much, but I also didn't want them to not know that this violence took place. I finished by telling them I never expected to tell them what happened but that I identified as a survivor during an interview I had just taped. I didn't want them to not know something about me that a lot of other folks would.

They had a lot of questions, and, admittedly, a few felt like they were victim-blaming. They backed away from and apologized for those questions as I shared with them why I didn't tell them or report this violence to anyone when it occurred. I told them I didn't want them or anyone else seeing me as a "fass-tailed girl" because of what happened. They understood and even agreed that we treat rape victims horribly. They commended me on sharing my truth in such a public way and told me what happened wasn't my fault. I felt relief and anger. I resented that I victim-blamed myself for what happened to me and that so many Black women and girls in my life then and now have a similar story. In addition to not trusting the police and the criminal punishment system, we didn't fully see ourselves as victims/survivors. The internalization of shame and blame kept many of us from seeking vital resources to support our posttrauma journeys. A trope invented to justify the rape of captive Africans and enslaved Black women had consequences for a 1980s baby Black girl who imbibed the belief that she was unrapeable. It makes me angry whenever I think about how this trope contributed to my self-silencing.

Including stereotypes and tropes in the broader struggle for justice acknowledges the roles that ideology and the internalization of injurious ideas can play in instilling hopelessness among Black women and girls. At its fullest and most dynamic, this struggle for justice centers on "crack whores," "fass-tailed girls," and "angry Black women." Criminalization, organized abandonment, and the politics of disposability rely on people, including those most directly affected by systemic harm, to buy into disparaging, shaming, and blaming rhetoric. Resisting the inhabiting and overtaking of our individual and collective psyches by hopelessness and self-silencing requires a full recognition of what we are up against. It necessitates a determination to imagine, envision, and build. The rejection of the status quo including stereotypes, tropes, and controlling images is an uphill battle in Black women and girls' struggle for justice.

7   *We Were Not Meant to Survive*

Hope is a discipline.

—MARIAME KABA

So what do we do with all this violence and unlivable living? How do we reckon with systems, institutions, and structures that too often feel indestructible? With death-dealing forces all around, what is the path to more just and liberatory futures for Black women and girls? Comprehending the burden and toll of specializing in the wholly impossible in the face of police violence, criminalization, intracommunal violence, medical violence, poverty, and the perpetuation of harmful and injurious tropes and stereotypes to justify injustice and unfreedom could understandably lead to a weighted sense of hopelessness. Since antiBlackness, misogynoir, racial capitalism, ableism, transphobia, queerphobia, and other oppressive forces are deeply entrenched and ever-present, is it futile to imagine and strive to create new worlds?

I come back to the words of Kaba whenever I want to "throw up both my hands" and fully bow out of the struggle for justice. To be disciplined with regard to this struggle is to remain tenaciously committed to envisioning new worlds. It is a call to proclaim "Goddam" when a new example of just how death-dealing this nation can be arises and to let the urgency and impassioned conviction inspired by injustice be a powerful catalyst for mobilization. The discipline is a part of a tradition that includes numerous campaigns, initiatives, strategies, ideologies, and forms of everyday resistance. For me, part of practicing hope as a discipline has meant returning to the archives in search of the terrain traversed by Black women and girls of past generations. It helps me to locate myself and those with whom I am in community within a robust and wide-ranging tradition of struggling for justice.

I think of Maria Stewart, the free-born African American who was the first known woman in the U.S. to speak in front of a mixed-raced and mixed-gender audience.[1] She lectured on women's rights and abolition, as she knew that without a commitment to both of these causes, Black women would continue to inhabit a subordinate status. She knew back in the 1830s that antiBlackness, racial capitalism in the form of chattel slavery, and patriarchy were inimical to Black women surviving, living, and thriving. More strikingly, she spoke out against Black people expecting white people to solve the problems that white supremacy, capitalism, and patriarchy created. It's not that she didn't hold white people and men responsible for the conditions of unfreedom; she firmly believed in Black autonomy and self-determination for Black people of all genders. In her writings and speeches, "she had no time for platitudes" that would have made her beliefs or ideas more palatable for her mixed race and gender audiences.[2] In quite a few ways, Stewart was before her time in terms of a Black nationalist politics that did not promote gender subordination.[3] Stewart is undeniably a progenitor in a centuries-long history in the U.S.

of Black women nationalists who opposed gender inequity and white supremacy.[4]

Stewart is one of many Black women who railed against white supremacist and patriarchal norms that dictated that Black women were prohibited from expressing their ideas and beliefs in public spaces. Black women such as Stewart, Sojourner Truth, Sarah Redmond, Mary Ann Shadd Cary, and Ellen Craft demolished existing conventions regarding "Black women's place" and struck out into the world demanding liberation.[5] But even before these more formal calls for abolition and women's rights, the captive Africans marked as women and girls aboard slave ships crossing the Atlantic to the Americas set a precedent for freedom under the most vile and perverse conditions. "An archive of Black women's freedom" in the United States commences at the point of capture. Their refusal of bondage included resistance during their transport on the route of terror. When captive Africans enslaved at sea resisted bondage, Black women—particularly those left unshackled owing to assumptions about gender, age, and the ability to be subdued—played a "crucial" role in shipboard revolts.[6] Reminding myself of this history refuels my hope. Those on board slave ships, and eventually those enslaved in the Americas, had few *reasons* to believe in worlds in which they would not be enslaved. This discipline of hope counters a world in which they weren't and now we aren't meant to survive beyond our capacity for laboring and exploitation.

I imagine someone like Harriet Tubman possessed this discipline of hope. In many ways, Tubman is renowned as a historic figure who heroically organized and led dozens of enslaved people to freedom. She also strategized and co-led the raid at the Combahee River in South Carolina during the Civil War, which effectively liberated more than seven hundred enslaved people.[7] Tubman was an enemy of the state during her lifetime and will now possibly be the face on the U.S. twenty-dollar bill. While I won't debate here why I have reservations about putting Tubman on any U.S. currency, it is truly something to witness this disabled Black woman who was criminalized for freedom-fighting become a widely celebrated historical figure. This celebration too often sanitizes what really happened and softens what is a story of fierce opposition to death-dealing systems.

It's befitting that when a group of radical queer Black feminist women formed a collective in the 1970s, they named themselves after the Tubman-led Combahee River Raid.[8] The founders and members of the Combahee River Collective channeled a formidable act of resistance led by a Black woman who dedicated much of her life to literally emancipating enslaved people, to abolition as the law of the land, and to women's rights—especially the elective franchise. Like Tubman, the Collective mobilized around combatting "the manifold and simultaneous oppressions that all women of color face."[9] The Combahee River Collective's statement also located the Collective in a tradition of Black women activists who understood and organized against white supremacy and systemic misogyny and sexism. Furthermore, the Collective understood themselves and their contemporaries committed to Black feminism as an "outgrowth of countless generations of personal sacrifice, militancy, and work by our mothers and sisters."[10]

There are many ways to view this tradition and the early twenty-first-century iteration of this "outgrowth." As a survivor of multiple forms of violence, a Black feminist, and a person deeply and distinctively committed to warring against the combined force of antiBlackness, misogynoir, and multiple jeopardy in the lives of

Black women and girls, I tend to think of the ways hope anchors a tradition of Black women and girls struggling for justice. What Kaba clarifies in her concept of hope is that it's not an emotion or even optimism. In a podcast published by Beyond Prisons in 2018, Kaba explained that "grounded hope" is an everyday practice that pivots around the fundamental belief in the "potential for transformation and for change."[11] The Black women named in the Combahee River Collective statement—Sojourner Truth, Harriet Tubman, Frances E. W. Harper, Ida B. Wells-Barnett, and Mary Church Terrell, as well as "thousands upon thousands unknown"—believed another world is possible.[12] They were frustrated, saddened, enraged, and even discouraged on their respective paths of fighting for a new world in which Black women and girls could survive, live, and thrive, yet they chose hope.

This choice didn't and doesn't come without an acute recognition of just how much was and is stacked against those who dreamt and dream of and worked and work to build new worlds.[13] After writing an entire book about just *some* of the ways that violence and unlivable living manifests in the lives of Black women and girls in the U.S., it would be foolish to discount the perspectives of those who embrace hopelessness and a worldview that dictates the impossibility for radical change. Too few of the stories told in this book have a "joyous ending." In fact, most of what I've presented here arguably supports that dismantling antiBlackness, misogynoir, and the numerous facets of multiple jeopardy that many Black women and girls face is wholly impossible. In many ways, these death-dealing systems seem impervious and intractably entrenched. These systems are so good at what they do that beyond spectacular events like the killing of Breonna or the "caught-on-tape" police assault of Sandra Bland that preceded her death in police custody, we rarely if ever get a clear picture of how they operate with the intent to assail and kill. The efficacy of these systems is undeniable. Among many things, this book offers receipt after receipt for the pervasiveness of antiBlackness, misogynoir, and several other oppressive forces in the lives of Black women and girls. From these accounts alone, it was a challenge to move beyond "Goddam." And I bet that quite a few folks reading this will conclude that nothing can or will change. I get that standpoint and comprehend it as a well-informed perspective.

Like Kaba, however, in the face of incalculable losses, I *choose* hope. I return to the words of Assata Shakur in *Assata: An Autobiography,* "It is our duty to fight for our freedom. It is our duty to win. We must love each other and support each other. We have nothing to lose but our chains."[14] I heard these words chanted repeatedly on the streets of Ferguson during the uprising in 2014. I heard them again at multiple protests pivoting around police violence against Black people since that time as well. Duty and discipline ground my sense of hope. I imagine it guided the sense of hope embodied by thousands upon thousands of known and unknown Black women and girls of previous generations who dared to believe that they would be victorious against death-dealing systems. Their hopes fuel mine, too.

I return to hope because I see the work of Black women and girls here and across the world who dream, plan, and build. It's the work of #SayHerName, #BlackTransLivesMatter, #MeToo, the Movement for Black Lives, and localized Black-led campaigns, initiatives, and organizing. I am charged by the Tubmanesque efforts of organizations led and heavily populated by Black women and girls based in the U.S., such as BYP100, Assata's Daughters, Trans Women of Color Ohio, Black Women's Blueprint, the Marsha

P. Johnson Institute, INCITE!, Black Mamas Matter Alliance, Critical Resistance, Survived and Punished, A Long Walk Home, Good Kid, M.A.A.D. City, Southerners on New Ground, UndocuBlack Network, Black Feminist Future, National Black Midwives Alliance, Grantmakers for Girls of Color, Blackout Collective, Solutions Not Punishment Collaborative, Black Queer and Intersectional Collective, The Audre Lorde Project, The Knights and Orchids Society, Black Women Radicals, New Voices for Reproductive Justice, The Dream Defenders, Organization for Black Struggle, the National Domestic Workers Alliance, The Nap Ministry, Black Alliance for Just Immigration, The Black Sex Workers Collective, Lead to Life, the Abolitionist Teaching Network, DecrimNow, National Black Disability Coalition, the Black Alliance for Peace, Black Voters Matter, the Electoral Justice Project, National Black Women's Justice Institute, Project NIA, Moms 4 Housing, National Black Food and Justice Alliance, SisterLove, SisterSong, and Project Nia. To be clear, this list isn't even remotely exhaustive. It's the tip of an organizing iceberg in which Black women and girls resist oppression in its numerous forms. Many of us aren't even in organizations and still find ways to be integral parts of the struggle for justice.

This collective energy of struggle bends toward freedom and justice. Those working for substantive reform, transformation, or even abolition may appear to be specializing in the wholly impossible. In reality however, what they specialize in is envisioning despite the odds stacked against us. I don't believe that the worlds I imagine will come into existence during my lifetime, but that's not a deterrent. Although my enslaved ancestors dreamt and fought for slavery abolition and bodily autonomy, I can't imagine they are at peace with how ravaging antiBlackness continues to be. We work toward a goal from which we may not directly benefit because we understand that the "our" in "our freedom" is unbound by time or borders.

My faith in us, Black people, is unconditional. My hope pivots around an active imagining of and working toward liberatory futures without the violence captured on these pages and occurring as you read these words. My faith emanates from my unflappable belief in the power of those rendered vulnerable, marginalized, dispossessed, exploited, and violated to resist, envision, and build. I bet on us because we intimately know how high the stakes are and that it is our lives we must protect and save. I hope that others will wrestle with the hard truths of this book and hear the multitude of voices of those on the margins demanding radical, transformative, or even revolutionary change. But I have faith that with or without you, we will find a way to get free. Hope propels me to embrace what scholar Ashon T. Crawley identifies as "otherwise possibilities."[15] My faith sustains me here and now because I know too often, we all we got, and *that's a hell of a lot to have.*

Knowing the enormity of what we are up against is one of the many tools at our disposal in the struggle as well. Although this book delves into the problem, it is my sincerest hope that there's more interest in and urgency around ending violence against Black women and girls. We also need an outright refusal of unlivable living. The politics of disposability are injurious at best and death-dealing at worst. When we look into the lives of Black women and girls, we can bear witness to the unbearable weight of multiple oppressive forces. *America, Goddam* is a small part of an ongoing call to action. We have been in the trenches fighting to save ourselves from this nation's penchant for criminalizing, violating, punishing, neglecting, stereotyping, and erasing us. In that fight, we offer paths to create a more just world. Getting free is still our North Star.

Epilogue

A Letter to Ma'Khia Bryant

Dear Ma'Khia,

You don't know me. To be perfectly honest, I don't really know you. I learned your name in late April 2021. I had just listened to the verdict in the Derek Chauvin trial, in which he was convicted of second-degree murder, third-degree murder, and second-degree manslaughter for the killing of George Floyd in Minneapolis on May 25, 2020. Almost immediately after hearing the verdict, I tweeted about another Black girl around your age, Darnella Frazier. Her cellphone video of Chauvin killing George catalyzed one of the biggest uprisings in U.S. history. Her video replayed on media outlets across the globe. Without this mortifying nearly ten-minute video, it would've been the word of primarily Black witnesses against that of Chauvin, his fellow officers, and a police report filled with lies about what transpired. Despite overwhelming evidence about the frequency with which police lie, far too many people still take police accounts as factual. It's an uphill and often losing battle to debunk their narrative. The word of a seventeen-year-old Black girl would carry little to no weight against that of a white police officer in a legal system hell-bent on criminalizing Black people.

Darnella's video provided incontrovertible proof of how fatally violent policing can be, yet I held my breath during the reading of the verdict knowing that a conviction wasn't a given. Even as it was read, I knew this wasn't justice either. The criminal punishment system cannibalized one of its own in a desperate act of self-preservation. Chauvin's conviction wasn't indicative of any systemic change; he was just the "bad apple" the system could afford to sacrifice for its unchecked perpetuation. Acknowledging that Chauvin's conviction wouldn't change the U.S. criminal punishment system, however, doesn't discount the significance of Darnella's brave act of witnessing. What she captured was a powerful confirmation of a truth I and a lot of Black folks knew. But what of the cost to her well-being?

Darnella still has nightmares about what she witnessed that fateful day. The acts of bearing witness and withness to violence for Black girls are soul-crushing and gut-wrenching. She lives with guilt, fear, and trauma I can't begin to imagine. She shouldn't have had to bear witness or withness. Yet without her practice of care for George, it's quite probable we wouldn't have known that George cried out for his mother as he took his last breaths. We may not have learned about the callous indifference of Chauvin's countenance as he kneeled on Floyd's neck for nine minutes and twenty-nine seconds.

I thought of Darnella more than I thought about what Chauvin's conviction did and didn't mean. I wondered what the guilty verdict meant for her. Would the verdict quiet the nightmares or alleviate her unwarranted guilt for not "doing more for George"? This Black girl's video changed the world, and her witnessing and withnessing changed her life forever as well. She deserved a world where she didn't have to be a star witness in a murder trial against an officer who kneeled on the neck of a Black man breathlessly begging for his mother for nearly ten minutes. In the immediate aftermath of the verdict, my thoughts were of a Black girl who witnessed and withnessed.

Less than an hour after the announcement of the verdict, scant details appeared on my Twitter timeline about police shooting someone just a few minutes from where I live in Columbus, Ohio. I didn't want to dig. I didn't think I could handle reading the details of yet another police killing. I couldn't stop myself from searching though. I felt a duty to bear witness. It was too close to home. A Black girl less than half my age resolved to witness; I could at least search for written details about a police killing in my city. Within minutes of scrolling and clicking, I learned that the victim of the shooting had died. A few minutes passed and I saw a tweet about the victim being a teenager. Soon, reports of it being a Black girl surfaced. Hot tears streamed down my face. Not again. Not another Black person. Not a Black child.

It was you.

Ma'Khia, I must apologize to you for a number of things. First and foremost, I am infuriated that we haven't yet built a world where Black girls are cared for and protected. A police officer killed you within moments of arriving on a scene where there were more than a few options for de-escalation. From what your family shared with us, you were fearful of being violated, either by persons who came to your foster home with the intent to harm you or perhaps by people within your foster home as well. You felt compelled to defend yourself against a recurring threat. You armed yourself with a knife. Early reports indicated that you called the police for help. Later reports suggested that person was your little sister, Ja'Niah. While I'm sure we will learn more about the moments before you were killed, I apologize for this being a world in which I wouldn't advise any Black person to call the police for help. Their penchant for criminalizing Black girls like you means that they can't see you or the other Black folks at the scene as vulnerable or as in need of help.

Let me be clear: I don't blame your sister for calling the police. She desperately sought help from those we pay to protect and serve. I just know all too well that police escalate violent situations, especially those involving Black people. Policing often snuffs out Black lives and livelihoods. According to the logics of U.S. policing, your Black skin renders you armed. Add a steak knife to the mix and the level of threat assigned to you in your last moments intensified. Additionally, we live in a world where millions of people don't believe a sixteen-year-old Black girl fearing for her life is worth caring for and protecting. The intertwined realities of antiBlackness, misogynoir, the adultification of Black girls, fatphobia, and poverty, combined with your attempt to defend yourself from multiple attackers, rendered you too easily disposable.

In the immediate aftermath of your killing, the city of Columbus quickly released body camera footage from the officer who took your life. Within minutes of the release of the footage, many people determined that you were a knife-wielding person deserving of having her life taken. People praised the officer for his swift action. More telling, some even posted about how his actions saved the lives of one of the persons with whom you had an altercation. Not even a few hours after the world learned the criminal punishment system's response to the murder of George Floyd, I watched and listened as people embraced death-dealing rationales for why a police officer had to kill you. I noted that even some of the folks who regularly called out the violence of policing worked overtime to justify the actions of the officer. They villainized you.

Many of us misspelled your name when we heard about what happened to you. The misspelling may seem like a "minor mistake," but given the tendency for folks to mispronounce and misspell the names of Black people, I owed you at least correctly spelling your beautiful Black-girl name in my tweets about your death. My initial tweet about you got thousands of retweets from folks equally enraged by what happened to you. Infuriatingly, I also got hundreds of replies celebrating your death. I also saw replies and tweets admonishing me for attempting to equate or connect what happened to you with what happened to George Floyd. While folks expressed sadness at your tragic death, it *only* took the release of less than twenty seconds of body camera footage for them to decide your death was justifiable. My heart broke.

Justifiable. It's truly something to watch folks argue so passionately about the necessity of killing a teenager. I felt rage pulsing throughout my body as I saw tweet after tweet of people doubling down on what was *legally* justifiable, as though the law has ever been a life-affirming mechanism for Black lives. Ma'Khia, I refused to engage in debates about the sanctity of your life. It's not that I am surprised that folks worked overtime to defend you being shot four times, center mass. We have yet to build a world in which the preservation of the lives of Black girls who make fly-as-fuck TikTok videos about their gorgeous hairstyles is prioritized by a vast majority. Instead, we live in a world in which people search for reasons to pontificate about what a scared Black girl child deserved. You were at once hypervisible as a potentially violent perpetrator and wholly invisible and illegible as a victim of tightly interconnected systems of marginalization and disposability. The comfort with which people concluded that your life "had to be taken" forced me to confront the gravity of the work that lies ahead, even as I remain entrenched in the discipline of hope.

I can't fathom what it was like to be moved around various foster homes in mid-Ohio over the last two years of your life, when all you wanted was to be with your mother. I know I couldn't bear listening to any of the recordings of your little sister's calls to 911 pleading for you and her to be removed from a foster home in which you felt unsafe. Unsurprisingly, officers who responded to a call from your terrified sister, fourteen-year-old Ja'Niah, just a few weeks before you were killed offered no protection. They told her "there was nothing they could do," despite Ja'Niah telling them about the fighting occurring at the home. This child feared that if she couldn't leave the home, "she was going to kill someone." I can't imagine how terrified and aggrieved your sister must've been to confess to police officers that she might kill someone if she couldn't leave this foster home. The officers coldly and dismissively wrote her off as "irate."

Just a little over three weeks later, Ja'Niah tried once more to get some help from the police. This time, however, someone was killed, a young Black girl who sought help. Police arrived on the scene to a fight and within less than a few moments, they killed you. Yes, you had a steak knife, but the arriving officers didn't even attempt to de-escalate the fight. Never mind that every damn day teachers, school counselors, assistant principals, coaches, social workers, and people who live in our neighborhoods intervene and de-escalate in similarly or even more volatile situations without anyone being killed. I am the daughter of two former teachers. Trust and believe, they and their colleagues found ways to calm their students down in the middle of violent encounters. My parents had not one hour of de-escalation training, yet they sought to preserve lives and to intervene in ways that refused any figuration of their students as disposable. They knew not one of their children was disposable, even when that student was actively causing harm. I wish you would've encountered at least one person committed to de-escalating and intervening to protect your life.

As I write this letter to you, I still can't fully wrap my mind around the pervasiveness of people fixing their mouths to say you shouldn't be here. With everything in me, I rail against a world in which the killing of Black girls is framed as justifiable, reasonable, or warranted. The other sickening reality is that there will never be justice for you, little sister. Even if we dismantled all these death-dealing systems tomorrow, you wouldn't be here. We failed you-time after time. I own the "we" of this because I can't help feeling a particular connection to all that you endured at the hands of system after system anchored in antiBlackness, misogynoir, fatphobia, and the criminalization of Black girls. I refuse to believe your killing was inevitable, but goddam, these systems made a violent death a strong possibility for you.

I promise to continue fighting alongside the many folks I mentioned in this book and those who read this book and may feel newly charged to make a better world for Ja'Niah and all the Black girls viewed by this world as disposable. I recommit to being a warrior for worlds in which Black girls are held warmly, lovingly, and in their/our fullness. I understand there's no such thing as *justice* for you. I can, however, struggle for the abolition of these death-dealing systems with the hope that you know your beautiful life is a propelling force. Ma'Khia, you now reside in my heart and in my spirit.

I will never forget to Say Your Name.

In Sisterly Love,
Treva B.

Acknowledgments

Writing this book was one of the most difficult and emotionally taxing things I've ever done. I've been thinking and writing about violence against Black women and girls for several years. It's hard, soul-crushing work. It's personal and powerfully undoing. I felt compelled to write through the pain, the screams, the unrelenting force of antiBlackness. And yet, I somewhat hesitantly began crafting this book through my own tears and the tears of too many girls like me. It would not have been possible without my village—loving on me as I researched, wrote, and revised.

I owe a debt of gratitude to my wonderful literary agent, Cherise Fisher. From the moment our dear friend Joan Morgan introduced us, I fell in awe of you. Your championing of my work and your unshakeable belief in its potency pulled me through the darkest moments of this process. I couldn't have asked for a better person with which to be on this journey.

My parents, the late Anthony Lindsey (the best #girldad ever) and my amazing mother Treva S. Lindsey, were/are my biggest cheerleaders. They always believed in my voice, and I am grateful for their unconditional love. My sister Talia has been a supportive and loving force throughout this process. My aunts, Sarah McCrae, the late Louise Hodge, and Linda Blunt, and my Uncle Hayves as well as my late grandmothers, Lula Pearl, Bertha Lindsey, and Ella Ruth Streeter, ground(ed) me in family. I've also been fortunate enough to have the best, chosen family: Cheryl and Kevin Brown, Cheryl George, Tony Santos, Sonnae Scott, Jackie and John Sherrod, Stan and Niecy Jackson cheer me on with an abundance of love and support. My godsisters and godbrothers Chenise, Miracle, Stanley, and Markus Jackson—I am grateful for all of you.

My Ohio State University community assisted me greatly in revising the book into what it became. My current and former colleagues in Women's, Gender, and Sexuality Studies at OSU have been with me at every step of researching and writing this book: Shannon Winnubst, Mary Thomas, Cricket Keating, Juno Parrenas, Wendy Smooth, Guisela Latorre, Jenny Suchland, Mytheli Srenivas, Lynn Itagaki, Ren Reczek, Linda Mizejewski, Katherine Marino, Jessica Delgado, Jian Chen, Azita Ranjbar, Lyn Tjon Soei Len, and Jill Byztydzienski are incredible colleagues who challenge me to be a better scholar. Our current and former departmental staff members Jackson Stotlar, Amber Williams, Lynaya Elliott, Tess Pugsley, and Elysse Jones are the best in the world. Colleagues across departments such as Daniel Rivers, Pranav Jani, Wendy Hesford, Koritha Mitchell, Hasan Jeffries, Kisha Radliff, and Elaine Richardson have been incredibly helpful in offering mentorship and providing feedback on my work. My exemplary students at OSU sharpened my work as well. I am particularly grateful to Deja Beamon, Mahaliah Little, and Sai Isoke for their close work with me as graduate research assistants.

Finding community outside of my employing institution helped me push through the more challenging aspects of completing *America, Goddam*. I want to thank Sandra Enimil, Erica Butler, Tyiesha Radford Shorts, Marshall Shorts, David Butler, Kaleem Musa, Tiffany Williams, Damia Smoot, Brittney Gray, Darrell Gray, Kristen Yates, Joanne Devaney, Michael Mandel, Amna Akbar, Melissa Crum, Sheri Neal, Jasmine Triplet, Carnell Willoughby, Krate Digga, and Barbara Fant for your friendship and love. I never expected to meet such a creative and warm community at this stage in my life.

I have had the pleasure of being part of two amazing collectives of scholars throughout my career. My S.P.A.C.E. folks: Angelique Nixon, Marlo David, Marlon Moore, C. Riley Snorton, L. H. Stallings, Mecca Jamilah Sullivan, and Darius Bost—you have my eternal gratitude for your friendship and brilliance. To my Pleasure Ninjas, Joan Morgan, Brittney Cooper, Esther Armah, Yaba Blay, and Kaila Story, thank you for being so amazing, brilliant, fly, and wonderful. This book exists in part because these collectives/friends ensured I had a pleasure practice as I mined these horrific archives and endured some of the worst moments of my life.

The academy has taught me many things, but I am most grateful for the friendships it gave me. To my scholar squad and friends, Jessica M. Johnson, Bettina Love, Marc Lamont Hill, Regina Bradley, Tanisha Ford, Uri McMillan,

TJ Chester, Sarah Diem, Bryana French, Zakiya Adair, Scott Heath, Nadia Brown, Vanessa Perez, Guthrie Ramsey, Alisha Jones, Nikki Greene, Christian Crouch, Akissi Britton, Bakari Kitwana, Charles Davis, Natanya Duncan, KT Ewing, Yomaira Figueroa-Vásquez, L'Heureux Lewis-McCoy, Erica Williams, Michael Eric Dyson, Susana Morris, Amanda Boston, Kristal Clemmons, Charisse Burden-Stelly, and the entire *Feminist Studies* journal editorial collective and staff: Ashwini Tambe, Attiya Ahmad, Judith Kegan Gardiner, Alexis Pauline Gumbs, Karla Mantilla, Kathryn Moeller, Bibiana Obler, Priti Ramamurthy, Matt Richardson, Lisa Rofel, Brittany Fremaux, Duy-Khuong Van, Megan Sweeney, and Neha Vora—thank you for being all the things. Our friendships may have started because of the academy—they thrive because y'all are amazing.

To the senior scholars, mentors, and advisers who gave me tools and the inspiration to do good and meaningful work: Mark Anthony Neal, Martha Jones, Carol Anderson, Laura Edwards, Davarian Baldwin, Adriane Lentz-Smith, Carol Lasser, Meredith Gadsby, Caroline Jackson-Smith, Monique Burgdorf, Derrick White, Michelle Scott, Shanna Benjamin, Pamela Brooks, Maurice Wallace, Barbara Ransby, Kaye Whitehead, Kali Gross, Stephanie Evans, Cynthia Dillard, Gwendolyn Pough, and E. Patrick Johnson—thank you, thank you, THANK YOU.

To my framily: Sia Barnes, Olivia Fenty, Amir Jenkins, Nyia Noel, Robynn Nichols, Rebeca Wolfe Balbuena, Britney Williams, Laura Williams, Brookes Gore, Sara Madavo Jean-Jacques, Shaba Lightfoot, Jose Balbuena, Maya Jackson, Charlene Blake, Marco Harris, Yendelela Neely, Michelle Bartley, Lynn Pitts, Chelsey Love, Nicole Moore, Rebecca Williams, Wade Davis, Darnell Moore, Marshall Greene, Patrick Douthit, Sophia Chang, Aisha Lewis-McCoy, Tef Poe, Julius Hill, Lauren Madlock, Marco Hardie, Trey Stanback, Derecka Purnell, Shaun Koiner, and Amber Coleman-Mortley—I love you all unconditionally and fiercely.

To my god babies: Aliyah, Elijah, Nona, Brooklyn, Kamiyah, August, Akeen, Aminah, and Anaya—you are my hearts outside of my body.

This project received support from numerous institutions and foundations. This book would not have been possible without considerable financial and research support from the Hutchins Center for African & African American Research, the American Council of Learned Societies, the Andrew W. Mellon Foundation, Women's Media Center, the Coca-Cola Critical Difference Grant

Program, and the Ohio State University Arts and Humanities Large Grants Program.

My heartfelt thanks go to the entire staff I worked with at the University of California Press. Naomi Schneider, your editorial insights, thorough engagement, passion, and championing of my work was a gift. You believed in my voice, and I couldn't be more grateful. Summer Farah, Teresa Iafolla, Katryce Lassle, Julie Van Pelt, Emilia Thiuri, and Alex Dahne—thank you all for your hard work helping bring *America, Goddam* to life. To my copyeditor, Joe Abbot, and my indexer, Do Mi Stauber, thank you for what is often thankless though without question, essential work. I also had the pleasure of working with an amazing publicist, Kathleen Carter, on this book. Her steadfast investment in my work was a gift from the moment we connected.

Finally, I would like to thank all Black girls, women, gender nonbinary, genderfluid, agender, gender expansive, and genderqueer people for being YOU. This book is for you and to help others see you and your stories. Thank you for being the heartbeat of our worlds—past, present, and future.

Notes

Introduction

1. Hauck, G., et al. (2021, March 30). "Updates from Day 2 of the Derek Chauvin Trial: 9-Year-Old, Teen Who Recorded Video of George Floyd's Death among Witnesses," *USA Today*, www.usatoday.com/story/news/nation/2021/03/30/derek-chauvin-trial-live-tuesday-witnesses-take-stand-donald-williams/7018720002/, retrieved March 31, 2021.

2. Hauck.

3. Guiton, C. (2019, December 2). "Nina Simone: An Artist's Duty Is to Reflect the Times," www.culturematters.org.uk/index.php/arts/music/item/3208-nina-simone-an-artist-s-duty-is-to-reflect-the-times, retrieved August 19, 2020.

4. Loudermilk, A. (2013). "Nina Simone & the Civil Rights Movement: Protest at Her Piano, Audience at Her Feet," *Journal of International Women's Studies, 14*(3), 121–136.

5. Kernodle, T. (2008). "'I Wish I Knew How It Would Feel to Be Free': Nina Simone and the Redefining of the Freedom Song of the 1960s," *Journal of the Society for American Music, 2*(3), 304.

6. Kernodle, 304.

7. Williams, M.V. (2013). *Medgar Evers: Mississippi Martyr.* Little Rock: University of Arkansas Press.

8. Simone, N. (2003). *I Put a Spell on You: The Autobiography of Nina Simone.* Cambridge, MA: De Capo Press, 90.

9. Evers-Williams, M., with Marable, M. (2006). *The Autobiography of Medgar Evers: A Hero's Life and Legacy Revealed through His Writings, Letters, and Speeches.* New York: Civitas.

10. Vollers, M. (1995). *Ghost of Mississippi: The Murder of Medgar Evers, the Trials of Byron De La Beckwith and the Haunting of the New South.* New York: Back Bay Books.

11. McKinstry, C., & George, D. (2013). *While the World Watched: A Birmingham Bombing Survivor Comes of Age during the Civil Rights Movement.* Carol Stream, IL: Tyndale House, 61.

12. Trent, S. (2020, March 6). "Sarah Collins Rudolph, Birmingham's Fifth Girl," *Washington Post,* www.washingtonpost.com/history/2020/03/06/sarah-collins-rudolph-birmingham-church-bombing-fifth-girl/, retrieved August 23, 2020.

13. Gado, M. (2015). "The Birmingham Church Bombing: Bombingham," www.crimelibrary.com/terrorists_spies/terrorists/birmingham_church/4.html, retrieved February 28, 2021; English, T. (2020). "Four Girls Forever Lost: 57 Years Ago, 16th Street Baptist Church Bombing Awakened Nation to Deadly Consequences of Hate," Southern Poverty Law Center, Montgomery, AL.

14. Simone (2003), 90.

15. Amelia Boynton was a U.S. activist who led the civil rights movement in Selma, Alabama. On March 7, 1965, as she attempted to cross the Edmund Pettus Bridge during a march from Selma to Montgomery, Alabama, law enforcement beat her unconscious. The media present at the march captured images of her bloodied and wounded body. Those images were publicized around the world, exemplifying the level of brutality to which Black people were subjected in their struggle for civil rights.

16. Pratt, R.A. (2016). *Selma's Bloody Sunday (Witness to History).* Baltimore, MD: Johns Hopkins University Press.

17. Oppel, R.A., Jr., Taylor, D.B., & Bogel-Burroughs, N. (2021, April 26). "What to Know about Breonna Taylor's Death," *New York Times,* www.nytimes.com/article/breonna-taylor-police.html, retrieved March 19, 2021.

18. Hansen, C. (2020, September 23). "No Officers Charged in Breonna Taylor Killing; One Indicted on Related Offense," *US World News and Business Report,* www.usnews.com/news/national-news/articles/2020-09-23/no-officers-charged-in-breonna-taylor-killing-one-indicted-on-related-offense, retrieved March 19, 2021.

19. *Recently* is an appropriate word here because the death of Sandra Bland in police custody galvanized widespread outrage in 2015. Bland's death in police custody is discussed at greater length in the second chapter of this book in my discussion of the violence against Black women and girls in the custody of the criminal punishment system.

20. Butler, J. (2004). *Undoing Gender.* New York: Routledge, 3.

21. Westbrook, L. (2020). *Unlivable Lives: Violence and Identity in Transgender Activism.* Berkeley: University of California Press, 4.

22. For many, violence only encompasses behavior involving physical force intended to hurt, damage, or kill. Violence also includes economic, political and institutional, and cultural forms of harm that individually and systemically hurt, damage, or kill. Gentrification, inadequate housing, unclean water, and food insecurity harm and sometimes kill people and disproportionately impact Black women and girls.

23. Hartman, S. (2008). *Lose Your Mother: A Journey along the Atlantic Slave Route.* New York: Farrar, Straus, and Giroux, 6.

24. Lindsey, T. (2017a). *Colored No More: Reinventing Black Womanhood in Washington, D.C.* Urbana-Champaign: University of Illinois Press, 12.

25. Threadcraft, S. (2018). *Intimate Justice: The Black Female Body and the Body Politic.* London: Oxford University Press, xi.

26. Walcott, R. (2015). "The Problem of the Human: Black Ontologies and 'the Coloniality of Our Being,'" in S. Broeck & C. Junker (Eds.), *Postcoloniality-Decoloniality-Black Critique: Joints and Fissures.* Frankfurt: Campus Verlag, 102.

27. Davis. A., et al. (2021). *Abolition. Feminism. Now.* New York: Haymarket Books.

28. #BlackLivesMatter is attributed to Patrisse Cullors, Alicia Garza, and Opal Tometi. #SayHerName was coined by Kimberlé Crenshaw and the African American Policy Forum. #MeToo was created by Tarana Burke.

29. Jones, M. (2020). *Vanguard: How Black Women Broke Barriers, Won the Vote, and Insisted on Equality for All.* New York: Basic Books.

30. Shakur, A. (2001). *Assata: An Autobiography.* Chicago: Lawrence Hill, 52.

31. Cohen, C. (1999). *The Boundaries of Blackness: AIDS and the Breakdown of Black Politics.* Chicago: University of Chicago Press, 63.

32. Emmett Till's murder emerged as and remains one of the most well-known examples of antiBlack violence in modern U.S. history. The fourteen-year-old boy was kidnapped, brutally assaulted, and lynched in Money,

Mississippi, on August 28, 1955, by a group of white men after being extralegally accused of offending a white woman. In 2008 the woman, Carolyn Bryant, admitted to historian and author Tim Tyson that she fabricated most of her testimony regarding her encounter with Till. Mamie Till's insistence on an open-casket funeral to show the world what these men did to her son made the image of Till's brutalized and unrecognizable body one of the most iconic images of the twentieth century and of this nation's history of antiBlack violence.

33. Recy Taylor was an African American woman who was kidnapped and gang-raped by six white men on September 3, 1944. Taylor reported the rape, and many African Americans organized around her case at the time. Despite this mobilization, two grand juries declined to indict the men who confessed to the attack. No charges were ever brought. Her case garnered nationwide attention in the immediate aftermath from organizers, but her story became increasingly less well-known very soon after the case resulted in no charges. Taylor's story was more recently recollected in both Danielle McGuire's book *At the Dark End of the Street: Black Women, Rape, and Resistance—A New History of the Civil Rights Movement from Rosa Parks to the Rise of Black Power* (New York: Vintage, 2011) and the award-winning documentary *The Rape of Recy Taylor* (Augusta Films, 2017).

34. Cohen (1999), 63.

35. Criminalization, as concisely defined by historian Carl Suddler in his book *Presumed Criminal: Black Youth and the Justice System in Postwar New York,* is "the means by which one is criminalized or prevented from being law-abiding, and its practices and processes extend further than the U.S. criminal and juvenile justice systems" (5). Suddler points out that criminalization occurs both within and outside of the criminal punishment system.

36. Morgan, J. L. (2004). *Laboring Women: Reproduction and Gender in New World Slavery.* Philadelphia: University of Pennsylvania Press, 50–69, 56. Morgan's groundbreaking book brings into sharp focus how race and "racial slavery" developed. More specifically, she centers on how racial slavery relied on "the real and imaginary reproductive potential of women whose 'blackness' was produced by and produced their enslavability" (1). Morgan drives home the fictive logics undergirding racial slavery in the New World fixated on the bodies of women as a primary site for establishing the status of the enslaved.

37. Morgan, 200.

38. Gross, K. N. (2015). "African American Women, Mass Incarceration, and the Politics of Protection," *Journal of American History*, 102(1), 25–26.

39. Berry, D. (2017). *The Price for Their Pound of Flesh: The Value of the Enslaved, from Womb to Grave, in the Building of a Nation*. New York: Beacon. Berry details in-depth some horrific examples of the kinds of violence captive and enslaved Africans endured. One specific example provided is a four-year-old being ripped away from his parent.

40. Haley, S. (2013) "'Like I Was a Man': Chain Gangs, Gender, and the Domestic Carceral Sphere in Jim Crow Georgia," *Signs*, 39(1), 55.

41. Feimster, C. (2009). *Southern Horrors: Women and the Politics of Rape and Lynching*. Cambridge, MA: Harvard University Press, 164.

42. I intentionally use *punishment* here instead of *justice* because the system more often than not fails to address harm through just practices; it doles out punishment. There is a lack of justice in our current system, particularly for Black girls and women, and a penchant for punishment.

43. Muhammad, K. (2019). *The Condemnation of Blackness: Race, Crime, and the Making of Modern Urban America* (2nd ed.). Cambridge, MA: Harvard University Press, 3.

44. Muhammad, 4.

45. Gross (2015), 26.

46. Gilmore, R. W. (2007). *Golden Gulag: Prisons, Surplus, Crisis, and Opposition in Globalizing California*. Berkeley: University of California Press, 28.

47. Roeder, A. (2019). "America Is Failing Its Black Mothers," www.hsph.harvard.edu, retrieved December 2, 2020.

48. On their groundbreaking Tumblr, #Antiblackness-is-a-Theory, L'Nassh (so_treu) pointedly etches out what antiBlackness is and how it operates. Their work was among the first to unpack the specificity of antiBlackness and its historical and contemporary operating praxes.

49. ross, k. m. (2020, June 4). "Call It What It Is: Anti-Blackness," *New York Times*, www.nytimes.com/2020/06/04/opinion/george-floyd-anti-blackness.html, retrieved August 20, 2021.

50. Jeffries, M. (2014, November 28). "Ferguson Must Force Us to Face Anti-Blackness," *Boston Globe*, www.bostonglobe.com/opinion/2014/11/28/ferguson-must-force-face-anti-blackness/pKVMpGxwUYpMDyHRWPln2M/story.html, retrieved March 15, 2020.

51. Walcott, R. (2021). *ANTIBLACKNESS*. Durham, NC: Duke University Press, *back cover*.

52. Bailey, M., & Trudz. (2018). "On Misogynoir: Citation, Erasure, and Plagiarism," *Feminist Media Studies, 18*(4), 762.

53. Morris, M. W. (2016). *PUSHOUT: The Criminalization of Black Girls in Schools*. New York: New Press.

54. Green, E. L., Walker, M., & Shapiro, E. (2020, October 1). "A Battle for the Souls of Black Girls," *New York Times,* www.nytimes.com/2020/10/01/us /politics/black-girls-school-discipline.html, retrieved October 15, 2020.

55. ACLU. (2017). "Black-White Girl School Arrest Risk," www.aclu.org /issues/racial-justice/race-and-inequality-education/black-white-girl-school- arrest-risk, retrieved October 15, 2020.

56. Skiba, R. J., & Williams, N. T. (2014). "Are Black Kids Worse? Myths and Facts about Racial Differences in Behavior: A Summary of the Literature," Bloomington: Equity Project at Indiana University, 4.

57. Quoted in Morris (2016), 5.

58. Owen, G. (2017). "I Have a Story That Needs to Be Told: Tangerine, Storytelling, and Public Space," *Queer Foundation Scholar,* 1.

59. Jones, Z. C. (2020, December 1). "Laverne Cox Says She and a Friend Were Targeted in Transphobic Attack," CBS News, www.cbsnews.com/news /laverne-cox-transphobic-attack-los-angeles-griffith-park/, retrieved December 3, 2020.

60. Bibi, E. (2020, October 6). "Human Rights Campaign President Alphonso David on the Unprecedented Fatal Violence against the Transgender and Gender Non-conforming Community in 2020," www.hrc.org/press-releases/human- rights-campaign-president-alphonso-david-on-the-unprecedented-fatal- violence-against-the-transgender-and-gender-non-conforming-commu- nity-in-2020, retrieved October 31, 2020.

61. Bibi.

62. King, D. (1988). "Multiple Jeopardy, Multiple Consciousness: The Context of a Black Feminist Ideology," *Signs, 14*(1), 47.

63. In *The Dawning of the Apocalypse: The Roots of Slavery, White Supremacy, Settler Colonialism, and Capitalism in the Long Sixteenth Century,* historian Gerald Horne examines the arrival of enslaved Africans to what would become South Carolina in the 1520s. During the century before the arrival of settlers in

Jamestown, enslaved people absconded to local Indigenous populations. Notably, Horne argues that during the sixteenth century, U.S. whiteness transformed into white supremacy as an oppositional force to enslaved Africans' and Indigenous resistance to slavery and settler colonialism.

64. Crenshaw, K. (1991). "Mapping the Margins: Intersectionality, Identity Politics, and Violence against Women of Color," *Stanford Law Review, 43*(6), 1241–1299.

65. Shange, N. (1976). *For Colored Girls Who Have Considered Suicide When the Rainbow Is Enuf.* Berkeley, CA: Shameless Hussy Press, 18–19.

66. Shange, 18–19.

67. Shedd, C. (2011). "Countering the Carceral Continuum," *Criminology and Public Policy, 10*(3), 851–863.

68. Gilmore, R. W. (2011). "What Is to Be Done?" *American Quarterly, 63*(2), 257.

69. King (1988), 50.

Chapter 1. Say Her Name

1. Ice Cube, MC Ren, D.O.C. (1988). "Fuck Tha Police," Ruthless/Priority Records.

2. King, Martin Luther, Jr. (1967). "The Other America," www.crmvet.org /docs/otheram.htm.

3. Threadcraft, S. (2017). "North American Necropolitics and Gender: On #BlackLivesMatter and Black Femicide," *South Atlantic Quarterly, 116*(3), 553.

4. Schwartz, J. (2016). "How Governments Pay: Lawsuits, Budgets, and Police Reform," *UCLA Review, 63*(1144), 15–23.

5. Lopez, G. (2020, August 28). "How Violent Protests against Police Brutality in the '60s and '90s Changed Public Opinion," Vox, www.vox.com/2020 /6/2/21275901/police-violence-riots-jacob-blake-kenosha-wisconsin, retrieved October 1, 2020.

6. Hill, M.L. (2017). *Nobody: Casualties of America's War on the Vulnerable from Ferguson to Flint and Beyond.* New York: Atria, 11.

7. Crenshaw, K., et al. (2015). *Say Her Name: Resisting Police Brutality against Black Women.* African American Policy Forum and the Center for Intersectionality and Policy Studies.

8. Lindsey, T. (2015, September 5). "Race in the US: Herstory," *Al Jazeera*, www.aljazeera.com/features/2015/09/05/race-in-the-us-herstory/, retrieved September 20, 2020.

9. James, J. (1996). *Resisting State Violence: Radicalism, Gender, and Race in U.S. Culture.* Minneapolis: University of Minnesota Press, 31.

10. Threadcraft (2017), 553.

11. Edwards, F., et al. (2019). "Risk of Being Killed by Police Use of Force in the United States by Age, Race–Ethnicity, and Sex," *Proceedings of the National Academy of Sciences of the United States of America, 116*(34), 16793–16798.

12. Morris. M. (2016). *Pushout: The Criminalization of Black Girls in Schools.* New York: New Press, 3, 56–57.

13. On the night of August 6, 2018, San Antonio police officers forced Natalie Simms to comply with a car and cavity search for suspicion of possession of drugs. During the search, the officer asked if Natalie had anything in her pants. Natalie informed the officer that she was on her period. The officer shined a light on her underwear and reached in and removed Natalie's tampon. This all occurred on the side of a San Antonio street. No drugs were found during this invasive and unnecessary search.

14. Reichel, P.L. (1988). "Southern Slave Patrols as a Transitional Police Type," *American Journal of Police, 7*(2), 51–77.

15. Hassett-Walker, C. (2020, June 2). "The Racist Roots of American Policing," The Conversation, https://theconversation.com/the-racist-roots-of-american-policing-from-slave-patrols-to-traffic-stops-112816, retrieved July 20, 2020.

16. Racial capitalism, a concept coined by Cedric Robinson, refers to the process of extracting social and economic value from a person of a different racial identity, referring, predominantly, to the extraction of value from Black people, Indigenous people, and people of color.

17. Robinson, C. (1983). *Black Marxism: The Making of the Black Radical Tradition.* Chapel Hill: University of North Carolina Press.

18. Melamed, J. (2015). "Racial Capitalism," *Critical Ethnic Studies, 1*(1), 76–85.

19. A slave society, as defined by historian David Blight, is "any society where slave labor—where the definition of labor, where the definition of the relationship between ownership and labor—is defined by slavery. By a cradle to grave—and some would've even said a cradle to grave and beyond—human

bondage." Blight, D. (n.d.). "The Civil War and Reconstruction Era, 1845–1877: Lecture 3 Transcript," Open Media: Yale University, http://openmedia.yale .edu/projects/iphone/departments/hist/hist119/transcript03.html, retrieved August 1, 2021.

20. Ralph, L. (2019). "The Logic of the Slave Patrol: The Fantasy of Black Predatory Violence and the Use of Force by the Police," *Palgrave Communications, 5*, 130.

21. Dulaney, W. (1996). *Black Police in America*. Bloomington: Indiana University Press, 2.

22. Waxman, O. (2017, May 18). "How the U.S. Got Its Police Force," *Time,* https://time.com/4779112/police-history-origins/, retrieved July 19, 2020.

23. Potter, G. (2017). "The History of Policing in the United States," *Eastern Kentucky University: Police Studies Online,* https://plsonline.eku.edu/insidelook /history-policing-united-states-part-3, retrieved August 18, 2020.

24. American Civil Liberties Union. (2020). "ICE and Border Patrol Abuses," ACLU.org, retrieved September 25, 2020.

25. French, L. (2018). *The History of Policing America: From Militias and Military to the Law Enforcement of Today.* Lanham, MD: Rowman and Littlefield, 83–106.

26. Flamm, M. (2007). *Law and Order: Street Crime, Civil Unrest, and the Crisis of Liberalism in the 1960s.* New York: Columbia University Press, 1–12.

27. U.S. Government Publishing Office. (1968). "Omnibus Crime Control and Safe Streets Act of 1968."

28. Hinton, E. (2017). *From the War on Poverty to the War on Crime: The Making of Mass Incarceration in America.* Cambridge, MA: Harvard University Press, 2.

29. Hinton, 2.

30. Davis, E., et al. (2018). "Contacts between Police and the Public, 2015," U.S. Department of Justice, Office of Justice Programs and Bureau of Justice Statistics, 1.

31. Alexander, M. (2014, April 29). "Michelle Alexander: A System of Racial and Social Control," interview by S. Childress, *Frontline,* www.pbs.org/wgbh /frontline/article/michelle-alexander-a-system-of-racial-and-social-control /, retrieved July 22, 2021.

32. Alexander.

33. James (1996), 143.

34. Giddings, P. (1984). *When and Where I Enter: The Impact of Black Women on Race and Sex in America.* New York: William Morrow, 37.

35. Weinbaum, E. (2019). *The Afterlife of Reproductive Slavery: Biocapitalism and Black Feminism's Philosophy of History.* Durham, NC: Duke University Press, 2–5; Morgan, J. (2004). *Laboring Women: Reproduction and Gender in New World Slavery.* Philadelphia: University of Pennsylvania Press.

36. Hadden, S. (2003). *Slave Patrols: Law and Violence in Virginia and the Carolinas.* Cambridge, MA: Harvard University Press.

37. Weinbaum (2019), 7.

38. Feder-Haugabook, A. (2017, October 21). "Eula Mae Love (1939–1979)," BlackPast.org, www.blackpast.org/african-american-history/love-eula-mae-1939–1979/, retrieved October 1, 2020.

39. Feder-Haugabook.

40. Feder-Haugabook.

41. Hill, G. (1979, October 7). "Los Angeles Police Criticized in Killing," *New York Times,* 24.

42. Felker-Kantor, M. (2016). "The Coalition against Police Abuse: CAPA's Resistance Struggle in 1970s Los Angeles," *Journal of Civil and Human Rights,* 2(1), 67.

43. Feder-Haugabook (2017).

44. Feder-Haugabook.

45. Feder-Haugabook.

46. Feder-Haugabook.

47. Hill (1979).

48. Feder-Haugabook (2017).

49. Hill (1979).

50. Feder-Haugabook (2017).

51. Leary, J. (2016, September 1). "Officer-Involved Obfuscation," *Jacobin,* www.jacobinmag.com/2016/09/eula-love-officer-involved-shooting-black-lives-matter, retrieved August 30, 2020.

52. Feder-Haugabook (2017).

53. Leary (2016).

54. Feder-Haugabook (2017).

55. Scott, J. A. (1998). *The City: Los Angeles and Urban Theory at the End of the Twentieth Century.* Berkeley: University of California Press, 355.

56. Feder-Haugabook (2017).

57. Leary (2016).

58. Hill (1979).

59. Center for Law and Social Justice. (1988). "Black Women under Siege by the New York City Police," Brooklyn, NY: Medgar Evers College Center for Law and Justice.

60. James (1996), 31.

61. Budur, L. (1984, October 30). "Police Kill Woman Being Evicted; Officers Say She Wielded a Knife," *New York Times.*

62. Prial, F. (1987, January 28). "Daughter Cites Bumpurs's Stay in State Hospital," *New York Times.*

63. Merola, M. (1988). *Big City D.A.* New York: Random House, 7-27.

64. Prial (1987).

65. Noel, P. (1987, January 31). "Group Decries 'Sham' Bumpurs Murder Trial," *New York Amsterdam News,* 10.

66. "The People of the State of New York against Stephen Sullivan," New York Court of Appeals Records and Brief, 68 NY2D 495, Appellants Appendix, part 1, People v. Sullivan (June 1986).

67. Harris, L. (2018). "Beyond the Shooting: Eleanor Gray Bumpurs, Identity Erasure, and Family Activism against Police Violence," *Souls,* 20(1), 86.

68. Budur (1984).

69. Harris (2018), 87.

70. Budur (1984).

71. Harris (2018), 87.

72. Raab, S. (1985, April 13). "State Judge Dismisses Indictment of Officer in the Bumpurs Killing," *New York Times,* www.nytimes.com/1985/04/13 /nyregion/state-judge-dismisses-indictment-of-officer-in-the-bumpurs-killing.html, retrieved August 16, 2020.

73. Raab.

74. Raab, S. (1985, February 1). "Officer Indicted in Bumpurs Case," *New York Times* www.nytimes.com/1985/02/01/nyregion/officer-indicted-in-bumpurs-case.html, August 16, 2020.

75. Scardino, A., & Finder, A. (1985, April 14). "Judge Dismisses Indictment in Bumpurs Case," *New York Times,* www.nytimes.com/1985/04/13/nyregion

/state-judge-dismisses-indictment-of-officer-in-the-bumpurs-killing.html, retrieved April 4, 2017.

76. Hevesi, D. (1986, November 26). "Court Allows Bumpurs Case to Be Tried," *New York Times*, www.nytimes.com/1986/11/26/nyregion/court-allows-bumpurs-case-to-be-tried.html, retrieved April 4, 2017.

77. Raab, S. (1987, January 12). "Trial of Officer in Bumpurs Case Starting with Request for No Jury," *New York Times*, www.nytimes.com/1987/01/12/nyregion/trial-of-officer-in-bumpurs-case-starting-with-request-for-no-jury.html, retrieved April 6, 2017.

78. Prial, F. J. (1987, February 27). "Judge Acquits Sullivan in Shotgun Slaying of Bumpurs," *New York Times*, www.nytimes.com/1987/02/27/nyregion/judge-acquits-sullivan-in-shotgun-slaying-of-bumpurs.html, retrieved April 6, 2017.

79. Associated Press. (1991, March 29). "New York City to Pay Heirs in Bumpurs Case," *New York Times*, www.nytimes.com/1991/03/29/nyregion/new-york-city-to-pay-heirs-in-bumpurs-case.html, retrieved April 7, 2017.

80. Raab, S. (1984, November 21). "Eviction Death Leads City to Demote Two," *New York Times*.

81. Harris (2018), 100.

82. Feuer, A. (2016, October 19). "Fatal Police Shooting in Bronx Echoes One from 32 Years Ago," *New York Times*, www.nytimes.com/2016/10/20/nyregion/fatal-police-shooting-in-bronx-echoes-one-from-32-years-ago.html, retrieved August 17, 2020.

83. Perry, D., & Carter-Long, L. (2016). "The Ruderman White Paper on Media Coverage of Law Enforcement Use of Force and Disability," Boston: Ruderman Family Foundation, 1.

84. Feuer (2016).

85. Kanno-Youngs, Z. (2018, February 1). "EMT Recounts Moments before Mentally Ill Woman Was Shot by Police Sergeant," *Wall Street Journal*, www.wsj.com/articles/emt-recounts-moments-before-mentally-ill-woman-was-shot-by-police-sergeant-1517536679, retrieved September 15, 2019.

86. Feuer (2016).

87. Allen, R. (2020). "Deborah J. Danner, 1950–2016," www.blackpast.org/african-american-history/people-african-american-history/deborah-j-danner-1950-2016/, retrieved August 18, 2020.

88. Allen.

89. BBC News. (2016, October 19). "New York Police Officer Kills Mentally Ill Black Woman," *BBC News*, www.bbc.com/news/world-us-canada-37707892, retrieved February 8, 2019.

90. Allen (2020).

91. Danner, D. (2012, January 28). "Living with Schizophrenia," New York: Self-Published, 4. https://s3.documentcloud.org/documents/3146953/Living-With-Schizophrenia-by-Deborah-Danner.pdf.

92. Danner.

93. Crenshaw et al. (2015).

94. "Gender-expansive" is when a person's identity or behavior is broader than the commonly held definitions of gender and gender expression in one or more aspects of their life.

95. Ritchie, A. (2017). *Invisible No More: Police Violence against Black Women and Women of Color.* Boston: Beacon Press, 91.

96. Pulrang, A. (2020, August 24). "Disabled People Are Afraid for Their Lives. Candidates Need to Listen," Forbes, www.forbes.com/sites/andrew pulrang/2020/08/14/disabled-people-are-afraid-for-their-lives-candidates-need-to-listen/?sh=5f389397301a, retrieved July 23, 2021.

97. Pulrang.

98. Dean, M. (2015, June 5). "'Black Women Unnamed': How Tanisha Anderson's Bad Day Turned into Her Last," *The Guardian,* www.theguardian .com/us-news/2015/jun/05/black-women-police-killing-tanisha-anderson, retrieved September 30, 2020.

99. Shaffer, C. (2015, January 2). "Tanisha Anderson Was Restrained in Prone Position; Death Ruled Homicide," Cleveland.com, www.cleveland.com /metro/2015/01/tanisha_anderson_was_restraine.html, retrieved July 23, 2021.

100. Shaffer.

101. Dean (2015).

102. Gallek, P. (2018, February 2). "No Indictment for Cleveland Police Officers in Tanisha Anderson's Death," Fox 8, fox8.com/news/no-indictment-for-cleveland-police-officers-in-tanisha-andersons-death/, retrieved July 23, 2021.

103. Cooper, B. (2020, June 4). "Why Are Black Women and Girls Still an Afterthought in Our Outrage over Police Violence?" *Time,* time.com/5847970 /police-brutality-black-women-girls/, retrieved July 23, 2021.

104. de la Cretaz, B. (2020, June 5). "Breonna Taylor Should Be Turning 27 Today. Here's How to Demand Justice for Her Death," Yahoo!, www.yahoo .com/lifestyle/breonna-taylor-turning-27-today-100003960.html, retrieved July 23, 2021.

105. Lovan, D. (2020, September 15). "'Say Her Name': City to Pay $12m to Breonna Taylor's Family," Associated Press, www.usnews.com/news/us/articles /2020-09-15/multi-million-settlement-reached-in-breonna-taylor-lawsuit, retrieved September 25, 2020.

106. Blay, Z. (2020). "The Memeification of Breonna Taylor's Death," *Huffington Post,* www.huffpost.com/entry/memes-breonna-taylor-arrest-the-cops_n_5efcf975c5b6acab284a93aa, retrieved August 1, 2020. Memeification is the conscious design of a meme for delivering information through effective, contagious messages. One can make someone into a meme. Breonna's name and image became tied to various campaigns. This process can make her more symbolic and evacuate her personhood.

107. Leduff, C. (2010, November/December). "What Killed Aiyana Stanley-Jones?" *Mother Jones,* motherjones.com/politics/2010/09/aiyana-stanley-jones-detroit/, retrieved July 14, 2019.

108. CBS News. (2019, October 12). "Fort Worth Police Officer Fatally Shoots Woman in Her Own Home," CBS News, cbsnews.com/news/police-officer-shooting-white-fort-worth-police-officer-fatally-shoots-black-woman-in-her-own-home-today-2019-10-12/, retrieved December 28, 2019.

109. Howland, J. (2020, October 11). "'She Won't Be Forgotten.' Atatiana Jefferson's Neighbor, 1 Year Later, Has New Purpose," *Fort Worth Star-Telegram,* www.star-telegram.com/news/local/fort-worth/article246367970.html, retrieved October 12, 2020.

110. Ortiz, E. (2019, December 20). "Fort Worth Police Officer Who Fatally Shot Atatiana Jefferson Indicted on Murder Charge," NBC News, www .nbcnews.com/news/us-news/fort-worth-police-officer-who-fatally-shot-atatiana-jefferson-indicted-n1105916, retrieved January 10, 2020.

111. Overton, I. (2020, June 1). "What Is Missing in the Debate about Police Violence in the US," *Byline Times,* https://bylinetimes.com/2020/06/01/what-is-missing-in-the-debate-about-police-violence-in-the-us/, retrieved July 15, 2020.

112. Lindsey, T. (2015b). "The Rape Trial Everyone in America Should Be Watching," *Cosmopolitan,* www.cosmopolitan.com/politics/a49050/daniel-holtzclaw-trial-oklahoma/, retrieved November 10, 2017.

113. Sedensky, M. (2015). "Hundreds of Officers Lose Licenses over Sex Misconduct," Associated Press, https://apnews.com/article/oklahoma-police-archive-oklahoma-city-fd1d4d05e561462a85abe50e7eaed4ec, retrieved November 10, 2017.

114. Sedensky.

115. Lindsey (2015b).

116. News 9. (2014, August 21). "Woman Who Sparked OCPD Officer Investigation Speaks Out," News 9, www.news9.com/story/5e34cd28e0c96e774b350177/woman-who-sparked-ocpd-officer-investigation-speaks-out, retrieved July 23, 2021.

117. Lindsey (2015b).

118. Testa, J. (2014, September 5). "How Police Caught the Cop Who Allegedly Sexually Abused Black Women," BuzzFeed News, www.buzzfeednews.com/article/jtes/daniel-holtzclaw-alleged-sexual-assault-oklahoma-city, retrieved October 30, 2017.

119. Dingler, M. (2014, November 18). "Oklahoma City Police Officer Faces Trial on 36 Counts, Including Rape," *The Oklahoman*, www.oklahoman.com/article/5368114/oklahoma-city-police-officer-faces-trial-on-36-counts-including-rape, retrieved October 30, 2017.

120. Lindsey, T. (2015). "Post-Ferguson: A 'Herstorical' Approach to Black Violability," *Feminist Studies, 41*(1), 232–237.

121. Lindsey, T. (2016, January 26). "A Serial Rapist Is in Jail, but the Healing for Victims Has Just Begun," *Cosmopolitan*, www.cosmopolitan.com/politics/news/a52708/daniel-holtzclaw-is-in-jail-but-the-healing-has-just-begun/, retrieved October 20, 2017.

122. See, e.g., Associated Press. (2016, September 2). "Deputy Who Tossed a S.C. High School Student Won't Be Charged," *New York Times*, www.nytimes.com/2016/09/03/afternoonupdate/deputy-who-tossed-a-sc-high-school-student-wont-be-charged.html, retrieved October 15, 2020.

123. Craven, J. (2016, June 23). "Texas Police Officer Who Manhandled Black Teens at Pool Party Will Not Face Charges," *Huffington Post*, www.huffpost.com/entry/texas-teen-pool-party-police-charges_n_576c3e97e4b0dbb1bbb9ef1a, retrieved October 15, 2020.

124. Lockhart, P. R. (2019, October 24). "Police Officer Resigns after Video Shows Him Using Excessive Force on an 11-Year-Old Girl," Vox, www.vox

.com/identities/2019/10/24/20929397/police-officer-excessive-force-school-11-year-old-girl-new-mexico, retrieved October 16, 2020.

125. Agorist, M. (2015, February 24). "High School Girl Has Jaw Broken by School Cop after Being Falsely Accused of Having Mace," Free Thought Project, https://thefreethoughtproject.com/high-school-girl-jaw-broken-school-cop-falsely-accused-mace/, retrieved October 15, 2020.

126. Jeltsen, M. (2020, October 21). "Police Are Cutting Ties with Domestic Violence Programs That Support Black Lives Matter," *Huffington Post,* www.huffpost.com/entry/domestic-violence-black-lives-matter-police_n_5f88c8a1c5b66ee9a5ee43d7, retrieved October 17, 2020.

127. Jeltsen.

Chapter 2. The Caged Bird Sings

1. Editorial Board. (2015, July 25). "Sandra Bland: Suspicion and Mistrust Flourish amid Official Inconsistencies," *The Guardian,* www.theguardian.com/us-news/2015/jul/25/sandra-bland-suspicion-mistrust-official-inconsistencies, retrieved December 9, 2017.

2. Lartey, J. (2018, December 3). "Sandra Bland: Behind a Poignant Documentary of Her Life and Death," *The Guardian,* www.theguardian.com/tv-and-radio/2018/dec/03/sandra-bland-behind-a-poignant-documentary-of-her-life-and-death, retrieved January 19, 2019.

3. Booth, J. (2019). "Capitalism, Anti-Blackness, and the Law: A Very Short History," *Harvard BlackLetter Law Journal, 35,* 5–9.

4. Hill, M. L. (2017). *Nobody: Casualties of America's War on the Vulnerable, from Ferguson to Flint and Beyond.* New York: Simon and Schuster, 66.

5. Sharpe, C. (2016). *In the Wake: On Blackness and Being.* Durham, NC: Duke University Press, 7.

6. Perry, I. (2018). *Vexy Thing: On Gender and Liberation.* Durham, NC: Duke University Press, 41.

7. Perry, 21.

8. Guion, P. (2015, July 24). "Sandra Bland: Twitter Erupts over Theory That Hanged Woman Was Already Dead in Her Mugshot," *Independent,* www.independent.co.uk/news/world/americas/sandra-bland-twitter-erupts-over-theory-hanged-woman-was-already-dead-her-mugshot-10411761.html, retrieved September 9, 2016.

9. Editorial Board. (2015, July 21). "Dashcam Footage of Sandra Bland's Arrest during a Traffic Stop before Her Death in Police Custody—Video," *The Guardian,* www.theguardian.com/us-news/video/2015/jul/22/dash-cam-sandra-bland-arrest-video.

10. Hassan, A. (2019, May 7). "The Sandra Bland Video: What We Know," *New York Times,* www.nytimes.com/2019/05/07/us/sandra-bland-brian-encinia.html, retrieved April 30, 2020.

11. Lartey, J. (2015, July 23). "Sandra Bland Dashcam Video Raises Doubts about Officer's Basis for Arrest," *The Guardian,* www.theguardian.com/us-news/2015/jul/23/sandra-bland-dashcam-video-analysis, retrieved September 9, 2016.

12. Davis, K., & Heilbroner, D. (2018). *Say Her Name: The Life and Death of Sandra Bland.* HBO Films.

13. Lartey (2018).

14. Edwards, B. (2015, July 30). "At Least 5 Black Women Have Died in Police Custody in July; WTF?!" The Root, www.theroot.com/at-least-5-black-women-have-died-in-police-custody-in-j-1790860695, retrieved October 15, 2016.

15. Survived and Punished. (2016). "S&P Analysis & Vision," https://survivedandpunished.org/analysis/, retrieved September 7, 2021.

16. Gross, K. (2015). "African American Women, Mass Incarceration, and the Politics of Protection," *Journal of American History, 102*(1), 25.

17. Bureau of Justice Statistics. (2020). "Total Correctional Population," Washington, D.C.: U.S. Department of Justice.

18. Fedock, J. (2018). "Number of Women in Jails and Prisons Soars," *University of Chicago School of Social Service Administration Magazine, 25*(1).

19. Kajstura, A. (2019). "Women's Mass Incarceration: The Whole Pie 2019," Northampton: Prison Policy Initiative.

20. Kajstura.

21. Kajstura.

22. Saar, M., et al. (2019). *The Sexual Abuse to Prison Pipeline: The Girls' Story.* Washington, D.C.: Center for Poverty and Inequality, Georgetown Law Center, 22.

23. Richie, B. (2012). *Arrested Justice: Black Women, Violence, and America's Prison Nation.* New York: New York University Press, 3.

24. Richie.

25. Sudbury, J. (2005). "Celling Black Bodies: Black Women in the Global Prison Industrial Complex," *Feminist Review,* no. 80, 177.

26. Sudbury, 177.

27. Sentencing Project. (2019). *Incarcerated Women and Girls.* Washington, D.C.: Sentencing Project.

28. Kajstura (2019).

29. Sudbury (2005), 162.

30. Sudbury, 177.

31. Smallwood, S. (2008). *Saltwater Slavery: A Middle Passage from Africa to American Diaspora.* Cambridge, MA: Harvard University Press, 6.

32. Gaspar, B., & Hine, D.C. (1996). *More Than Chattel: Black Women and Slavery in the Americas.* Bloomington: Indiana University Press.

33. Benjamin, R. (2016). "Catching Our Breath: Critical Race STS and the Carceral Imagination," *Engaging Science, Technology and Society,* no. 2, 153, 146.

34. LeFlouria, Talitha. (2016). *Chained in Silence: Black Women and Convict Labor in the New South.* Chapel Hill: University of North Carolina Press.

35. Davey, M., & Bosman, J. (2014, November 24). "Protests Flare after Ferguson Police Officer Is Not Indicted," *New York Times,* www.nytimes.com/2014/11/25/us/ferguson-darren-wilson-shooting-michael-brown-grand-jury.html, retrieved September 5, 2021.

36. Crenshaw, K., et al. (2015). "#SayHerName: Black Women Are Killed by Police Too." *African American Policy Forum.* www.aapf.org/sayhername.

37. Harris-Perry, M. (2011). *Sister Citizen: Shame, Stereotypes, and Black Women in America.* New Haven, CT: Yale University Press, 86–96.

38. Lacey-Bordeaux, E. (2014, June 30). "Arizona Professor's Jaywalking Arrest Gets Out of Hand," www.cnn.com/2014/06/30/justice/arizona-jaywalking-arrest/index.html, retrieved March 5, 2020.

39. Elfrink, T. (2019, May 7). "'Open Up the Case, Period': Sandra Bland's Family Demands Answers over New Video of Her Arrest," *Washington Post,* www.washingtonpost.com/nation/2019/05/07/open-up-case-period-sandra-blands-family-demands-answers-over-new-video-her-arrest/, retrieved July 26, 2021.

40. Lockhart, P.H. (2019, May 7). "Sandra Bland Recorded Her Traffic Stop. The Video Is Finally Public, Years after Her Death," Vox, www.vox.com/2019/5/7/18535659/sandra-bland-video-traffic-stop-brian-encinia-texas-police, retrieved February 1, 2020.

41. Hinkle, J. (2018, March 16). "Trooper Fired for Sandra Bland Arrest: 'My Safety Was in Jeopardy,'" www.kxan.com/investigations/trooper-fired-for-sandra-bland-arrest-my-safety-was-in-jeopardy/, retrieved May 15, 2018.

42. Keneally, M. (2015, July 20). "Sandra Bland's Death Probe Being Treated like a Murder Investigation, DA Says," ABC News, https://abcnews.go.com/US/sandra-bland-supporters-call-independent-investigation/story?id=32572897, retrieved June 1, 2016.

43. Lockhart, P.H. (2019, May 7). "Sandra Bland Recorded Her Traffic Stop. the Video Is Finally Public, Years after Her Death," Vox, www.vox.com/2019/5/7/18535659/sandra-bland-video-traffic-stop-brian-encinia-texas-police, retrieved February 1, 2020.

44. Hassan, A. (2019, May 7). "The Sandra Bland Video: What We Know," *New York Times,* www.nytimes.com/2019/05/07/us/sandra-bland-brian-encinia.html, retrieved February 18, 2020.

45. Robinson, C. (2019, March 6). "Police Release Portion of Kindra Chapman Jail Video before Self-Inflicted Hanging," *Birmingham Real-Time News,* www.al.com/news/birmingham/2015/07/video_of_kindra_chapman_shows.html, retrieved January 2, 2020.

46. Robinson.

47. Cleek, A. (2015, July 23). "Holding Cell Death of Black Ala. Teen Ruled Suicide, but Questions Remain," Al Jazeera English, http://america.aljazeera.com/articles/2015/7/23/questions-surround-kindra-chapmans-death-in-alabama-holding-cell.html, retrieved August 30, 2017.

48. Robinson (2019).

49. Wood, J.D., et al. (2017). "The 'Gray Zone' of Police Work during Mental Health Encounters: Findings from an Observational Study in Chicago," *Police Quarterly, 20*(1), 81–105; Wood, J., & Watson, A.C. (2017). "Improving Police Interventions during Mental-Health Related Encounters: Past, Present, and Future," *Policing and Society: An International Journal, 26*(3), 289–299.

50. Ritchie, A.J., & Jones-Brown, D. (2017). "Policing Race, Gender, and Sex: A Review of Law Enforcement Policies," *Women & Criminal Justice, 27*(1): 21–50; Chesney-Lind, M. "Policing Women's Bodies: Law, Crime, Sexuality, and Reproduction," *Women & Criminal Justice, 27*(1), 1–3.

51. Robinson (2019).

52. Cleek (2015).

53. Coleman, C. (2015, July 25). "Family of Kindra Chapman, Teen Found Dead in Jail Cell, Says She Committed Suicide," *Washington Informer,* www.washingtoninformer.com/family-of-kindra-chapman-teen-found-dead-in-jail-cell-says-she-committed-suicide/, retrieved March 18, 2021.

54. Gettys, T. (2016, February 25). "Black Woman Dies of Thirst after She Was Dragged Out of SC Hospital to Jail over Unpaid Court Fines," Raw Story, www.rawstory.com/2016/02/black-woman-dies-of-thirst-after-she-was-dragged-out-of-sc-hospital-to-jail-over-unpaid-court-fines/, retrieved July 19, 2018.

55. Hogan, P. (2016, February 25). "South Carolina Woman 'Deprived of Water' Dies in Jail after Arrest on 4-Year-Old Charge," Splinter News, https://splinternews.com/south-carolina-woman-deprived-of-water-dies-in-jail-aft-1793854966, retrieved May 6, 2017.

56. Gettys (2016).

57. Gettys.

58. Hogan (2016).

59. Hogan.

60. Gettys (2016).

61. Bowers, B. (2016, February 24). "$2,200 in Shoplifting Fines Haunted Joyce Curnell until Her Death," *Charleston (SC) Post and Courier,* www.postandcourier.com/archives/2-200-in-shoplifting-fines-haunted-joyce-curnell-until-her-death/article_59cd59db-c047-5f70-bd55-486589469132.html, retrieved March 18, 2021.

62. Bowers.

63. Brennan, C. (2016, February 25). "Family Says South Carolina Woman Died in Jail Because She Was Not Given Water," *New York Daily News,* www.nydailynews.com/news/national/family-south-carolina-woman-died-jail-dehydration-article-1.2543228, retrieved May 3, 2017.

64. Knapp, A., & Munday, D. (2016, February 23). "Filing: Jailed Woman Left to Die[;] Ailing Inmate Untended, Deprived of Water as She Vomited All Night, Attorneys Say," *Charleston (SC) Post and Courier,* www.postandcourier.com/archives/filing-jailed-woman-left-to-die-ailing-inmate-untended-deprived-of-water-as-she-vomited/article_a23d27f7-abdd-52ae-8753-119aa0802413.html, retrieved May 3, 2017.

65. Brennan (2016).

66. FindLaw. (2017). "Rights of Inmates," FindLaw, www.findlaw.com/civilrights/other-constitutional-rights/rights-of-inmates.html.

67. Gettys (2016).

68. Rosenberg, E. (2016, February 26). "Family Says Death of Black Woman in South Carolina Jail Was Easily Preventable," *New York Times*, www.nytimes.com/2016/02/27/us/joyce-curnell-south-carolina-jail-death.html, retrieved May 5, 2017.

69. Joyner, J. (2018, May 25). "Nobody Believes That Black Women Are in Pain, and It's Killing Us," *Wear Your Voice Mag*, www.wearyourvoicemag.com/black-women-are-in-pain/, retrieved July 28, 2019.

70. Joyner.

71. Danyiko, R. (2019, January 11). "Cleveland Heights Police Release Body Cam Video Showing Arrest of Woman Who Died in Jail," Cleveland.com, www.cleveland.com/cleveland-heights/2015/08/cleveland_heights_police_relea_1.html, retrieved January 15, 2020.

72. Danyiko, R. (2015, August 10). "'I don't want to die in your cell': Police Release Video of Ralkina Jones Taken Prior to Death," Cleveland.com, www.cleveland.com/cleveland-heights/2015/08/i_dont_want_to_die_in_your_cel_1.html, retrieved January 15, 2020.

73. Danyiko.

74. Danyiko (2019).

75. Heisig, E. (2019, January 20). "Cleveland Heights Settles with Family of Ralkina Jones, Who Died in Jail Cell in 2015," Cleveland.com, www.cleveland.com/court-justice/2018/01/cleveland_heights_settles_with.html, retrieved March 20, 2020.

76. Heisig.

77. Spillane, M. (2015, October 20). "'Natural Causes,' Drug Use Cited in Raynette Turner Autopsy," *Journal News*, www.lohud.com/story/news/local/westchester/2015/10/20/raynette-turner-mount-vernon/74256162/, retrieved April 4, 2017.

78. Spillane.

79. Gershman, B. L. (2016, August 6). "On the Death of Raynette Turner," *Huffington Post*, www.huffpost.com/entry/on-the-death-of-raynette-turner_b_7933426, retrieved October 1, 2020.

80. Lerner, J., Coyne, M., & Spillane, M. (2015, July 28). "Raynette Turner's Family Seeks Answers in Jail Death," *Journal News*, www.lohud.com/story/news/2015/07/28/woman-dies-mount-vernon-holding-cell/30773979/, retrieved April 4, 2017.

81. Spillane (2015).

82. Lerner, Coyne, & Spillane (2015).

83. Materese, J. (2016, March 3). "Mount Vernon Inmate's Death Caused by Enlarged Heart," ABC News, https://abc7ny.com/raynette-turner-mount-vernon-inmate-death-mother-of-eight/1041482/, retrieved April 6, 2017.

84. Whitford, E. (2016, Mach 3). "AG Finds 'No Criminal Culpability' in Holding Cell Death of Westchester County Woman Arrested for Shoplifting," *Gothamist,* https://gothamist.com/news/ag-finds-no-criminal-culpability-in-holding-cell-death-of-westchester-county-woman-arrested-for-shoplifting, retrieved April 6, 2017.

85. Lopez, R. (2019, November 27). "'I think her last heartbeat was when we got her out of the car': Dallas Police Failed to Give Medical Treatment to Woman Who Died in Custody," wfaa.com, www.wfaa.com/article/news/i-think-her-last-heartbeat-was-when-we-got-her-out-of-the-car-dallas-police-failed-to-render-aid-to-woman-in-custody/287-c27afd2d-ae42-4ed1-8fdf-02fc7c268668, retrieved June 24, 2020.

86. Baker, M., et al. (2020, June 28). "Three Words. 70 Cases. The Tragic History of 'I Can't Breathe,'" *New York Times,* www.nytimes.com/interactive/2020/06/28/us/i-cant-breathe-police-arrest.html, retrieved August 25, 2020.

87. Lopez (2019).

88. Bonvillian, C. (2020). "Lawsuit: Dallas Woman Died of Drug Overdose after Cops and Paramedics Failed to Provide Medical Aid," www.wftv.com, retrieved August 29, 2020.

89. Lopez (2019).

90. Bonvillian (2020).

91. Lennard, N. (2019, June 13). "How New York's Criminal Justice System Killed a Transgender Woman at Rikers Island," The Intercept, https://theintercept.com/2019/06/13/layleen-polanco-death-rikers-trans-woman-sex-work/, retrieved July 1, 2019.

92. Bullock, M. (2018, October 26). "From Paris Is Burning to Pose: The House of Xtravaganza," The Cut, www.thecut.com/2018/10/the-house-of-xtravaganza-at-35.html, retrieved March 30, 2021.

93. Gold, H. (2020, August 31). "What Really Happened to Layleen Polanco?" The Cut, www.thecut.com/2020/08/what-really-happened-to-layleen-polanco.html, retrieved March 5, 2021.

94. Feller, M., Walsh, S., & Weaver, H. (2020, August 31). "Activists Demand Justice and Cash Bail Reform for Layleen Polanco a Year after Her Death in Solitary," *Elle,* www.elle.com/culture/career-politics/a27921290 /who-is-layleen-polanco-transgender-woman-died-solitary-confinement/, retrieved October 6, 2020.

95. Fitzgerald, E., et al. (2015). *Meaningful Work: Transgender Experiences in the Sex Trade.* Washington, D.C.: National Center for Transgender Equality.

96. Sosin, K. (2020, June 13). "New Video Reveals Layleen Polanco's Death at Rikers Was Preventable, Family Says," NBC News, www.nbcnews.com /feature/nbc-out/new-video-reveals-layleen-polanco-s-death-rikers-was-pre-ventable-n1230951, retrieved August 26, 2020.

97. Paz, I.G., & Astor, M. (2020, June 28). "Black Trans Women Seek More Space in the Movement They Helped Start," *New York Times,* www.nytimes .com/2020/06/27/us/politics/black-trans-lives-matter.html, November 6, 2020.

98. Herskovitz, J. (2015, July 28). "Second Suspect in 10 Days Dies in Custody of Houston Police," Reuters, https://cn.reuters.com/article/us-usa-police-houston/second-suspect-in-10-days-dies-in-custody-of-houston-police-idUSKCN0Q229E20150728, retrieved August 23, 2021.

99. Crenshaw, K. (1989). "Mapping the Margins: Intersectionality, Identity Politics, and Violence against Women of Color," *Stanford Law Review, 43*(6), 1242.

100. Hinton, E., Henderson, L., & Reed, C. (2018). "An Unjust Burden: The Disparate Treatment of Black Americans in the Criminal Justice System," New York: Vera Institute of Justice, 6.

101. National Institute of Justice. (2019). "Police Use of Force," https://nij .ojp.gov/topics/law-enforcement/use-of-force, retrieved November 1, 2020.

102. Lee, J.C., & Park, H. (2018, October 5). "15 Black Lives Ended in Confrontations with Police. 3 Officers Convicted," *New York Times,* www.nytimes .com/interactive/2017/05/17/us/black-deaths-police.html, retrieved March 22, 2019.

103. Wines, M., & Robles, F. (2014, August 22). "Key Factor in Police Shootings: 'Reasonable Fear,'" *New York Times,* www.nytimes.com/2014/08/23/us /ferguson-mo-key-factor-in-police-shootings-reasonable-fear.html, retrieved March 22, 2019.

104. Farrell, P. (2020, April 20). "Garion McGlothen: 5 Fast Facts You Need to Know," Heavy.com, https://heavy.com/news/2019/08/cyntoia-brown-pimp-garion-mcglothen/, retrieved October 25, 2019.

105. Love146. (2020, January 3). "CHILD TRAFFICKING: SOME FACTS & STATS," https://love146.org/child-trafficking-some-facts-stats/, retrieved February 4, 2020.

106. Silva, C. (2017, November 22). "Cyntoia Brown Laughed about Killing Man, Threatened to Shoot Nurse after Arrest," *Newsweek,* www.newsweek.com/cyntoia-brown-laughed-killing-man-threatened-shoot-720363, retrieved June 22, 2018.

107. Farrell (2020).

108. Garcia, J. (2019, January 7). "Who Was Cyntoia Brown Convicted of Killing? A Look at Johnny Allen," *The Tennessean,* www.tennessean.com/story/news/2019/01/07/cyntoia-brown-clemency-johnny-allen-case-story/2503198002/, retrieved February 1, 2020.

109. Garcia.

110. Goggin, B. (2019, January 8). "Cyntoia Brown, a Trafficking Victim Jailed for Killing a Man Using Her for Sex, Was Granted Clemency Following a Social-Media Campaign. Here's Everything You Need to Know," *Insider,* www.insider.com/cyntoia-brown-timeline-clemency-story-kim-kardashian-2019-1, retrieved February 2, 2020.

111. Ortiz, E. (2019, January 10). "Celebrities Rallied around Cyntoia Brown, but Some Worry about 'Kardashian Effect,'" NBC News, www.nbcnews.com/pop-culture/celebrity/celebrities-rallied-around-cyntoia-brown-some-worry-about-kardashian-effect-n956871, retrieved March 30, 2019.

112. Hauser, C. (2018, May 3). "Cyntoia Brown, Trafficking Victim Serving Life Sentence for Murder, Will Get Clemency Hearing," *New York Times,* www.nytimes.com/2018/05/03/us/cyntoia-brown-clemency-hearing-.html, retrieved September 23, 2018.

113. Andone, D. (2018, May 24). "Parole Board Splits on Clemency for Trafficking Victim Serving Life for Killing a Man Who Picked Her Up for Sex," CNN, www.cnn.com/2018/05/24/us/cyntoia-brown-clemency-request/index.html, retrieved March 30, 2019.

114. Wadhwani, A. (2018, December 11). "Cyntoia Brown: Parole Panel Split during Clemency Hearing for Nashville Woman Sentenced to Life," *The*

Tennessean, www.tennessean.com/story/news/2018/05/23/cyntoia-brown-hearing-nashville-parole-panel-split-granting-clemency/622627002/, retrieved November 19, 2018.

115. Hauser, C. (2019, August 7). "Cyntoia Brown Is Freed from Prison in Tennessee," *New York Times*, www.nytimes.com/2019/08/07/us/cyntoia-brown-release.html, retrieved January 10, 2020.

116. Global Network of Sex Work Projects. (2011). "Sex Work Is Not Trafficking," NSWP, www.nswp.org/sites/default/files/SW%20is%20Not%20Trafficking.pdf.

117. George, A., Vindhya, U., & Ray, S. (2010). "Sex Trafficking and Sex Work: Definitions, Debates and Dynamics—A Review of Literature," *Economic and Political Weekly*, 45(17), 64–73.

118. Kelly, C. (2019, July 30). "13 Sex Trafficking Statistics That Explain the Enormity of the Global Sex Trade," *USA Today*, www.usatoday.com/story/news/investigations/2019/07/29/12-trafficking-statistics-enormity-global-sex-trade/1755192001/, retrieved January 15, 2020.

119. Walker, L. E. A. (2016). *The Battered Woman Syndrome*. New York: Springer.

120. Allard, S. A. (1991). "Rethinking Battered Woman Syndrome: A Black Feminist Perspective," *UCLA Women's Law Journal*, 1, 191.

121. Lugo-Sanchez, W., Wortzel, H. S., & Martinez, R. (2013). "Appropriate Use of a Defense of Extreme Emotional Distress," *Journal of the American Academy of Psychiatry and the Law Online*, 41(3), 461–463.

122. Bromwich, J. E. (2017, May 5). "Bresha Meadows, an Ohio Teenager Accused of Killing Father, Seeks Release before Trial," *New York Times*, www.nytimes.com/2017/05/05/us/bresha-meadows-father-killing.html, retrieved August 6, 2018.

123. Bromwich.

124. Caniglia, J. (2016, August 12). "Murder or Self Defense? Bresha Meadows Accused of Killing Father," Cleveland.com, www.cleveland.com/metro/2016/08/murder-or-self-defense-bresha-meadows.html, retrieved August 6, 2018.

125. O'Hara, M. E. (2017, May 22). "Bresha Meadows Case: Teen Who Killed Father Gets Deal That Spares Jail Time," NBC News, www.nbcnews.com/news/us-news/bresha-meadows-case-teen-who-killed-father-gets-deal-spares-n762906, retrieved August 6, 2018.

126. Meadows, B. (2020, July 14). "Love, Bresha: Letters to My Younger Selves," *Essence*, www.essence.com/feature/bresha-meadows-letters-survival/, retrieved October 3, 2020.

127. Caniglia (2016).

128. Jeltsen, M. (2017, August 14). "When Surviving Childhood Means Killing Your Father," *Huffington Post*, www.huffpost.com/entry/bresha-meadows-abuse-case_n_589501cbe4b0406131370b40, retrieved August 6, 2018.

129. Mouffitt, T. (2013). "Childhood Exposure to Violence and Lifelong Health: Clinical Intervention Science and Stress Biology Research Join Forces," *Development and Psychopathology*, 25(4), 1619–1634.

130. Law, V. (2017, January 23). "'I'll Be Able to Lay in the Grass': Bresha Meadows to Be Transferred to Treatment Facility," Rewire News Group, https://rewirenewsgroup.com/article/2017/01/23/ill-able-lay-grass-bresha-meadows-transferred-treatment-facility/, retrieved August 8, 2018.

131. Caniglia (2016).

132. Law (2017).

133. Alexander, M. (2019, August 26). "'Stand Your Ground' Laws Must Be Repealed before Another Innocent Black Man Is Killed," NBC News, www.nbcnews.com/think/opinion/stand-your-ground-laws-must-be-repealed-another-innocent-black-ncna1046211, retrieved February 18, 2020.

134. Hauser, C. (2017, February 7). "Florida Woman Whose 'Stand Your Ground' Defense Was Rejected Is Released," *New York Times*, www.nytimes.com/2017/02/07/us/marissa-alexander-released-stand-your-ground.html, retrieved May 25, 2018.

135. Green, S. (2017). "Violence against Black Women—Many Types, Far-Reaching Effects," Washington, D.C.: Institute for Women's Policy Research.

136. McClean, K. (2013). "Marissa Alexander: A Miscarriage of Justice," National Lawyers Guild, Guild Notes, www.nlg.org/guild-notes/article/marissa-alexander-a-miscarriage-of-justice/, retrieved July 5, 2018.

137. Nelson, S. (2014, March 3). "Marissa Alexander Now Faces 60 Years for 'Warning Shot' at Abusive Husband," *US News and World Report*, www.usnews.com/news/articles/2014/03/03/marissa-alexander-now-faces-60-years-for-warning-shot-at-abusive-husband, retrieved July 5, 2018.

138. Armah, E. (2013, December 5). "Convicting Marissa Alexander Would Be a Form of Emotional Terrorism," Salon, www.salon.com/2013/12/05

/convicting_marisa_alexander_would_be_a_form_of_emotional_terrorism_
partner/, retrieved July 5, 2018.

139. Frumin, A. (2014, November 24). "Marissa Alexander Accepts Plea Deal,"
MSNBC, www.msnbc.com/msnbc/marissa-alexander-accepts-plea-deal-
msna465976, retrieved July 5, 2018.

140. CNN Editorial Team. (2021, February 17). "Trayvon Martin Shooting
Fast Facts," CNN, www.cnn.com/2013/06/05/us/trayvon-martin-shooting-
fast-facts/index.html, retrieved April 8, 2021.

141. CNN Editorial Team.

142. Teeman, T. (2017, August 4). "Why Are So Many Transgender Women
of Color Being Killed in America?" *Daily Beast*, www.thedailybeast.com/why-
are-so-many-trans-women-of-color-being-killed-in-america, retrieved April 1,
2019.

143. Avery, D. (2012, January 4). "Trans Woman Chrishaun 'CeCe' McDonald
Sentenced to 41 Months for Slaying Attacker," *Queerty*, www.queerty.com
/trans-woman-chrishaun-cece-mcdonald-sentenced-to-41-months-for-slaying-
attacker-20120604, retrieved June 1, 2020.

144. Avery.

145. Pasulka, N. (2012, May 22). "The Case of CeCe McDonald: Murder—or
Self-Defense against a Hate Crime?" *Mother Jones*, www.motherjones.com
/politics/2012/05/cece-mcdonald-transgender-hate-crime-murder/, retrieved
July 16, 2019.

146. Avery (2012).

147. Pasulka (2012).

148. Yuen, L. (2012, May 3). "Transgender Woman Gave Up Self-Defense
Claim in Plea Deal," MPR News, www.mprnews.org/story/2012/05/03
/cece-plea, retrieved October 19, 2019.

149. Perry, B., & Dyck, D. R. (2014). "'I Don't Know Where It Is Safe': Trans
Women's Experiences of Violence," *Critical Criminology, 22*, 49–63.

150. Mannix, A. (2012, May 9). "CeCe McDonald Murder Trial," Internet
Archive WayBack Machine, https://web.archive.org/web/20140122144811
/http://www.citypages.com/2012-05-09/news/cece-mcdonald-murder-trial/,
retrieved June 2, 2020.

151. Graham, L.F. (2014). "Navigating Community Institutions: Black
Transgender Women's Experiences in Schools, the Criminal Justice System,
and Churches," *Sexuality Research and Social Policy, 11*, 274–287.

152. Yuen (2012).

153. Avery (2012).

154. Pasulka (2012).

155. Erderly, S. R. (2014, July 30). "The Transgender Crucible," *Rolling Stone,* www.rollingstone.com/culture/culture-news/the-transgender-crucible-114095/, retrieved October 18, 2019.

156. Movement Advancement Project and Center for American Progress. (2016). "Unjust: How the Broken Criminal Justice System Fails Transgender People," www.lgbtmap.org, retrieved May 15, 2020.

157. Hunter, L.A. (2015, February 6). "Every Breath a Black Trans Woman Takes Is an Act of Revolution," *Huffington Post,* www.huffpost.com/entry /every-breath-a-black-tran_b_6631124, retrieved May 20, 2020.

158. Torres, I., Hopper, J., & Chang, J. (2019, November 20). "For Trans Women of Color Facing 'Epidemic' of Violence, Each Day Is a Fight for Survival: 'I'm an Endangered Species... but I Cannot Stop Living,'" ABC News, https://abcnews.go.com/US/trans-women-color-facing-epidemic-violence-day-fight/story?id=66015811, retrieved May 30, 2020.

Chapter 3. Up against the Wind

1. *Montana* is a pseudonym.

2. Commenters of Twitter, TikTok, and other popular social media platforms hypothesized that Tory shot Megan because he found out she was "really" a man. Megan does not identify as a Black trans woman, yet people justified violence against her because of the normalization of violence against Black trans women. These hypotheses about what "caused the shooting" rely on a collective complicity with cisgender, heterosexual men attacking trans women because they are trans. In these hypotheses, Megan's lack of "disclosure" prompted violence against her. There is a normalization of violence against Black trans women, particularly in moments of consensual or forced disclosure. The hypotheses that circulated in August 2020 both misgendered and masculinized Meg as well as reified the normalcy of violence against Black trans women.

3. FBI. (2018). *2018: Crime in the United States,* https://ucr.fbi.gov/crime-in-the-u.s/2018/crime-in-the-u.s.-2018.

4. FBI.

5. Morgan, R. (2017). *Race and Hispanic Origins of Victims and Offenders, 2012-2015.* Bureau of Justice Statistics.

6. Atkins, S. (2009). "Racial Segregation, Concentrated Disadvantage, and Violent Crime," *Journal of Ethnicity in Criminal Justice, 7*(1), 30–52.

7. Parker, P. (1972). "Brother," in *Child of Myself.* San Francisco: Women's Press Collective, 4.

8. The statistics I provide in this paragraph are from the Violence Policy Center. (2018). *When Men Murder Women: An Analysis of 2016 Homicide Data, 6.*

9. U.S. Department of Justice Office on Violence against Women. (2018). *Myths and Facts about Sexual Violence.* Washington, D.C.: Office on Violence against Women.

10. Black Women's Blueprint. (2012). "The Truth Commission on Black Women and Sexual Violence." New York: Black Women's Blueprint.

11. Blackburn Center. (2019). "Black Women and Domestic Violence." Greensburg, PA: Blackburn Center.

12. Devin-Norelle. (2020). "Six Black Trans Women Were Found Dead in Nine Days," www.them.us/story/six-black-trans-women-were-found-dead-in-nine-days, retrieved August 31, 2020.

13. Mic. (2016). *Unerased: Counting Transgender Lives.* New York: Mic Network.

14. Human Rights Campaign. (2017, 2018, 2019). *Violence against the Transgender Community.* Washington, D.C.: Human Rights Campaign.

15. National Center for Transgender Equality. (2020). "Murders of Transgender People in 2020 Surpasses Total for Last Year in Just Seven Months," transequality.org, retrieved August 30, 2020.

16. Davis, A. (1983). *Women, Race, & Class.* New York: Vintage, 7.

17. Davis, A. (1971). "Reflections on the Black Woman's Role in the Community of Slaves," *Black Scholar, 3*(4), 2–15.

18. Bay, M. (2010). *To Tell the Truth Freely: The Life of Ida B. Wells.* New York: Hill and Wang, 112.

19. Foster, T. (2019). *Rethinking Rufus: Sexual Violations of Enslaved Men.* Athens: University of Georgia Press.

20. West, E. (2018). "Reflections on the History and Historians of the Black Woman's Role in the Community of Slaves: Enslaved Women and Intimate Partner Sexual Violence," *American Nineteenth Century History, 18*(1), 1.

21. Berry, D.R. (2017). *The Price for Their Pound of Flesh: The Value of the Enslaved, from Womb to Grave, in the Building of a Nation.* Boston: Beacon, 79.

22. Berry, 114. Enslaved women and children not only participated in the rebellion, which is more commonly known as the Nat Turner rebellion; enslaved women played an integral role in this most famous slave rebellion in U.S. history. Historians such as Vanessa Holden document the importance of moving the story of the 1831 rebellion from a tale of singular heroism and execution to one of community resistance.

23. Turner, S. (2019). *Contested Bodies: Pregnancy, Childrearing, and Slavery in Jamaica.* Philadelphia: University of Pennsylvania Press, 63.

24. West (2018), 6.

25. White, D.G. (1999). *Ar'n't I a Woman? Female Slaves in the Plantation South.* New York: Norton, 152.

26. Turner (2019), 63.

27. Turner, 64.

28. Turner, 64.

29. Edwards, L. (2015). *A Legal History of the Civil War and Reconstruction.* Cambridge, UK: Cambridge University Press. The Reconstruction Amendments include the Thirteenth, Fourteenth, and Fifteenth Amendments to the Constitution. Passed, ratified, and adopted between 1865 and 1870, these amendments sought to guarantee the liberty of formerly enslaved people and to establish and prevent some civil rights discrimination against them and all citizens of the United States. Broadly, these amendments were part of a large-scale effort to reconstruct the American South in the aftermath of the Civil War. The efficacy of these amendments was thwarted and eroded by state laws and federal court decisions throughout the late nineteenth century. These laws and decisions set the table for the Jim Crow era, which formally legalized racial segregation.

30. Packard, J. (2003). *American Nightmare: The History of Jim Crow.* Amarillo, TX: St. Martin's Griffin.

31. Wood, A. (2011). *Lynching and Spectacle: Witnessing Racial Violence in America, 1890-1940.* Chapel Hill: University of North Carolina Press.

32. Hine, D.C. (1989). "Rape and the Inner Lives of Black Women in the Middle West," *Signs, 14*(1), 912-920. In this groundbreaking article, Hine defines dissemblance as "the behavior and attitudes of Black women that cre-

ated the appearance of openness and disclosure but actually shielded the truth of their inner lives and selves from their oppressors" (912).

33. Hine, 912.

34. Hine, 914.

35. Hine, 914.

36. Hine, 914.

37. Russell, D.E.H. (1977). "Report on the International Tribunal on Crimes against Women," *Frontiers: A Journal of Women's Studies*, 2(1), 1–6.

38. Staples, R. (1979). "The Myth of Black Macho: A Response to Angry Black Feminists," *Black Scholar*, 10(6/7), 24–33.

39. Shipp, E.R. (1986, January 27). "Blacks in Heated Debate over 'The Color Purple,'" *New York Times*.

40. Cole, J., & Guy-Sheftall, B. (2003). *Gender Talk: The Struggle for Women's Equality in African American Communities*. New York: One World, xxvii, xxx.

41. Ramsey, D. (2012). "Rapper Too Short, in XXL Column, Gives Boys Advice to 'Turn Girls Out,'" www.grio.com, retrieved August 19, 2020. "Turning out" is transitive slang for a coercive, sometimes violent, process of convincing someone to become very sexually active. It often refers to the process by which pimps engage sex workers but can also refer to non-sex-work-related contexts.

42. We Are the 44% Coalition. (2012). "'We Are the 44%' Coalition Challenges Sexual Violence against Black and Latina Teens," NewBlackMan (in Exile), www.newblackmaninexile.net/2012/02/we-are-44-coalition-challenges-sexual.html, retrieved August 19, 2020.

43. National Center on Violence against Women in the Black Community. (2018). *Black Women and Sexual Assault*. Washington, D.C.: Ujima. The report uses data from the U.S. Department of Justice, Bureau of Justice Statistics Special Report, *Female Victims of Sexual Violence* (2013). More recent reports on Black women and girls and sexual violence have been released by organizations such as Black Women's Blueprint and RAINN.

44. National Center on Violence against Women in the Black Community. (2018).

45. National Center on Violence against Women in the Black Community.

46. Rose, T. (2003). *Longing to Tell: Black Women's Stories of Sexuality and Intimacy*. New York: Farrar, Straus and Giroux.

47. McDonald, N. (2019). "All Your Questions about R. Kelly's Alleged Sex Crimes, Answered," Vulture.com, retrieved September 1, 2020.

48. Hopper, J. (2013, December 16). "Read the 'Stomach-Churning' Sexual Assault Accusations against R. Kelly in Full," *Village Voice*.

49. Taylor, G. (2013). "#FastTailedGirls: Hashtag Has a Painful History behind It," *The Grio*, www.thegrio.com, retrieved September 1, 2020. *Fass* is commonly used within Black communities as a way to talk about Black girls who are perceived to be prematurely sexually active.

50. Brown, R. N. (2008). *Black Girlhood Celebration: Toward a Hip-Hop Feminist Pedagogy*. New York: Peter Lang, 24.

51. Taylor (2013).

52. National Center on Violence against Women in the Black Community. (2018).

53. National Center on Violence against Women in the Black Community.

54. Banks, D., & Kyckelhahn, T. (2011). *Characteristics of Suspected Human Trafficking Incidents, 2008–2010*. Department of Justice, Bureau of Justice Statistics, https://bjs.ojp.gov/content/pub/pdf/cshti0810.pdf, retrieved July 27, 2021.

55. National Coalition against Domestic Violence. (2020). "National Statistics Domestic Violence Fact Sheet," Denver, CO: NCADV.

56. National Criminal Justice Reference Service. (2015). *Intimate Partner Violence*. Washington, D.C.: National Center for Victims of Crime.

57. National Criminal Justice Reference Service.

58. Blackburn Center (2019).

59. Beh, A. (2009). "Police Suspect Boyfriend in Triple Murder Case," NBC News, www.nbcwashington.com/news/local/police-suspect-boyfriend-in-triple-murder/2099125/, retrieved September 15, 2020.

60. Bet.com news staff. (2009). "D.C. Mother, Sons Stabbed to Death by Live-in Boyfriend," BET, www.bet.com/news/news/2009/03/23/news articledcmothersonskilledbyboyfriend.html, retrieved October 8, 2016.

61. Cherkis, J. (2009). "Three Murders, Three Questions," *Washington City Paper*, https://washingtoncitypaper.com, retrieved October 8, 2016.

62. Cherkis.

63. Cherkis.

64. The most dangerous time for battered women is when they leave an abusive relationship. According to the Justice Department, domestic assaults and potentially fatal violence intensify after a woman leaves her partner.

65. Degraffinried, R. (2018). "Woman Allegedly Killed by Ex-Husband Who Had Been Hired by Mayor of Cleveland Despite Domestic Violence History," The Root, www.theroot.com, retrieved May 5, 2019.

66. Goist, R. (2018). "Vigil Is Monday for Slain Shaker Heights Teacher, Estranged Wife of Former Judge Accused in Her Death," Cleveland.com, www .cleveland.com/news/2018/11/vigil-is-monday-for-slain-shaker-heights-teacher-estranged-wife-of-former-judge-accused-in-her-death.html, retrieved September 12, 2020.

67. Schladabeck, J. (2020). "South Carolina Man Was in Jealous Rage When He Killed Ex-Girlfriend, Two Daughters in Murder-Suicide, Cops Say," *Daily News*, www.nydailynews.com/news/crime/ny-south-carolina-man-jealous-rage-killed-ex-children-suicide-20200520-zsim76hxkvbmnclalel3uweoie-story.html, retrieved September 15, 2020.

68. Schladabeck.

69. Wray, D. (2016). "Larry Cosby Convicted for Murder of Daughter and Her Girlfriend," *Houston Press*, www.houstonpress.com/news/larry-cosby-convicted-for-murder-of-daughter-and-her-girlfriend-8658352, retrieved September 16, 2020.

70. Goldstein, S. (2014). "Texas Dad Killed Daughter, Her Lesbian Lover Because He Disliked That She Was Gay: Mom," *Daily News*, www.dailynews .com, retrieved August 5, 2020.

71. Daily Mail Reporter. (2014). "Did Dad Kill Daughter and Her Girlfriend Because They Were Gay? Relatives Say 'Devout Muslim' Father Couldn't Get His Head around Her Sexuality," *Daily Mail*, www.dailymail.co.uk/news/article-2581508/Did-dad-kill-daughter-girlfriend-GAY-Relatives-say-devout-Muslim-father-head-sexuality.html, retrieved August 5, 2020.

72. Fitzsimons, T. (2020). "Minnesota Trans Woman Said She Thought She Was Going to Die in Beating," NBC News, www.nbcnews.com, retrieved November 15, 2020.

73. Peiser, J. (2020). "L.A. Officials Blast 'Callous' Bystanders Who Filmed Attack on Trans YouTube Star and Her Friends," *Washington Post*, www .washingtonpost.com/nation/2020/08/21/eden-doll-hate-crime-la/, retrieved September 12, 2020.

74. Patill, A. (2020). "How a March for Black Trans Lives Became a Huge Event," *New York Times*, www.nytimes.com/2020/06/15/nyregion/brooklyn-black-trans-parade.html, retrieved August 29, 2020.

75. Jones, I. (2019). "Confronting Black Men's Roles in the Murders of Black Transgender Women May Be the Only Way to Save Our Lives," *The Grio,* www .grio.com, retrieved November 28, 2020.

76. Salau, T. (2020, June 14). 247 Live Culture, https://twitter.com/247LC /status/1272402383797018627, retrieved August 20, 2020.

77. Ahmaud Arbery was an unarmed twenty-five-year-old black man who was pursued and fatally shot while jogging near Brunswick in Glynn County, Georgia, on February 23, 2020. Arbery had been pursued by three white residents—Travis McMichael and his father, Gregory, and William "Roddie" Bryan. Arbery was confronted and fatally shot by Travis McMichael. The footage of their pursuit and killing of Arbery went viral in early May. Although not killed by police, Arbery's killing exemplifies the violence of antiBlackness and of white supremacy.

78. Mogul, J., Ritchie, A., & Whitlock, K. (2012). *Queer (In)Justice: The Criminalization of LGBT People in the United States.* Boston: Beacon, 41–54.

79. Salau, T. https://twitter.com/virgingrltoyin/status/1269341695558275072, retrieved August 20, 2020.

80. Clarke, S. (2019). "There Are 64,000 Missing Black Women in the USA: So Why Aren't We Seeing Their Cases Reported in the Media?" *Medium,* https://medium.com/the-blight/there-are-64-000-missing-black-women-in-the-usa-222001806a6e, retrieved August 19, 2020.

Chapter 4. Violability Is a Preexisting Condition

1. APM Research Lab. (2020). "The Color of Coronavirus: Covid-19 Deaths by Race and Ethnicity in the U.S.," retrieved October 15, 2020.

2. APM Research Lab Staff. (2021). "The Color of Coronavirus: Covid-19 Deaths by Race and Ethnicity in the U.S.," APM Research Lab, www .apmresearchlab.org/covid/deaths-by-race, retrieved February 15, 2021.

3. Schindo, B. (2020, October 21). "These Pre-Existing Conditions Could Triple Your Risk of Dying from COVID-19," World Economic Forum, www .weforum.org/agenda/2020/10/pre-existing-conditions-risk-death-covid19-coronavirus/?utm_source=sfmc&utm_medium=email&utm_campaign=2734373_Agenda_weekly-23October2020&utm_term=&emailType=Newsletter, retrieved October 25, 2020.

4. Centers for Disease Control and Prevention. (2020b). "People with Certain Medical Conditions," CDC, www.cdc.gov/coronavirus/2019-ncov/need-extra-precautions/people-with-medical-conditions.html, retrieved October 20, 2020.

5. Hill, M. L. (2020). *We Still Here: Pandemic, Policing, Protest, & Possibility*. New York: Haymarket Books, 18.

6. Centers for Disease Control and Prevention. (2020). "Overweight and Obesity," retrieved October 20, 2020.

7. Byrne, C. (2020, October 3). "Weight Isn't the Problem with COVID-19. How We Talk about It Is," *Huffington Post*, www.huffpost.com/entry/fat-covid-19-pandemic-obesity_l_5f736f60c5b6e99dc3336e3e, retrieved October 5, 2020.

8. Centers for Disease Control and Prevention (2020b).

9. Summers, J. (2020, April 10). "U.S. Surgeon General: People of Color 'Socially Predisposed' to Coronavirus Exposure," NPR, www.npr.org/sections/coronavirus-live-updates/2020/04/10/832026070/u-s-surgeon-general-people-of-color-socially-predisposed-to-coronavirus-exposure, retrieved September 6, 2021.

10. Summers.

11. Bonhomme, E. (2020, April 16). "Racism: The Most Dangerous 'Pre-existing Condition,'" *Al Jazeera*, www.aljazeera.com/opinions/2020/4/16/racism-the-most-dangerous-pre-existing-condition, retrieved October 1, 2020.

12. Lindsey, T. (2020, April 17). "Why COVID-19 Is Hitting Black Women So Hard," Women's Media Center, https://womensmediacenter.com/news-features/why-covid-19-is-hitting-black-women-so-hard, retrieved September 20, 2020.

13. Hill (2020), 66.

14. Matthew, D. B. (2018). *Just Medicine: A Cure for Racial Inequality in American Health Care*. New York: New York University Press, 2.

15. Washington, H. A. (2008). *Medical Apartheid: The Dark History of Medical Experimentation on Black Americans from Colonial Times to the Present*. Norwell, MA: Anchor, 2. The medical industrial complex includes the vast network of corporations and entities supplying healthcare services and products for a profit. The concept was first introduced in the 1971 book *The American Health Empire*. The concept conveys how profit emerges as the primary function of the U.S. healthcare system.

16. Shapiro, J. (2018). "'Violence' in Medicine: Necessary and Unnecessary, Intentional and Unintentional," *Philosophy, Humanities, and Ethics in Medicine*, 13(7).

17. Mustakeem, S. (2016). *Slavery at Sea: Terror, Sex, and Sickness in the Middle Passage*. Urbana: University of Illinois Press.

18. Mustakeem, S. (2011). "'She Must Go Overboard & Shall Go Overboard': Diseased Bodies and the Spectacle of Murder at Sea," *Atlantic Studies*, 8(3), 302.

19. Mustakeem (2016), 55–75.

20. Mustakeem, 58.

21. Mustakeem, 58.

22. Mustakeem, 16.

23. Johnson, J. M. (2020). *Wicked Flesh: Black Women, Intimacy, and Freedom in the Atlantic World*. Philadelphia: University of Pennsylvania Press, 78, 97, 119.

24. *Able* here refers to persons perceived to be physically capable of productive and reproductive labor. Racial capitalism has deeply ableist logics whereby persons deemed unfit for labor via disabilities are perceived as less valuable and potentially disposable. Ableist logics continue to undergird economically exploitative systems and disproportionately render Black women and girls as unfit. The combined force of misogynoir, ableism, and antiBlackness is particularly evident in race science and how it is manifested in the field of medicine.

25. Spillers, H. (1987). "Mama's Baby, Papa's Maybe: An American Grammar Book," *Diacritics*, 17(2), 68.

26. Fisher, W. (1968). "Physicians and Slavery in the Antebellum Southern Medical Journal," *Journal of the History of Medicine and Allied Sciences*, 23(1), 39.

27. Washington (2008), 26.

28. King, P. A. (2004). "Reflections on Race and Bioethics in the United States," *Health Matrix*, 14(1), 150.

29. Washington (2008), 29.

30. I use *gestational capacity* here to include people who do not identify as women or girls but can become pregnant. Not all who give birth are women.

31. Savitt, T. L. (1981). *Medicine and Slavery: The Diseases and Health Care of Blacks in Antebellum Virginia*. Urbana: University of Illinois Press, 14.

32. Severby, S. M. (2013). *Examining Tuskegee: The Infamous Syphilis Study and Its Legacy*. Chapel Hill: University of North Carolina Press, 1–2. The "Tuskegee Study of Untreated Syphilis in the Negro Male" initially involved six hundred black men—399 with syphilis, 201 who did not have the disease. The study was conducted without the patients' informed consent. Researchers told the men they were being treated for "bad blood," a local term used to describe several ailments, including syphilis, anemia, and fatigue. In truth, they did not receive the proper treatment needed to cure their illness. In exchange for taking part in the study, the men received free medical exams, free meals, and burial insurance. Although originally projected to last six months, the study actually went on for forty years (see "The Tuskegee Timeline," www.cdc.gov/tuskegee/timeline.htm).

33. Severby (2013), 2.

34. Severby, S. M. (2000). *Tuskegee's Truths: Rethinking the Tuskegee Syphilis Study*. Chapel Hill: University of North Carolina Press, 3.

35. Ingram, J. (2018, June 19). "Why Are Black Men Afraid of the Doctor?" Black America Web, https://blackamericaweb.com/2018/06/19/why-are-black-men-afraid-of-the-doctor/, retrieved October 25, 2020.

36. Washington (2008), 61, 62.

37. Washington, 64–65. Vesicovaginal fistula is an abnormal fistulous tract extending between the bladder and the vagina that allows the continuous involuntary discharge of urine into the vaginal vault.

38. Pernick, M. S. (1996). *The Black Stork: Eugenics and the Death of "Defective" Babies in American Medicine and Motion Pictures since 1915*. New York: Oxford University Press.

39. Washington (2008), 67.

40. Washington, 70.

41. Washington, 70.

42. Skloot, R. (2001). "Cells That Save Lives Are a Mother's Legacy," *New York Times*, November 17.

43. Skloot, R. (2010). *The Immortal Life of Henrietta Lacks*. New York: Crown, 13.

44. Skloot, 102, 172. Adenocarcinoma is a type of cancer that starts in mucus-producing glandular cells of one's body.

45. Skloot, 33, 30, 1.

46. Johns Hopkins Medicine. (2020). "The Legacy of Henrietta Lacks," www.hopkinsmedicine.org, retrieved October 31, 2020.

47. Zielinski, S. (2010, January 22). "Cracking the Code of the Human Genome: Henrietta Lacks' 'Immortal' Cells," *Smithsonian Magazine,* www.smithsonianmag .com/science-nature/henrietta-lacks-immortal-cells-6421299/, retrieved October 30, 2020.

48. Johns Hopkins Medicine (2020).

49. Owens, D.C. (2017). *Medical Bondage: Race, Gender, and the Origins of American Gynecology.* Athens: University of Georgia Press, 107.

50. Goodman, A., & Moynihan, D. (2020, September 24). "ICE's 'Uterus Collector' and Trump's Racist Immigration Policies," Democracy Now!, www .democracynow.org/2020/9/24/ices_uterus_collector_and_trumps_racist, retrieved September 25, 2020.

51. Yeo, P.K. (2020, September 15). "ICE Whistleblower Complaint Alleges 'Uterus Collector' Doctor Performed Mass Hysterectomies," *Daily Beast,* www .thedailybeast.com/ice-whistleblower-complaint-alleges-uterus-collector-doctor-performed-mass-hysterectomies-11, retrieved September 30, 2020.

52. International Rescue Committee. (2020, August 3). "COVID-19 Escalating in ICE Detention Centers as States Hit Highest Daily Records—and ICE Deportation Flights into Northern Triangle Continue," International Rescue Committee, www.rescue.org/press-release/covid-19-escalating-ice-detention-centers-states-hit-highest-daily-records-and-ice, retrieved August 30, 2020.

53. Yeo (2020).

54. Refugee and Immigrant Center for Education and Legal Services. (2020, July 22). "Black Immigrant Lives Are under Attack," Refugee and Immigrant Center for Education and Legal Services, www.raicestexas.org/2020/07/22 /black-immigrant-lives-are-under-attack/, retrieved October 31, 2020.

55. Merchant, M. (2020). "US Deports Migrant Women Who Alleged Abuse by Georgia Doctor," *Boston Globe,* www.bostonglobe.com, retrieved November 11, 2020.

56. Washington (2008), 202–203.

57. Washington, 202.

58. Ladd-Taylor, M. (2020). *Fixing the Poor: Eugenic Sterilization and Child Welfare in the Twentieth Century.* Baltimore: Johns Hopkins University Press, 5.

59. Black, E. (2012). *War against the Weak: Eugenics and America's Campaign to Create a Master Race.* Washington, D.C.: Dialog Press, xv.

60. Massey, D.S., & Denton, N.A. (1993). *American Apartheid: Segregation and the Making of the Underclass.* Cambridge, MA: Harvard University Press.

61. Black (2012), xvi.

62. Washington (2008), 203.

63. Lee, C.K. (2000). *For Freedom's Sake: The Life of Fannie Lou Hamer.* Urbana: University of Illinois Press, x.

64. Lee, 21.

65. Briggs, L. (2002). *Reproducing Empire: Race, Sex, Science, and U.S. Imperialism in Puerto Rico.* Berkeley: University of California Press, 142–161.

66. Safford, K. (1984). "*La Operación:* Forced Sterilization," *Jump Cut: A Review of Contemporary Media, 29*(1), 37.

67. Walden, R. (2013, July 10). "CIR Prison Investigation Opens Another Chapter on Sterilization of Women in U.S.," Our Bodies, Ourselves, www.ourbodiesourselves.org/2013/07/cir-prison-investigation-opens-another-chapter-on-sterilization-of-women-in-u-s/, retrieved August 10, 2020.

68. Roberts, D. (2011). *Fatal Invention: How Science, Politics, and Big Business Re-create Race in the Twenty-First Century.* New York: New Press, 37.

69. Washington (2008), 203.

70. Lindsey, T. (2017b). "Why You So Angry? Serena Williams, Black Girl Pain, and the Pernicious Power of Stereotypes," in G. Sirrakos & C. Emdin (Eds.), *Between the World and the Urban Classroom* (pp. 43–52). Rotterdam, Netherlands: Sense.

71. Kulp, P. (2016, September 1). "Nike Calls Serena Williams the 'Greatest Athlete Ever' in New Ad," Mashable, https://mashable.com/article/serena-williams-nike-ad-goat, retrieved October 8, 2020.

72. Richards, K. (2017, April 24). "These Responses to Serena Williams's Pregnancy Are Sexist as Hell," *Allure,* www.allure.com/story/serena-williams-pregnancy-sexist-responses, retrieved October 8, 2020.

73. Lockhart, P.R. (2018, January 11). "What Serena Williams's Scary Childbirth Story Says about Medical Treatment of Black Women," Vox, www.vox.com/identities/2018/1/11/16879984/serena-williams-childbirth-scare-black-women, retrieved October 6, 2020.

74. Haskell, R. (2018). "Serena Williams on Motherhood, Marriage, and Making Her Comeback," *Vogue,* www.vogue.com/article/serena-williams-vogue-cover-interview-february-2018, retrieved October 6, 2020.

75. Centers for Disease Control and Prevention. (2019c). "Racial and Ethnic Disparities Continue in Pregnancy-Related Deaths," CDC, www.cdc.gov /media/releases/2019/p0905-racial-ethnic-disparities-pregnancy-deaths .html, retrieved October 4, 2020.

76. World Health Organization. (2019). "Maternal mortality," WHO, www .who.int/news-room/fact-sheets/detail/maternal-mortality, retrieved October 4, 2020.

77. Centers for Disease Control and Prevention. (2019). "Maternal Mortality," www.cdc.gov/reproductivehealth/maternal-mortality/index.html, retrieved October 4, 2020.

78. Oparah, J.C., et al. (2017). *Battling over Birth: Black Women and the Maternal Health Care Crisis.* Amarillo, TX: Praeclarus Press, 27.

79. Lister, R., et al. (2019). "Black Maternal Mortality—The Elephant in the Room," *World Journey of Gynecology & Women's Health,* 3(1), 1–8.

80. Miller, A.M. (2020, October 27). "A Black Doctor Died in Childbirth, Highlighting a Tragic Trend That Affects Pregnant Women of Color in the US," *Insider,* www.insider.com/dr-chaniece-wallace-died-in-childbirth-black-women-maternal-mortality-2020-10, retrieved October 28, 2020. Preeclampsia is a pregnancy complication characterized by high blood pressure and signs of damage to another organ system, most often the liver and kidneys. Preeclampsia usually begins after twenty weeks of pregnancy in women whose blood pressure had been normal.

81. Harvard Health Publishing. (2018, October 26). "Preeclampsia and Eclampsia: What Is It?" Harvard Medical School, www.health.harvard.edu/a_to_z/preeclampsia-and-eclampsia-a-to-z, retrieved October 28, 2020.

82. Healthcare Costs and Utilization Project. (2017, April 1). "Delivery Hospitalizations Involving Preeclampsia and Eclampsia, 2005–2014," Agency for Healthcare Research and Quality, www.hcup-us.ahrq.gov/reports/statbriefs /sb222-Preeclampsia-Eclampsia-Delivery-Trends.pdf, retrieved October 28, 2020.

83. Shannon-Karasik, C. (2019, April 17). "Beyoncé Reveals More Details about 'Extremely Difficult Pregnancy' in Netflix's 'Homecoming,'" *Women's*

Health,   www.womenshealthmag.com/health/a22654228/what-is-toxemia-preeclampsia/, retrieved May 31, 2019.

84. Roberts (2011), 3.

85. Saini, A. (2019). *Superior: The Return of Race Science.* Boston: Beacon.

86. Centers for Disease Control and Prevention. (2019, May 7). "Pregnancy-Related Deaths: Saving Women's Lives before, during and after Delivery," CDC, www.cdc.gov/media/releases/2019/p0507-pregnancy-related-deaths.html, retrieved August 20, 2019.

87. Lockhart, P.R. (2018, January 10). "Too Many Black Women like Erica Garner Are Dying in America's Maternal Mortality Crisis," Vox, www.vox.com/identities/2018/1/10/16865750/black-women-maternal-mortality-erica-garner, retrieved September 15, 2019.

88. Smith, C. (2018, January 5). "The Fallout of Police Violence Is Killing Black Women like Erica Garner," PBS, www.pbs.org/newshour/nation/the-fallout-of-police-violence-is-killing-black-women-like-erica-garner, retrieved February 23, 2018.

89. Smith.

90. Centers for Disease Control and Prevention (2019).

91. Centers for Disease Control and Prevention. (2019d). "Racial/Ethnic Disparities in Pregnancy-Related Deaths—United States, 2007–2016," www.cdc.gov, retrieved November 13, 2020.

92. Chuck, E. (2020, January 29). "The U.S. Finally Has Better Maternal Mortality Data. Black Mothers Still Fare the Worst," NBC News, www.nbcnews.com/health/womens-health/u-s-finally-has-better-maternal-mortality-data-black-mothers-n1125896, retrieved November 13, 2020.

93. Howard, J. (2020, February 22). "When Women Die in Childbirth, These Are the Fathers Left Behind," CNN, www.cnn.com/2020/02/21/health/maternal-mortality-fathers-grief/index.html, retrieved May 15, 2020.

94. Mauch, A. (2020, July 10). "Death of Pregnant Black Woman, Sha-Asia Washington, Highlights Racial Disparities in Maternal Mortality," *People,* https://people.com/health/death-of-pregnant-black-woman-sha-asia-washington-highlights-racial-disparities-in-maternal-mortality/, retrieved August 20, 2020.

95. Dickson, E.J. (2020, July 9). "Death of Sha-Asia Washington, Pregnant 26-Year-Old Black Woman, Highlights Devastating Trend," *Rolling Stone,*

www.rollingstone.com/culture/culture-features/shaasia-washington-death-woodhull-hospital-black-maternal-mortality-rate-1026069/, retrieved August 20, 2020.

96. Roberts (2011), 23.

97. Centers for Disease Control and Prevention. (2016, October 14). "Breast Cancer Rates among Black Women and White Women," www.cdc.gov/mmwr/volumes/65/wr/mm6540a1.htm, retrieved October 13, 2020; Lupus Foundation of America. (2018, October 24). "Black Women Develop Lupus at Younger Age with More Life-Threatening Complications," www.lupus.org/news/black-women-develop-lupus-at-younger-age-with-more-lifethreatening-complications, retrieved October 13, 2020.

98. Lewally, A. (2020, October 30). "As a Black Woman, I Had to Beg Doctors to Take Me Seriously When My Brain Was Leaking," *Los Angeles Times,* www.latimes.com/lifestyle/story/2020-10-30/amira-lewally-i-begged-doctors-to-take-me-seriously-when-my-brain-was-leaking, retrieved November 2, 2020.

99. Lewally.

100. Lewally.

101. Lewally.

102. Rao, V. (2020, July 27). "'You Are Not Listening to Me': Black Women on Pain and Implicit Bias in Medicine," *Today,* www.today.com/health/implicit-bias-medicine-how-it-hurts-black-women-t187866, retrieved August 5, 2020.

103. U.S. Department of Health and Human Services. (2020, June 12). "HHS Finalizes Rule on Section 1557 Protecting Civil Rights in Healthcare, Restoring the Rule of Law, and Relieving Americans of Billions in Excessive Costs," www.hhs.gov/guidance/document/hhs-finalizes-rule-section-1557-protecting-civil-rights-healthcare-restoring-rule-law-and, retrieved July 16, 2020.

104. U.S. Department of Health and Human Services. (2010). "Section 1557 of the Patient Protection and Affordable Care Act," www.hhs.gov/civil-rights/for-individuals/section-1557/index.html, retrieved July 16, 2020.

105. U.S. Department of Health and Human Services. (2020).

106. Servai, S. (2020, July 10). "Transgender Americans Just Lost Health Protections. Now What?" *The Dose,* https://doi.org/10.26099/dofh-nc60, retrieved July 15, 2020.

107. Association of Schools & Programs of Public Health. (2017, November 21). "Harvard, NPR & RWJF: Poll Finds a Majority of LGBTQ Americans Report Violence, Threats, or Sexual Harassment Related to Sexual Orientation

or Gender Identity; One-Third Report Bathroom Harassment," www.aspph .org/harvard-npr-one-third-report-bathroom-harassment/, retrieved October 15, 2019.

108. James, S. E., Brown, C., & Wilson, I. (2017). *2015 U.S. Transgender Survey: Report on the Experiences of Black Respondents*. Washington, D.C.: National Center for Transgender Equality, Black Trans Advocacy, and National Black Justice Coalition.

109. Rosellini, S., & Coursolle, A. (2020, August 20). "Changes Are Needed in the Health Care System to Meet the Needs of Black Transgender and Gender Non-Conforming People," *National Health Law Program*, https://healthlaw .org/changes-are-needed-in-the-health-care-system-to-meet-the-needs-of-black-transgender-and-gender-non-conforming-people/.

110. Samuels, E. A., Tape, C., Garber, N., Bowman, S., & Choo, E. K. (2018). "'Sometimes You Feel like the Freak Show': A Qualitative Assessment of Emergency Care Experiences among Transgender and Gender-Nonconforming Patients," *Annals of Emergency Medicine*, 71(2), 170–182.

111. James, Brown, & Wilson (2017).

112. Bauer, G. A., et al. (2009). "'I Don't Think This Is Theoretical; This Is Our Lives': How Erasure Impacts HealthCare for Transgender People," *Journal of the Association of Nurses in AIDS Care*, 20(5), 349.

113. Sevelius, J. M., et al. (2014, February 1). "Barriers and Facilitators to Engagement and Retention in Care among Transgender Women Living with Human Immunodeficiency Virus," National Center for Biotechnology Information, www.ncbi.nlm.nih.gov/pmc/articles/PMC3925767/, retrieved May 1, 2021.

114. LaMartine, S., Brennan-Ing, M., & Nakamura, N. (2018). "Transgender Women of Color and HIV," American Psychological Association, *Psychology and AIDS Exchange Newsletter*, www.apa.org/pi/aids/resources/exchange /2018/03/transgender-women-hiv, retrieved February 12, 2021.

115. Roberts (2011), 102.

Chapter 5. Unlivable

1. Gifford, B. (1994, December 9). "The Curse of D.C. General," *Washington City Paper*, https://washingtoncitypaper.com/article/290068/the-curse-of-dc-general/, retrieved November 1, 2020.

2. I prefer using the term *unhoused* to describe unhoused people and families. Unhoused people often create homes and home spaces even without permanent residences. Most research on unhoused people still uses the term *homeless* to describe unhoused people. It's an ongoing debate among housing activists regarding preferred terminology for identifying unhoused people. Some within housing justice movements see moves toward "unhoused" as an identifier as a distraction. Ultimately, within justice spaces, unhoused and homeless are more often than not used interchangeably.

3. Gifford (1994).

4. Brown, D.L. (2015, March 16). "Relisha Rudd's Brothers to Remain in Foster Care for Now, Court Rules," *Washington Post,* www.washingtonpost.com /local/relisha-rudds-brothers-to-remain-in-foster-care-for-now-court-rules/2015/03/16/5a321b84-cc17-11e4-8c54-ffb5ba6f2f69_story.html, retrieved October 1, 2019.

5. Barnes, M. (2017, March 30). "Remembering Relisha Rudd, Missing Black Girl from DC," *Rolling Out,* https://rollingout.com/2017/03/30/remembering-black-missing-girl-relisha-rudd-dc/, retrieved October 1, 2019.

6. Barnes.

7. The Charley Project. (2020, February 28). "Relisha Tenau Rudd," The Charley Project, https://charleyproject.org/case/relisha-tenau-rudd, retrieved October 19, 2020.

8. The Charley Project.

9. The Charley Project.

10. The Charley Project.

11. The Charley Project.

12. Li, J. (2020, March 17). "Six Years On, Family of Relisha Rudd Still Has Many Unanswered Questions about 8-Year-Old's Disappearance," *Inside Edition,* www.insideedition.com/six-years-on-family-of-relisha-rudd-still-has-many-unanswered-questions-about-8-year-olds-58704, retrieved March 30, 2020.

13. Li.

14. The Charley Project (2020).

15. Li (2020).

16. Li.

17. Li.

18. Li.

19. Li.

20. The Charley Project (2020).

21. Li (2020).

22. Li (2020).

23. The Charley Project (2020).

24. The Charley Project.

25. The Charley Project.

26. Li (2020).

27. NBC News Washington. (2014, March 25). "Police: Man Sought in Girl's Disappearance Had Contact with Other Girls," NBC News, www.nbcwashington.com/news/local/kahlil-tatum-with-missing-girl-relisha-rudd-criminal-past/79187/, retrieved April 25, 2017.

28. The Charley Project (2020).

29. Li (2020).

30. Li.

31. Li.

32. Browne, T. E. (2014, April 14). "Relisha Rudd and the Horrors of Human Trafficking," *Ebony,* https://www.google.com/search?client=firefox-b-1-e&q=Relisha+Rudd+and+the+Horrors+of+Human+Trafficking, retrieved April 18, 2016.

33. Hill, J. (2021). *Through the Cracks.* Podcast. National Public Radio, www.npr.org/podcasts/959614430/through-the-cracks.

34. Gaines, A. C. (2008). "The Straight Facts on Women in Poverty," Washington, D.C.: Center for American Progress.

35. Ransby, B. (2006). "Katrina, Black Women, and the Deadly Discourse on Black Poverty in America," *Du Bois Review, 3*(1), 216.

36. Peterson, J. (1987). "The Feminization of Poverty," *Journal of Economic Issues, 21*(1), 329.

37. Ransby (2006), 216.

38. Gilman, M. E. (2014). "The Return of the Welfare Queen," *Journal of Gender, Social Policy, & the Law, 22*(2), 247.

39. Bleiweis, R., Boesch, D., & Gaines, A. C. (2020, August 3). "The Basic Facts about Women in Poverty," Washington, D.C.: Center for American Progress.

40. Delaney, A., & Edwards-Levy, A. (2018, February 5). "Americans Are Mistaken about Who Gets Welfare," Center for Law and Social Policy, www

.clasp.org/press-room/news-clips/americans-are-mistaken-about-who-gets-welfare, retrieved September 6, 2021.

41. Delaney & Edwards-Levy.

42. Collins, P.H. (2000). *Black Feminist Thought.* New York: Routledge, 87–90.

43. Moses, J. (2018). "Demographic Data Project: Race, Ethnicity, and Homelessness," Washington, D.C.: Homelessness Research Institute / National Alliance to End Homelessness, https://endhomelessness.org/wp-content /uploads/2019/07/3rd-Demo-Brief-Race.pdf.

44. Wiltz, T. (2019, March 29). "'A Pileup of Inequities': Why People of Color Are Hit Hardest by Homelessness," PEW, www.pewtrusts.org/en /research-and-analysis/blogs/stateline/2019/03/29/a-pileup-of-inequities-why-people-of-color-are-hit-hardest-by-homelessness, retrieved January 19, 2020.

45. Desmond, M. (2012). "Eviction and the Reproduction of Urban Poverty," *American Journal of Sociology, 118*(1), 103–104.

46. Desmond, M. (2017). *Evicted: Poverty and Profit in the American City.* New York: Crown.

47. Desmond (2012), 121.

48. Desmond, 117.

49. Desmond, 120.

50. U.S. Department of Housing and Urban Development. (2007). *Annual Homeless Assessment Report to Congress.* Washington, D.C.: U.S. Department of Housing and Urban Development.

51. Roschelle, A. (2017). "Our Lives Matter: The Racialized Violence of Poverty among Homeless Mothers of Color," *Sociological Forum, 32*(S1), 998–1017, 1001.

52. Roschelle, 1002.

53. Roschelle, 1001.

54. Roschelle, 1011.

55. Hahn, R. (2020). "These Moms Fought for a Home—And Started a Movement," *Vogue,* www.vogue.com, retrieved November 23, 2020.

56. Paulas, R. (2020, January 15). "The Black Moms Who Occupied a Vacant House and Became Icons of the Homelessness Crisis," *Vice,* www.vice .com/en/article/bvgnmm/moms-4-housing-occupied-a-vacant-house-in-oakland-eviction, retrieved November 23, 2020.

57. Moms 4 Housing. (2020). "Moms 4 Housing," moms4housing.org, retrieved November 24, 2020.

58. Paulas (2020).

59. Hahn (2020).

60. Paulas (2020).

61. Vo, L.T. (2020, January 14). "A Group of Women Occupying an Empty House in a Gentrified Neighborhood Because 'Housing Is a Human Right' Were Forcibly Evicted," Buzzfeed News, www.buzzfeednews.com/article/lamvo/activist-woman-moms-house-evicted-oakland-gentrification, retrieved November 24, 2020.

62. Hahn (2020).

63. Paulas (2020).

64. Hahn (2020).

65. Bott, M., & Myers, S. (2019, December 31). "Examining Wedgewood: A Look at the Home-Flipping Giant in Battle with Homeless Mothers," NBC Bay Area News, www.nbcbayarea.com/investigations/examining-wedgewood-a-look-at-the-home-flipping-giant-in-battle-with-homeless-mothers/2208119/, retrieved November 24, 2020.

66. Paulas (2020).

67. Kendall, M. (2020, January 10). "Moms 4 Housing Loses Court Case, Still Refuses to Move Out," *Mercury News,* www.mercurynews.com/2020/01/10/moms-4-housing-loses-court-case-must-vacate-west-oakland-home/, retrieved November 24, 2020.

68. Paulas (2020).

69. Paulas (2020).

70. Leong, A. (@anthonyleong). (2020, January 14). Twitter, https://twitter.com/anthonyleong83/status/1217080646465572864?s = 21.

71. Bauman, T., et al. (2014). *No Safe Place: The Criminalization of Homelessness in U.S. Cities.* Washington, D.C.: National Law Center on Homelessness and Poverty.

72. Hunt, J., & Moodie-Mills, A. (2012, June 29). "The Unfair Criminalization of Gay and Transgender Youth: An Overview of the Experiences of LGBT Youth in the Juvenile Justice System," Center for American Progress, www.americanprogress.org/issues/lgbtq-rights/reports/2012/06/29/11730/the-unfair-criminalization-of-gay-and-transgender-youth/, retrieved September 6, 2021.

73. Prison Policy Initiative. (2019, January 22). "LGBTQ Youth Are at Greater Risk of Homelessness and Incarceration," *Prison Policy Initiative,* www.prison policy.org/blog/2019/01/22/lgbtq_youth/, retrieved January 30, 2020.

74. Choi, S. K., et al. (2015). "Serving Our Youth: The Needs and Experiences of Lesbian, Gay, Bisexual, Transgender, and Questioning Youth Experiencing Homelessness," Los Angeles: UCLA School of Law, Williams Institute.

75. Prison Policy Initiative (2019).

76. Grant, J. M., Mottet, L. A., & Tanis, J., with others (2017). "Injustice at Every Turn: A Report of the National Transgender Discrimination Survey," National Center for Transgender Equality/National Gay and Lesbian Task Force, https://transequality.org/sites/default/files/docs/resources/NTDS_ Exec_Summary.pdf.

77. Grant, Mottet, & Tanis, [2].

78. Economic Research Service. (2020). "Definitions of Food Security," U.S. Department of Agriculture.

79. Mock, B. (2016, January 26). "If You Want Clean Water, Don't Be Black in America," Bloomberg, www.bloomberg.com/news/articles/2016-01-26 /why-michigan-governor-snyder-can-t-rule-out-racism-in-flint-water-crisis, retrieved November 23, 2020.

80. Mock.

81. Du Bois, W. E. B. (1899). *The Philadelphia Negro: A Social Study.* New York: Ginn, 162.

82. Bread for the World. (2018, September). "Hunger and Poverty in the African American Community," Bread for the World, www.bread.org/sites /default/files/hunger-poverty-african-american-september-2018.pdf, retrieved November 25, 2020.

83. Bread for the World.

84. Bread for the World.

85. Natural Resources Defense Council, Coming Clean, & Environmental Justice Health Alliance. (2019, September). *Watered Down Justice.* www.nrdc .org/sites/default/files/watered-down-justice-report.pdf, retrieved November 24, 2020.

86. Florida, R., & Tran, C. (2019, August 6). "Where Americans Lack Running Water, Mapped," Bloomberg CityLab, www.bloomberg.com/news/articles /2019-08-06/where-americans-lack-running-water-mapped, retrieved November 24, 2020.

87. Covert, B. (2016, February 18). "Race Best Predicts Whether You Live Near Pollution," *The Nation,* www.thenation.com/article/archive/race-best-predicts-whether-you-live-near-pollution/, retrieved November 24, 2020.

88. Bread for the World (2018).

89. Hill (2017), xxi.

90. Hill, 161.

91. Copeny, M. (2019). "The Flint Water Crisis Began 5 Years Ago. This 11-Year-Old Activist Knows It's Still Not Over," *Elle,* www.elle.com/culture/career-politics/a27253797/little-miss-flint-water-crisis-five-years/, retrieved November 23, 2020.

92. Beeler, C. (2016, January 20). "Flint's Lead Problem Extreme Example of Chronic Global Problem," *The World,* www.pri.org/stories/2016-01-20/flints-lead-problem-extreme-example-chronic-global-problem, retrieved November 23, 2020.

93. Ruble, K., et al. (2019, April 25). "Five Years In, the Flint Water Crisis Continues Its Deadly Toll," PBS, www.pbs.org/wgbh/frontline/article/flint-water-crisis-legionnaires-disease-deaths/, retrieved August 9, 2020.

94. In Our Own Voice, et al. (2020, July). "Clean Water and Reproductive Justice: LACK OF ACCESS HARMS WOMEN OF COLOR," National Partnership for Women & Families, www.nationalpartnership.org/our-work/repro/reports/clean-water-and-reproductive-health.html, retrieved November 24, 2020, 3.

95. In Our Own Voice, et al.

96. In Our Own Voice, et al.

97. March of Dimes. (2016). "Lead Poisoning," March of Dimes, www.marchofdimes.org/lead-poisoning.aspx, retrieved November 24, 2020.

98. In Our Own Voice, et al. (2020).

99. In Our Own Voice, et al.

100. Brones, A. (2018, May 15). "Food Apartheid: The Root of the Problem with America's Groceries," *The Guardian,* www.theguardian.com/society/2018/may/15/food-apartheid-food-deserts-racism-inequality-america-karen-washington-interview, retrieved November 25, 2020.

101. Brones.

102. Tucker, J., & Ewing-Nelson, C. (2020, November). "One in Six Latinas and One in Five Black, Non-Hispanic Women Don't Have Enough to Eat,"

National Women's Law Center, https://nwlc.org/wp-content/uploads/2020/11/pulseFS11.pdf, retrieved November 24, 2020.

103. Vesoulis, A. (2020, November 20). "Families Strained by the Pandemic Are Turning to Food Banks Struggling to Keep Up," *Time,* https://time.com/5914551/food-banks-covid-19-photos/, retrieved November 24, 2020.

104. Simien, E. (2020). "COVID-19 and the 'Strong Black Woman,'" Gender Policy Report, genderpolicyreport.umn.edu, retrieved November 24, 2020.

105. Reese, A. (2019). *Black Food Geographies: Race, Self-Reliance, and Food Access in Washington, D.C.* Chapel Hill: University of North Carolina Press, 34.

106. Roberts, D. (2017). *Killing the Black Body: Race, Reproduction, and the Meaning of Liberty.* New York: Vintage, xvi.

107. Roberts, 18, 23.

108. Giroux, H.A. (2006). "Reading Hurricane Katrina: Race, Class, and the Biopolitics of Disposability," *College Literature, 33*(3), 171–196.

Chapter 6. They Say I'm Hopeless

1. Gillum, T.L. (2019). "The Intersection of Intimate Partner Violence and Poverty in Black Communities," *Aggression and Violent Behavior, 46,* 37–44.

2. Ransby, B. (2006). "Katrina, Black Women, and the Deadly Discourse on Black Poverty in America," *Du Bois Review, 3*(1), 219.

3. Shange, S. (2019). *Progressive Dystopia: Abolition, Anti-Blackness, and Schooling in San Francisco.* Durham, NC: Duke University Press, 21.

4. Harley, S. (1996). "Nannie Helen Burroughs: 'The Black Goddess of Liberty,'" *Journal of Negro History, 81*(1), 63.

5. Hartman, S. (1997). *Scenes of Subjection: Terror, Slavery, and Self-Making in Nineteenth-Century America.* London: Oxford University Press, 112.

6. Ransby (2006), 220.

7. Collins, P.H. (2000). *Black Feminist Thought.* New York: Routledge, 76–77.

8. Windsor, L.C., Dunlap, E., & Golub, A. (2011). "Challenging Controlling Images, Oppression, Poverty, and Other Structural Constraints: Survival Strategies among African–American Women in Distressed Households," *Journal of African American Studies, 15*(1), 292.

9. Moynihan, D. (1965). *The Negro Family: The Case for National Action*. Santa Barbara, CA: Praeger.

10. Not all Black mothers are people who identify as Black women and girls. The trope of the bad Black mother does, however, emerge out of misogynoir and racist, classist, ableist, and sexist ideas about Black femininity and Black feminine personhood.

11. Collins (2000), 84.

12. Collins, 76.

13. Windsor, Dunlap, & Golub (2011), 292.

14. Windsor, Dunlap, & Golub, 292.

15. Cooper, B. (2018). *Eloquent Rage: A Black Feminist Discovers Her Superpower*. New York: St. Martin's, 3–4.

16. Lorde, A. (1981). "The Uses of Anger: Women Responding to Racism," *Women's Studies Quarterly*, 25(1–2), 278–285.

17. Centers for Disease Control and Prevention. (2020). "Understanding the Epidemic," CDC, www.cdc.gov/opioids/basics/epidemic.html, retrieved December 8, 2020.

18. Frakt, A., & Monkovic, T. (2019, December 2). "A 'Rare Case Where Racial Biases' Protected African-Americans," *New York Times*, www.nytimes.com/2019/11/25/upshot/opioid-epidemic-blacks.html, retrieved December 29, 2019.

19. Alexander, M. J., Kiang, M. V., & Barbieri, M. (2018). "Trends in Black and White Opioid Mortality in the United States, 1979–2015," *Epidemiology*, 29(5), 707–715.

20. Frakt & Monkovic (2019).

21. Netherland, J., & Hansen, H. B. (2016). "The War on Drugs That Wasn't: Wasted Whiteness, 'Dirty Doctors,' and Race in Media Coverage of Prescription Opioid Misuse," *Culture, Medicine, and Psychiatry*, 40(1), 664–686.

22. Frakt & Monkovic (2019).

23. Frakt & Monkovic.

24. Alexander, M. (2012). *The New Jim Crow: Mass Incarceration in the Age of Colorblindness*. New York: New Press, x.

25. Windsor, Dunlap, & Golub (2011), 293.

26. Windsor, Dunlap, & Golub, 292.

27. In 1991, the hip-hop group The Dogs released a song titled "Yo' Mama's on Crack Rock." The song is harsh and demeaning toward those living with

addiction. Furthermore, the mother in the music video for the derisive song is a Black woman.

28. Lejuez, C.W., et al. (2007). "Risk Factors in the Relationship between Gender and Crack/Cocaine," *Experimental and Clinical Psychopharmacology*, 15(2), 165–175.

29. Keneally, M., & Parkinson, J. (2017, November 15). "What Roy Moore's 8 Accusers Have Said and His Responses," ABC News, https://abcnews .go.com/US/roy-moores-accusers-responses/story?id=51138718, retrieved November 25, 2020.

30. BBC News. (2018, May 1). "Roy Moore Sues Women Who Accused Him of Sexual Misconduct," www.bbc.com/news/world-us-canada-43964909, retrieved November 25, 2020.

31. St. Felix, D. (2017, December 14). "How the Alabama Senate Election Sanctified Black Women Voters," *New Yorker*, www.newyorker.com/news /daily-comment/how-the-alabama-senate-election-sanctified-black-women-voters, retrieved November 25, 2020.

32. St. Felix.

33. Lindsey, T. (2017, December 18). "Just a Reminder: Black Women Saved Alabama but Not for the Reasons You Think," *The Grio*, https://thegrio .com/2017/12/18/alabama-black-women-voters/, retrieved November 25, 2020.

34. Graham, R. (2017, April 30). "Black Women Aren't Here to Save America from Itself," *Boston Globe*, www.bostonglobe.com/opinion/2019/04/30 /black-women-aren-here-save-america-from-itself/GmP5RedfNptOzOm EoUyAJP/story.html, retrieved November 25, 2020.

35. Graham.

36. In Tamara Beauboeuf-Lafontant's book *Behind the Mask of the Strong Black Woman: Voice and the Embodiment of a Costly Performance* (Temple University Press, 2009), Beauboeuf-Lafontant identifies the "strong black woman" as characters in a redemptive narrative in which the personal actions and agency of Black women "trump all manner of social abuses" (3). It's a trope that aligns with specializing in the "wholly impossible," while systems producing contexts for harm are left intact and unaccountable. Beauboeuf-Lafontant and other Black feminist and womanist scholars trace this trope from slavery to segregation to contemporary antiBlack racism and intracommunal sexism.

37. hooks, b. (1999). *Ain't I a Woman*. Boston: South End Press.

38. Windsor, Dunlap, & Golub (2011).

39. Lomax, T. (2018). *Jezebel Unhinged: Loosing the Black Female Body in Religion and Culture*. Durham, NC: Duke University Press, 2.

40. Lomax, 37.

41. Epstein, R., Blake, J. J., & González, T. (2017). *Girlhood Interrupted: The Erasure of Black Girls' Childhood*. Washington, D.C.: Georgetown Law Center on Poverty and Inequality.

42. Cohan, W. D. (2016, March 10). "Remembering (and Misremembering) the Duke Lacrosse Case," *Vanity Fair*, www.vanityfair.com/news/2016/03 /duke-lacrosse-case-fantastic-lies-documentary, December 3, 2020.

Chapter 7. We Were Not Meant to Survive

1. Stewart, M. W. (1987). *Maria W. Stewart: America's First Black Woman Political Writer*. Bloomington: Indiana University Press.

2. Hine, D. C., & Thompson, K. (1998). *A Shining Thread of Hope: The History of Black Women in America*. New York: Broadway Books, 106.

3. Collins, P. H. (2006). *From Black Power to Hip Hop: Racism, Nationalism, and Feminism*. Philadelphia, PA: Temple University Press, 17.

4. Blain, K. (2019). *Set the World on Fire: Black Nationalist Women and the Global Struggle for Freedom*. Philadelphia: University of Pennsylvania Press, 9.

5. Hine & Thompson (1998), 104–109.

6. Johnson, J. M. (2020). *Wicked Flesh: Black Women, Intimacy, and Freedom in the Atlantic World*. Philadelphia: University of Pennsylvania Press, 155, 93–94.

7. The Combahee River Raid (Raid on Combahee Ferry) was a military operation during the American Civil War conducted on June 1 and June 2, 1863. Tubman led an expedition of 150 African American soldiers of the Fifty-Fourth Massachusetts Infantry Regiment alongside elements of the Union Army. Tubman and Union ships and soldiers rescued and transported more than 750 formerly enslaved people who legally had been freed five months earlier by the Emancipation Proclamation.

8. Taylor, K-Y. (2017). *How We Get Free: Black Feminism and the Combahee River Collective*. New York: Haymarket Books, 3.

9. Combahee River Collective. (1977). "The Combahee River Collective Statement," BlackPast.org, www.blackpast.org/african-american-history /combahee-river-collective-statement-1977/, retrieved September 7, 2021.

10. Combahee River Collective.

11. Kaba, M., Sonenstein, B., & Wilson, K. (2020). "Hope Is a Discipline," Towardfreedom.org, retrieved December 2, 2020.

12. Combahee River Collective (1977).

13. Kaba, Sonenstein, & Wilson (2020).

14. Shakur, A. (2001). *Assata: An Autobiography*. Chicago: Lawrence Hill, 52.

15. Crawley, A. (2016). *Black Pentecostal Breath: The Aesthetics of Possibility*. New York: Fordham University Press.

Selected Bibliography

Alexander, M. J., Kiang, M. V., & Barbieri, M. (2018). "Trends in Black and White Opioid Mortality in the United States, 1979-2015." *Epidemiology, 29*(5), 707-715.

Allard, S. A. (1991). "Rethinking Battered Woman Syndrome: A Black Feminist Perspective." *UCLA Women's Law Journal, 1*, 191-208.

Atkins, S. (2009). "Racial Segregation, Concentrated Disadvantage, and Violent Crime." *Journal of Ethnicity in Criminal Justice, 7*(1), 30-52.

Bailey, M. (2021). *Misogynoir Transformed: Black Women's Digital Resistance.* New York: New York University Press.

Bailey, M., & Trudz. (2018). "On Misogynoir: Citation, Erasure, and Plagiarism." *Feminist Media Studies, 18*(4), 762-768.

Bauer, G. A., et al. (2009). "'I Don't Think This Is Theoretical; This Is Our Lives': How Erasure Impacts HealthCare for Transgender People." *Journal of the Association of Nurses in AIDS Care, 20*(5), 348-361.

Bauman, T., et al. (2014). *No Safe Place: The Criminalization of Homelessness in U.S. Cities.* Washington, D.C.: National Law Center on Homelessness and Poverty.

Bay, M. (2010). *To Tell the Truth Freely: The Life of Ida B. Wells.* New York: Hill and Wang.

Benjamin, R. (2016). "Catching Our Breath: Critical Race STS and the Carceral Imagination." *Engaging Science, Technology and Society*, no. 2, 145-156.

Berry, D. (2017). *The Price for Their Pound of Flesh: The Value of the Enslaved, from Womb to Grave, in the Building of a Nation.* New York: Beacon.

Black, E. (2012). *War against the Weak: Eugenics and America's Campaign to Create a Master Race.* Washington, D.C.: Dialog Press.

Blain, K. (2019). *Set the World on Fire: Black Nationalist Women and the Global Struggle for Freedom.* Philadelphia: University of Pennsylvania Press.

Bleiweis, R., Boesch, D., & Gaines, A.C. (2020). "The Basic Facts about Women in Poverty." Washington, D.C.: Center for American Progress.

Booth, J. (2019). "Capitalism, Anti-Blackness, and the Law: A Very Short History." *Harvard BlackLetter Law Journal*, 35(5), 5–10.

Briggs, L. (2002). *Reproducing Empire: Race, Sex, Science, and U.S. Imperialism in Puerto Rico.* Berkeley: University of California.

Brown, R.N. (2008). *Black Girlhood Celebration: Toward a Hip-Hop Feminist Pedagogy.* New York: Peter Lang.

Butler, J. (2004). *Undoing Gender.* New York: Routledge.

Carruthers, C. (2018). *Unapologetic: A Black, Queer, and Feminist Mandate for Radical Movements.* Boston: Beacon.

Center for Law and Social Justice. (1988). "Black Women under Siege by the New York City Police." Brooklyn, NY: Medgar Evers College Center for Law and Justice.

Chesney-Lind, M. (2017). "Policing Women's Bodies: Law, Crime, Sexuality, and Reproduction." *Women & Criminal Justice*, 27(1), 1–3.

Choi, S.K., et al. (2015). "Serving Our Youth: The Needs and Experiences of Lesbian, Gay, Bisexual, Transgender, and Questioning Youth Experiencing Homelessness." Los Angeles: UCLA School of Law, Williams Institute.

Cohen, C. (1999). *The Boundaries of Blackness: AIDS and the Breakdown of Black Politics.* Chicago: University of Chicago Press.

Cole, J., & Guy-Sheftall, B. (2003). *Gender Talk: The Struggle for Women's Equality in African American Communities.* New York: One World.

Collins, P.H. (2000). *Black Feminist Thought.* New York: Routledge.

Collins, P.H. (2006). *From Black Power to Hip Hop: Racism, Nationalism, and Feminism.* Philadelphia: Temple University Press.

Combahee River Collective. (1977). "The Combahee River Collective Statement." Zillah Eisenstein (self-published).

Cooper, B. (2018). *Eloquent Rage: A Black Feminist Discovers Her Superpower.* New York: St. Martin's.

Crawley, A. (2016). *Black Pentecostal Breath: The Aesthetics of Possibility.* New York: Fordham University Press.

Crenshaw, K. (1990). "Mapping the Margins: Intersectionality, Identity Politics, and Violence against Women of Color." *Stanford Law Review,* 43(6), 1241–1299.

Crenshaw, K., Ritchie, A., Anspach, R., Gilmer, R., & Harris, L. (2015). *Say Her Name: Resisting Police Brutality against Black Women.* African American Policy Forum and the Center for Intersectionality and Policy Studies.

Davis, A. (1983). *Women, Race, & Class.* New York: Vintage.

Davis. A., et al. (2021). *Abolition. Feminism. Now.* New York: Haymarket Books.

Desmond, M. (2012). "Eviction and the Reproduction of Urban Poverty." *American Journal of Sociology,* 118(1), 88–133.

Desmond, M. (2017). *Evicted: Poverty and Profit in the American City.* New York: Crown.

Du Bois, W. E. B. (1899). *The Philadelphia Negro: A Social Study.* New York: Ginn.

Dulaney, W. (1996). *Black Police in America.* Bloomington: Indiana University Press.

Edwards, L. (2015). *A Legal History of the Civil War and Reconstruction.* Cambridge: Cambridge University Press.

Evers-Williams, M., & Marable, M. (2006). *The Autobiography of Medgar Evers: A Hero's Life and Legacy Revealed through His Writings, Letters, and Speeches.* New York: Civitas.

Fedock, J. (2018). "Number of Women in Jails and Prisons Soars." *University of Chicago School of Social Service Administration Magazine,* 25(1).

Feimster, C. (2009). *Southern Horrors: Women and the Politics of Rape and Lynching.* Cambridge, MA: Harvard University Press.

Felker-Kantor, M. (2016). "The Coalition against Police Abuse: CAPA's Resistance Struggle in 1970s Los Angeles." *Journal of Civil and Human Rights,* 2(1), 52–88.

Fisher, W. (1968). "Physicians and Slavery in the Antebellum Southern Medical Journal." *Journal of the History of Medicine and Allied Sciences,* 23(1), 36–49.

Flamm, M. (2007). *Law and Order: Street Crime, Civil Unrest, and the Crisis of Liberalism in the 1960s.* New York: Columbia University Press.

Foster, T. (2019). *Rethinking Rufus: Sexual Violations of Enslaved Men.* Athens: University of Georgia Press.

French, L. (2018). *The History of Policing America: From Militias and Military to the Law Enforcement of Today.* Lanham, MD: Rowman and Littlefield.

Gaines, A.C. (2008). "The Straight Facts on Women in Poverty." Washington, D.C.: Center for American Progress.

Gaspar, B., & Hine, D.C. (1996). *More Than Chattel: Black Women and Slavery in the Americas.* Bloomington: Indiana University Press.

George, A., Vindhya, U., & Ray, S. (2010). "Sex Trafficking and Sex Work: Definitions, Debates and Dynamics—A Review of Literature." *Economic and Political Weekly, 45*(17), 64–73.

Georgetown Law's Center on Poverty and Inequality. (2017). *Girlhood Interrupted: The Erasure of Black Girls' Childhood.* Washington, D.C.: Georgetown Law School.

Giddings, P. (1984). *When and Where I Enter: The Impact of Black Women on Race and Sex in America.* New York: William Morrow.

Gilman, M.E. (2014). "The Return of the Welfare Queen." *Journal of Gender, Social Policy, & the Law, 22*(2), 247–280.

Gilmore, R.W. (2007). *Golden Gulag: Prisons, Surplus, Crisis, and Opposition in Globalizing California.* Berkeley: University of California Press.

Gilmore, R.W. (2011). "What Is to Be Done?" *American Quarterly, 63*(2), 245–265.

Giroux, H.A. (2006). "Reading Hurricane Katrina: Race, Class, and the Biopolitics of Disposability." *College Literature, 33*(3), 171–196.

Graham, L.F. (2014). "Navigating Community Institutions: Black Transgender Women's Experiences in Schools, the Criminal Justice System, and Churches." *Sexuality Research and Social Policy, 11,* 274–287.

Green, S. (2017). "Violence against Black Women—Many Types, Far-Reaching Effects." Washington, D.C.: Institute for Women's Policy Research.

Gross, K. (2015). "African American Women, Mass Incarceration, and the Politics of Protection." *Journal of American History, 102*(1), 25–33.

Hadden, S. (2003). *Slave Patrols: Law and Violence in Virginia and the Carolinas.* Cambridge, MA: Harvard University Press.

Haley, S. (2013). "'Like I Was a Man': Chain Gangs, Gender, and the Domestic Carceral Sphere in Jim Crow Georgia." *Signs, 39*(1), 53–77.

Haley, S. (2016). *No Mercy Here: Gender, Punishment, and the Making of Jim Crow Modernity.* Chapel Hill: University of North Carolina Press.

Harley, S. (1996). "Nannie Helen Burroughs: 'The Black Goddess of Liberty.'" *Journal of Negro History, 81*(1), 62–71.

Harris, L. (2018). "Beyond the Shooting: Eleanor Gray Bumpurs, Identity Erasure, and Family Activism against Police Violence." *Souls, 20*(1), 86–109.

Harris-Perry, M. (2011). *Sister Citizen: Shame, Stereotypes, and Black Women in America.* New Haven, CT: Yale University Press.

Hartman, S. (1997). *Scenes of Subjection: Terror, Slavery, and Self-Making in Nineteenth-Century America.* London: Oxford University Press.

Hartman, S. (2008). *Lose Your Mother: A Journey along the Atlantic Slave Route.* New York: Farrar, Straus and Giroux.

Hill, M. L. (2017). *Nobody: Casualties of America's War on the Vulnerable, from Ferguson to Flint and Beyond.* New York: Simon and Schuster.

Hill, M. L. (2020). *We Still Here: Pandemic, Policing, Protest, & Possibility.* New York: Haymarket Books.

Hine, D. C. (1989). "Rape and the Inner Lives of Black Women in the Middle West." *Signs, 14*(1), 912–920.

Hine, D. C., & Thompson, K. (1998). *A Shining Thread of Hope: The History of Black Women in America.* New York: Broadway Books.

Hinton, E. (2017). *From the War on Poverty to the War on Crime: The Making of Mass Incarceration in America.* Cambridge, MA: Harvard University Press.

Hinton, E. (2021). *America of Fire: The Untold History of Police Violence and Black Rebellion since the 1960s.* New York: Liveright.

Hinton, E., Henderson, L., & Reed, C. (2018). "An Unjust Burden: The Disparate Treatment of Black Americans in the Criminal Justice System." New York: Vera Institute of Justice.

hooks, b. (1999). *Ain't I a Woman.* Boston: South End.

Horne, G. (2020). *The Dawning of the Apocalypse: The Roots of Slavery, White Supremacy, Settler Colonialism, and Capitalism in the Long Sixteenth Century.* New York: Monthly Review Press.

Hunt, J., & Moodie-Mills, A. (2012). *The Unfair Criminalization of Gay and Transgender Youth: An Overview of the Experiences of LGBT Youth in the Juvenile Justice System.* Washington, D.C.: Center for American Progress.

James, J. (1996). *Resisting State Violence: Radicalism, Gender, and Race in U.S. Culture.* Minneapolis: University of Minnesota Press.

Johnson, J. M. (2020). *Wicked Flesh: Black Women, Intimacy, and Freedom in the Atlantic World*. Philadelphia: University of Pennsylvania Press.

Jones, M. (2020). *Vanguard: How Black Women Broke Barriers, Won the Vote, and Insisted on Equality for All*. New York: Basic Books.

Kaba, M. (2021). *We Do This 'til We Free Us*. Chicago: Haymarket Books.

Kernodle, T. (2008). "'I Wish I Knew How It Would Feel to Be Free': Nina Simone and the Redefining of the Freedom Song of the 1960s." *Journal of the Society for American Music, 2*(3), 295–317.

King, D. (1988). "Multiple Jeopardy, Multiple Consciousness: The Context of a Black Feminist Ideology." *Signs, 14*(1), 42–72.

King, P. A. (2004). "Reflections on Race and Bioethics in the United States." *Health Matrix, 14*(1), 149–154.

Ladd-Taylor, M. (2020). *Fixing the Poor: Eugenic Sterilization and Child Welfare in the Twentieth Century*. Baltimore: Johns Hopkins University Press.

LaMartine, S., Brennan-Ing, M., & Nakamura, N. (2018, March). "Transgender Women of Color and HIV." American Psychological Association, Psychology and AIDS Exchange Newsletter, www.apa.org/pi/aids/resources /exchange/2018/03/transgender-women-hiv.

Lee, C. K. (2000). *For Freedom's Sake: The Life of Fannie Lou Hamer*. Urbana: University of Illinois Press.

LeFlouria, T. (2016). *Chained in Silence: Black Women and Convict Labor in the New South*. Chapel Hill: University of North Carolina Press.

Lejuez, C. W., et al. (2007). "Risk Factors in the Relationship between Gender and Crack/Cocaine." *Experimental and Clinical Psychopharmacology, 15*(2), 165–175.

Lindsey, T. (2015). "Post-Ferguson: A 'Herstorical' Approach to Black Violability." *Feminist Studies, 41*(1), 232–237.

Lindsey, T. (2017a). *Colored No More: Reinventing Black Womanhood in Washington, D.C.* Urbana-Champaign: University of Illinois Press.

Lindsey, T. (2017b). "Why You So Angry? Serena Williams, Black Girl Pain, and the Pernicious Power of Stereotypes." In G. Sirrakos & C. Emdin (Eds.), *Between the World and the Urban Classroom* (pp. 43–52). Rotterdam, Netherlands: Sense.

Lister, R., et al. (2019). "Black Maternal Mortality—The Elephant in the Room." *World Journey of Gynecology & Women's Health, 3*(1), 1–8.

Lomax, T. (2018). *Jezebel Unhinged: Loosing the Black Female Body in Religion and Culture*. Durham, NC: Duke University Press.

Lorde, A. (1981). "The Uses of Anger: Women Responding to Racism." *Women's Studies Quarterly, 25*(1–2), 278–285.

Loudermilk, A. (2013). "Nina Simone & the Civil Rights Movement: Protest at Her Piano, Audience at Her Feet." *Journal of International Women's Studies, 14*(3), 121–136.

Love, B. (2019). *We Want to Do More Than Survive: Abolitionist Teaching and the Pursuit of Educational Freedom*. Boston: Beacon.

Lugo-Sanchez, W., Wortzel, H.S., & Martinez, R. (2013). "Appropriate Use of a Defense of Extreme Emotional Distress." *Journal of the American Academy of Psychiatry and the Law Online, 41*(3), 461–463.

Massey, D.S., & Denton, N.A. (1993). *American Apartheid: Segregation and the Making of the Underclass*. Cambridge, MA: Harvard University Press.

Matthew, D.B. (2018). *Just Medicine: A Cure for Racial Inequality in American Health Care*. New York: New York University Press.

McKinstry, C., & George, D. (2013). *While the World Watched: A Birmingham Bombing Survivor Comes of Age during the Civil Rights Movement*. Carol Stream, IL: Tyndale House.

Melamed, J. (2015). "Racial Capitalism." *Critical Ethnic Studies, 1*(1), 76–85.

Merola, M. (1988). *Big City D.A.* New York: Random House.

Mogul, J., Ritchie, A., & Whitlock, K. (2012). *Queer (In)Justice: The Criminalization of LGBT People in the United States*. Boston: Beacon.

Morgan, J.L. (2004). *Laboring Women: Reproduction and Gender in New World Slavery*. Philadelphia: University of Pennsylvania Press.

Morris, M.W. (2016). *PUSHOUT: The Criminalization of Black Girls in Schools*. New York: New Press.

Mouffitt, T. (2013). "Childhood Exposure to Violence and Lifelong Health: Clinical Intervention Science and Stress Biology Research Join Forces." *Development and Psychopathology, 25*(4), 1619–1634.

Moynihan, D. (1965). *The Negro Family: The Case for National Action*. Santa Barbara, CA: Praeger.

Muhammad, K. (2019). *The Condemnation of Blackness: Race, Crime, and the Making of Modern Urban America*. 2nd ed. Cambridge, MA: Harvard University Press.

Mustakeem, S. (2011). "'She Must Go Overboard & Shall Go Overboard': Diseased Bodies and the Spectacle of Murder at Sea." *Atlantic Studies, 8*(3), 301–316.

Mustakeem, S. (2016). *Slavery at Sea: Terror, Sex, and Sickness in the Middle Passage.* Urbana: University of Illinois Press.

Netherland, J., & Hansen, H. B. (2016). "The War on Drugs That Wasn't: Wasted Whiteness, 'Dirty Doctors,' and Race in Media Coverage of Prescription Opioid Misuse." *Culture, Medicine, and Psychiatry, 40*(1), 664–686.

Oparah, J. C., et al. (2017). *Battling over Birth: Black Women and the Maternal Health Care Crisis.* Amarillo, TX: Praeclarus Press.

Owens, D. C. (2017). *Medical Bondage: Race, Gender, and the Origins of American Gynecology.* Athens: University of Georgia Press.

Packard, J. (2002). *American Nightmare: The History of Jim Crow.* Amarillo, TX: St. Martin's Griffin.

Parker, P. (2016). "Brother." In J. Enszer (Ed.), *The Complete Works of Pat Parker.* New York: Midsummer's Night.

Pernick, M. S. (1996). *The Black Stork: Eugenics and the Death of "Defective" Babies in American Medicine and Motion Pictures since 1915.* New York: Oxford University.

Perry, I. (2018). *Vexy Thing: On Gender and Liberation.* Durham, NC: Duke University Press.

Peterson, J. (1987). "The Feminization of Poverty." *Journal of Economic Issues, 21*(1), 329–337.

Pratt, R. A. (2016). *Selma's Bloody Sunday (Witness to History).* Baltimore: Johns Hopkins University Press.

Purnell, D. (2021). *Becoming Abolitionists: Police, Protests, and the Pursuit of Freedom.* New York: Astra House.

Ralph, L. (2019). "The Logic of the Slave Patrol: The Fantasy of Black Predatory Violence and the Use of Force by the Police." *Palgrave Communications, 5*(130), 1–10.

Ransby, B. (2006). "Katrina, Black Women, and the Deadly Discourse on Black Poverty in America." *Du Bois Review, 3*(1), 215–222.

Reese, A. (2019). *Black Food Geographies: Race, Self-Reliance, and Food Access in Washington, D.C.* Chapel Hill: University of North Carolina Press.

Reichel, P. L. (1988). "Southern Slave Patrols as a Transitional Police Type." *American Journal of Police, 7*(2), 51–77.

Richie, B. (2012). *Arrested Justice: Black Women, Violence, and America's Prison Nation.* New York: New York University Press.

Ritchie, A. (2017). *Invisible No More: Police Violence against Black Women and Women of Color.* Boston: Beacon.

Ritchie, A. J., & Jones-Brown, D. (2017). "Policing Race, Gender, and Sex: A Review of Law Enforcement Policies." *Women & Criminal Justice, 27*(1), 21–50.

Roberts, D. (2011). *Fatal Invention: How Science, Politics, and Big Business Re-create Race in the Twenty-First Century.* New York: New Press.

Roberts, D. (2017). *Killing the Black Body: Race, Reproduction, and the Meaning of Liberty.* New York: Vintage.

Robinson, C. (1983). *Black Marxism: The Making of the Black Radical Tradition.* Chapel Hill: University of North Carolina Press.

Roschelle, A. (2017). "Our Lives Matter: The Racialized Violence of Poverty among Homeless Mothers of Color." *Sociological Forum, 32*(S1), 998–1017.

Rose, T. (2003). *Longing to Tell: Black Women's Stories of Sexuality and Intimacy.* New York: Farrar, Straus and Giroux.

Russell, D. E. H. (1977). "Report on the International Tribunal on Crimes against Women." *Frontiers: A Journal of Women's Studies, 2*(1), 1–6.

Saar, M., et al. (2019). *The Sexual Abuse to Prison Pipeline: The Girls' Story.* Washington, D.C.: Center for Poverty and Inequality, Georgetown Law Center.

Safford, K. (1984). "*La Operación:* Forced Sterilization." *Jump Cut: A Review of Contemporary Media, 29*(1), 37–38.

Saini, A. (2019). *Superior: The Return of Race Science.* Boston: Beacon.

Samuels, E. A., Tape, C., Garber, N., Bowman, S., & Choo, E. K. (2018). "'Sometimes You Feel like the Freak Show': A Qualitative Assessment of Emergency Care Experiences among Transgender and Gender-Nonconforming Patients." *Annals of Emergency Medicine, 71*(2), 170–182.

Savitt, T. L. (1981). *Medicine and Slavery: The Diseases and Health Care of Blacks in Antebellum Virginia.* Urbana: University of Illinois Press.

Schwartz, J. (2016). "How Governments Pay: Lawsuits, Budgets, and Police Reform." *UCLA Review, 63*(1144), 15–23.

Scott, J. A. (1998). *The City: Los Angeles and Urban Theory at the End of the Twentieth Century.* Berkeley: University of California Press.

Severby, S. M. (2000). *Tuskegee's Truths: Rethinking the Tuskegee Syphilis Study.* Chapel Hill: University of North Carolina Press.

Severby, S. M. (2013). *Examining Tuskegee: The Infamous Syphilis Study and Its Legacy.* Chapel Hill: University of North Carolina Press.

Shakur, A. (2001). *Assata: An Autobiography.* Chicago: Lawrence Hill.

Shange, N. (1976). *For Colored Girls Who Have Considered Suicide When the Rainbow Is Enuf.* Berkeley: Shameless Hussy Press.

Shange, S. (2019). *Progressive Dystopia: Abolition, Anti-Blackness, and Schooling in San Francisco.* Durham, NC: Duke University Press.

Shapiro, J. (2018). "'Violence' in Medicine: Necessary and Unnecessary, Intentional and Unintentional." *Philosophy, Humanities, and Ethics in Medicine, 13*(7), 1–8.

Sharpe, C. (2016). *In the Wake: On Blackness and Being.* Durham, NC: Duke University Press.

Shedd, C. (2011). "Countering the Carceral Continuum." *Criminology and Public Policy, 10*(3), 851–863.

Simone, N. (2003). *I Put a Spell on You: The Autobiography of Nina Simone.* Cambridge, MA: Da Capo.

Skloot, R. (2010). *The Immortal Life of Henrietta Lacks.* New York: Crown.

Smallwood, S. (2008). *Saltwater Slavery: A Middle Passage from Africa to American Diaspora.* Cambridge, MA: Harvard University Press.

Spillers, H. (1987). "Mama's Baby, Papa's Maybe: An American Grammar Book." *Diacritics, 17*(2), 64–81.

Staples, R. (1979). "The Myth of Black Macho: A Response to Angry Black Feminists." *Black Scholar, 10*(6/7), 24–33.

Stewart, M. W. (1987). *Maria W. Stewart: America's First Black Woman Political Writer.* Bloomington: Indiana University Press.

Sudbury, J. (2005). "Celling Black Bodies: Black Women in the Global Prison Industrial Complex." *Feminist Review,* no. 80, 162–179.

Suddler, C. (2020). *Presumed Criminal: Black Youth and the Justice System in Postwar New York.* New York: New York University.

Taylor, K-Y. (2017). *How We Get Free: Black Feminism and the Combahee River Collective.* New York: Haymarket Books.

Threadcraft, S. (2017). "North American Necropolitics and Gender: On #BlackLivesMatter and Black Femicide." *South Atlantic Quarterly, 116*(3), 553–579.

Threadcraft, S. (2018). *Intimate Justice: The Black Female Body and the Body Politic.* London: Oxford University Press.

Turner, S. (2019). *Contested Bodies: Pregnancy, Childrearing, and Slavery in Jamaica.* Philadelphia: University of Pennsylvania Press.

Vollers, M. (1995). *Ghost of Mississippi: The Murder of Medgar Evers, the Trials of Byron De La Beckwith and the Haunting of the New South.* New York: Back Bay.

Walcott, R. (2015). "The Problem of the Human: Black Ontologies and 'the Coloniality of Our Being.'" In S. Broeck & C. Junker (Eds.), *Postcoloniality-Decoloniality-Black Critique: Joints and Fissures* (pp. 93–105). Frankfurt: Campus Verlag.

Walcott, R. (2021). *ANTIBLACKNESS.* Durham, NC: Duke University Press.

Washington, H. A. (2008). *Medical Apartheid: The Dark History of Medical Experimentation on Black Americans from Colonial Times to the Present.* Norwell, MA: Anchor.

Weinbaum, E. (2019). *The Afterlife of Reproductive Slavery: Biocapitalism and Black Feminism's Philosophy of History.* Durham, NC: Duke University Press.

West, E. (2018). "Reflections on the History and Historians of the Black Woman's Role in the Community of Slaves: Enslaved Women and Intimate Partner Sexual Violence." *American Nineteenth Century History, 18*(1), 1–21.

Westbrook, L. (2020). *Unlivable Lives: Violence and Identity in Transgender Activism.* Berkeley: University of California Press.

White, D. G. (1999). *Ar'n't I a Woman? Female Slaves in the Plantation South.* New York: Norton.

Williams, M. V. (2013). *Medgar Evers: Mississippi Martyr.* Little Rock: University of Arkansas Press.

Windsor, L. C., Dunlap, E., & Golub, A. (2011). "Challenging Controlling Images, Oppression, Poverty, and Other Structural Constraints: Survival Strategies among African-American Women in Distressed Households." *Journal of African American Studies, 15*(1), 290–306.

Wood, A. (2011). *Lynching and Spectacle: Witnessing Racial Violence in America, 1890-1940.* Chapel Hill: University of North Carolina Press.

Wood, J., & Watson, A.C. (2017). "Improving Police Interventions during Mental-Health Related Encounters: Past, Present, and Future." *Policing and Society: An International Journal, 26*(3), 289-299.

Wood, J.D., et al. (2017). "The 'Gray Zone' of Police Work during Mental Health Encounters: Findings from an Observational Study in Chicago." *Police Quarterly, 20*(1), 81-105.

Index

Hine, Darlene Clark, 129–30, 276–77 (n. 32)
Hinton, Elizabeth, 44
HIV, 176–77
Holden, Vanessa, 276 (n. 22)
Holtzclaw, Daniel, 65–66, 72
homophobia, 144. *See also* lesbian and queer Black women
hooks, bell, 220
hope, 226–27, 230, 231, 233
hopelessness, 206–7, 209, 225, 230–31
Hopson, Edward, 46–47
Horne, Gerald, 252–53 (n. 63)
houselessness, 182, 189–97, 290 (n. 2)
House of Xtravaganza, 95
hypersexuality/unrapeability myth, 13, 16, 66–67, 128, 138, 221, 225

ICE (U.S. Immigration and Customs Enforcement), 43, 162–63
Ice Cube, 32–33
immigrants, 43, 162–63
imperialism/colonialism, 27, 165
INCITE!, 232
Indigenous experience, 16, 23, 80, 139, 150, 252–53 (n. 63)
interdependent control systems. *See* multiple jeopardy
internalization, 207, 208, 209, 222, 225
intersectionality, 23–24, 97. *See also* multiple jeopardy
In the Wake: On Blackness and Being (Sharpe), 73
intracommunal violence, 14–15, 113–49; Black community tensions and, 132–33; vs. "Black-on-Black crime," 119–20; Black trans women and, 122–23, 144–46; civil rights era, 130–31; criminal punishment system and, 14, 131, 132; dissemblance and, 129–30, 276–77 (n. 32); extent of, 121; invisibility of, 135–36, 137–38, 148–49; Jim Crow era, 127–29; lesbian and queer Black women and, 143–44; misogynoir and, 21; myths about Black men and, 121–22, 127, 128, 147, 149; myths about Black women and girls and, 136–37; popular culture and, 135–36; protection of Black men and, 116–18, 121–22, 123, 128, 130, 149; sexual violence, 133–38, 277 (n. 41); slavery and, 125–27; witnessing, 113–18. *See also* domestic violence
inviolability, 16. *See also* hypersexuality/unrapeability myth; pain tolerance myth
invisibility of violence against Black women and girls, 6–8, 12–13; disposability and, 18; intracommunal violence and, 135–36, 137–38, 148–49; Jim Crow era, 10; police custody deaths, 76–77, 81, 85; police violence and, 36–37, 39–40, 51, 66, 240; Relisha Rudd disappearance and, 186
Invisible No More: Police Violence against Black Women and Women of Color (Ritchie), 57
I Put a Spell on You (Simone), 3

Jackson, Crystal, murder of, 143–44
James, Joy, 40

maternal mortality, 169–72

Mattingly, Jonathan, 9

Mays, Joseph Randolph, 141, 143

McDade, Tony, 146–47

McDonald, CeCe, attack on, 98, 108–10, 145

McDowell, Ephraim, 159, 161

McGlothen, Garion "Kutthroat," 99

McGuire, Danielle, 250 (n. 33)

McKinney, Patrick, 195

McMichael, Gregory, 280 (n. 77)

McMichael, Travis, 280 (n. 77)

McNair, Carol Denise, 4–5, 6, 7

Meadows, Bresha, self-defense criminalization of, 98, 103–5

Medical Apartheid: The Dark History of Medical Experimentation on Black Americans from Colonial Times to the Present (Washington), 158, 163

medical/health-related violence, 150–80; care deprivation, 172–77, 178–79; COVID-19 deaths and, 150–54; experimentation, 156–61; fatphobia/fat-shaming and, 151; forced sterilization, 161–66; misogynoir and, 151, 169, 174; multiple jeopardy and, 153–54; pain tolerance myth and, 93, 212–13; personal experiences, 178–79; police custody deaths and, 90–91, 92, 93, 95; pregnancy/childbirth and, 166–68, 178, 286 (n. 80); slavery and, 154–56, 157–60, 161; stress and, 172, 177, 179

medical industrial complex: Black mistrust of, 156–57; defined, 281 (n. 15); slavery and, 155, 161; white

cis male domination of, 175–76. *See also* medical/health-related violence

Me Facing Life: Cyntoia's Story, 100

Megan Thee Stallion, 118–19, 274 (n. 2)

memeification, 62, 260 (n. 106)

mental illness: police violence and, 52–53, 56–57, 58–60; unlivable living and, 182–83. *See also* multiple jeopardy

#MeToo, 231

Meyers, Brian, 59–60

misogynoir, 19, 21–22; defined, 21; food and water insecurity and, 203; intracommunal violence and, 21; medical/health-related violence and, 151, 169, 174; police custody deaths and, 75, 77, 83, 86, 88, 91, 96–97; police violence and, 85, 86; self-defense criminalization and, 107–8, 111. *See also* myths about Black women and girls

misogyny: criminal punishment system and, 74, 79–80. *See also* misogynoir

"Mississippi Goddam" (Simone), 2–3, 5, 6, 7

Moms 4 Housing, 193–95, 232

monstrous Black womanhood, 17

Moore, Roy, 216–17, 218

Moreno, Daniel, 110

Morgan, J. L., 250 (n. 36)

Morris, Monique W., 21, 27, 40, 111

Movement for Black Lives, 85, 231

Muhammad, Khalil Gibran, 17

multiple jeopardy, 19, 22–24; criminal punishment system and,

Founded in 1893,
UNIVERSITY OF CALIFORNIA PRESS
publishes bold, progressive books and journals
on topics in the arts, humanities, social sciences,
and natural sciences—with a focus on social
justice issues—that inspire thought and action
among readers worldwide.

The UC PRESS FOUNDATION
raises funds to uphold the press's vital role
as an independent, nonprofit publisher, and
receives philanthropic support from a wide
range of individuals and institutions—and from
committed readers like you. To learn more, visit
ucpress.edu/supportus.